P9-ECQ-457

Language, Children and Society

Language, Children and Society

An Introduction to Linguistics and Language Development

David Lee
Senior Lecturer in English
University of Queensland

NEW YORK UNIVERSITY PRESS
Washington Square, New York

Manufactured in Great Britain

Library of Congress Cataloging-in-Publication Data

Lee, David (David A.)
Language, children, and society.

Bibliography: p. 212
Includes index.
1. Language acquisition. 2. Linguistics. I. Title.
P118.L39 1986 401′.9 86–8648
ISBN 0–8147–5025–7

First published in 1986 in the U.S.A. by
NEW YORK UNIVERSITY PRESS,
Washington Square, New York, N.Y. 10003

To Sheila, Vicky, Debbie and Cathy

Contents

List of phonetic symbols

Note: examples are based on RP pronunciations (see pp.120–1).

æ	p*a*t
ɑ	c*a*lm
ɒ	p*o*t
b	*b*at
d	*d*in
ð	*th*is
ɛ	p*e*t
ɜ	b*ir*d (no *r* sound)
ə	*a*bove
f	*f*at
g	*g*ot
h	*h*at
i	p*ea*t
ɪ	p*i*t
j	*y*es
k	*c*at
l	*l*ight
m	*m*at
n	*n*ight
ŋ	si*ng*
ɔ	l*aw*
p	*p*at
r	*r*at
s	*s*ip
ʃ	*sh*ip
t	*t*ap
θ	*th*ink
u	p*oo*l
ʊ	p*u*t
v	*v*at
ʌ	b*u*t
w	*w*et
z	*z*ip
ʒ	vi*si*on

Preface

The aim of this book is twofold. First, it sets out to introduce the reader to the field of general linguistics. It takes up such questions as: how do linguists approach the enormously complex task of describing (and perhaps ultimately explaining) language? What concepts do they need and what kind of methodology do they employ? The second aim is to introduce the reader to the study of child-language development. This is an area within the field of psycholinguistics and is one that has seen significant advances in the last twenty years or so. The rationale behind the linking of these aims is the belief that many readers may find the field of linguistics more approachable if they can see the relevance of linguistic concepts to a phenomenon such as child language.

The dual aim of this book is reflected in its structure. It consists of four pairs of chapters. The first member of each pair deals with one major area in general linguistics; the second is concerned with issues arising out of that area in the field of language development. Thus, Chapter 1 is concerned with semantics; Chapter 2 with semantic development in children. Chapter 3 deals with grammar and Chapter 4 with the child's construction of the grammatical system. Chapters 5 and 6 discuss phonology and phonological development, respectively. Chapter 7 introduces some of the major concepts in sociolinguistics, and Chapter 8 reviews issues connected with sociolinguistic variation as they affect the child in the educational process.

Inevitably, a short introductory book of this kind has to be highly selective. The chapters concerned with general linguistics concentrate on those concepts which have some relevance to child language. This means that there are topics in each area which are not covered. There is no discussion in Chapter 1 of formal semantics, for example, since it has had no appreciable impact on studies in language development. For similar reasons the short discussion of transformational grammar in Chapter 3 does not attempt to look at developments in the field since the 'standard model' associated with Chomksy 1965. The overall aim, then, is a fairly modest one—to provide those with a general interest in language with an informal introduction to what sometimes appears to be a rather forbidding and perhaps rather abstract subject, and to show the relevance of many basic concepts in linguistics to the study of language development in children.

I should like to acknowledge my debt to a number of individuals and institutions. I am especially indebted to my colleague, Rodney Huddleston. His influence will be apparent at many points in the book, particularly in the chapters dealing with semantics and grammar. I have also derived much benefit (and much pleasure) from discussions of material covered here with Bob Cochrane, John Ingram, Hank Kylstra, Bruce Rigsby and Anna Shnukal. I am also indebted to students taking courses in psycho- and sociolinguistics at the University of Queensland—their interest in these topics has been a constant source of stimulation. I am grateful to Athol and Lesley Chase, who most generously lent me their word-processing equipment at an early stage and initiated me into the mysteries of the art, and to Tony Bunney for helping me overcome numerous obstacles. Most of the book was written during a special-studies programme granted to me by the University of Queensland; I am also grateful to the University of Cambridge (particularly to Terry Moore) for being willing to put up with my presence for part of that programme. Finally, I should like to acknowledge my greatest debt—to my wife, Sheila, and daughters, Vicky, Debbie and Cathy. They allowed me to become a participant in, rather than merely a spectator of, the whole fascinating process of language development.

1 Semantics

INTRODUCTION

Until recently it would have seemed odd to many linguists to take semantics as the starting-point for a book on language and linguistics. To the layman, however, the decision would seem a rather natural one. Semantics is the study of meaning. And a language is after all primarily a code which allows meanings to be communicated from one person to another.

For linguists the problem with meaning is that it is a vague, intangible area. By contrast, the forms of a particular language—its sounds, vocabulary and grammar—constitute a relatively concrete domain, to which linguists can immediately apply their already well-developed analytic methods. It is a much more difficult task to describe the meanings which such a language expresses. Part of the problem has to do with the representational tools that we possess. Writing systems, which we have had for thousands of years, provide us with a reasonably satisfactory tool for representing at least the words and grammatical structures of a particular language, but what tools do we have for representing meanings? The one tool that we do have, of course, is words themselves. It is not difficult to demonstrate, however, that words are not always a very satisfactory way of representing meaning. Even a simple word like *give* can express different meanings, as the following sentences show:

(1) He gave me a book.
(2) He gave me a strange look.
(3) He gave me a hearing test.

In (1) *give* refers to a process in which ownership of an

object changes from person A to person B as the result of an action on the part of person A. In (2) it refers to another kind of action, in which no change of ownership is involved. In (3) it refers to a different kind of action again. The link between word and meaning, then, is far from straightforward, and this leaves us without an immediately obvious way of representing meaning.

It is because of the intangible nature of meaning that linguists tended for many years to shy away from semantics. It seemed much more profitable to concentrate on the description of the formal properties of the code itself. In the nineteenth century major efforts had been devoted to the problem of describing how languages change through time—how words change from one form into another, how grammatical systems are affected by change, ultimately how whole linguistic systems develop through time. Semantics was certainly not excluded from this domain and a good deal was discovered about how and why the meanings of particular words and expressions have changed from one period to another. But 'form' rather than meaning occupied the centre of the stage in this work.

The same is true of most work in linguistics in the twentieth century up to the mid–1960s. Although work on historical linguistics has continued up to the present time, twentieth-century linguistics has been concerned mainly with describing the grammatical systems of the world's languages. It is true that some languages, like English, have received much more attention than others, but there is now a vast body of knowledge available on human languages in general, including, for example, Amerindian languages, which have been intensively studied in the last fifty years by American scholars. Again, however, although meaning has not been excluded from study, the major emphasis has been on the formal properties of grammatical systems and on the development of the theoretical apparatus necessary for describing such systems.

This tradition has had an important influence on the study of the process of language development in children. This is a field which underwent very rapid expansion in the 1960s, for reasons that will be discussed in Chapters 3 and 4.

Because of the emphasis on form rather than on meaning in the study of adult languages, early work on child language also tended to follow the same pattern. However, as we shall see, there are major problems in concentrating on form to the virtual exclusion of meaning in this area. As this realisation grew through the 1960s, researchers in child-language development began to turn their attention more and more to the area of meaning. At the same time, linguists in general were becoming more and more conscious of the fact that semantics had been neglected for far too long. Indeed, it was becoming clear to everybody that if progress in linguistics was to be maintained, then major effort would have to be devoted to the area of meaning. Since the early 1970s there has been a fruitful interaction between the study of semantics in the area of adult languages and in the complementary area of child-language development. There are, of course, some topics in semantics which are of more interest to those working in the first area than to those in the second and these will not be dealt with in any detail here. There are, however, many topics of mutual concern. We will concentrate on these in the belief that they will be of particular interest to the kind of reader to whom this book is addressed, and that they will provide a useful introduction to the findings of recent work in semantics.

REFERENCE

We begin our discussion of meaning by looking at a process which is central to the expression of meaning in language—the process of reference. Clearly, in order to be able to talk to each other about the world around us, we need to be able to refer to the elements that make up that world. It would be very misleading to suggest that it is the function of every element in a language to 'refer' in this way, but it would be equally wrong to ignore the role of reference in the semantic system of a language. It is certainly an important process in the early stages of child-language development.

We can begin by identifying two major categories of entity in the world: I will call them 'objects' and 'processes'.

Objects include such things as trees, chairs, houses, grass as well as people, animals, birds and so on. Processes include the changes of state in which objects become involved—breaking, falling, appearing, disappearing, rolling, growing, cracking, getting up, sitting down, walking, running, eating, sleeping and so on. We can also include in this category psychological processes such as wanting, liking, hoping, thinking and many more. Although these are not as easily observable as the process of falling, for example, they are no less real to us, and they form an important domain of reference.

These two conceptual categories—objects and processes—have an important influence on the structure of language. Indeed, traditional approaches to language appeal to these concepts in the definition of two major word classes—nouns and verbs—the general idea being that nouns are those words which refer to objects in the real world and that verbs refer to processes. We will see in Chapter 3 that the situation is rather more complex than this, although there certainly is a relationship between conceptual categories such as 'object' and 'process' and word classes such as 'noun' and 'verb'.

The categories of 'object' and 'process' do not exhaust the set of conceptual categories. I will not attempt to provide here anything like a complete list, since this task is far from straightforward. I should, however, mention one other major category—that of 'attributes', which can be subdivided into the subcategories 'attributes of objects' (e.g. characteristics concerning colour, shape, size, texture etc.) and 'attributes of processes' (whether the process is habitual, non-habitual, complete, incomplete, gradual, sudden etc.). Again, we tend to think of these categories as corresponding to word classes, since in English, at least, attributes of objects are often represented by adjectives (*red*, *round*, *big*, *rough* etc.) and attributes of processes by adverbs (*slowly*, *quickly*, *harshly*, *noisily*, *often* etc.). This relationship too is far from straightforward. For the moment, however, it will suit our purposes to make the simplifying assumption that there are a limited set of conceptual categories and that the semantic function of many words in a language is to refer to those categories.

Having established that words can denote such categories as object, process, attribute and so on, our next task is to identify a number of ways in which this process of reference operates. Some words denote specific entities in the world. This is true of the names of places and particular people—*London*, *Sydney*, *Paris*, *Mary*, *Harry* and so on—with the minor proviso that a number of different places or individuals may carry the same name. Words which belong in this category have traditionally been called 'proper nouns'. As far as the infant is concerned, we should note that even the acquisition of proper nouns is not entirely straightforward. She first has to recognise that the various manifestations of a particular object are exactly that—different aspects of the same entity rather than different entities. In other words, an infant has to recognise that when she sees the family cat eating, then sleeping on the sofa, and later walking in the garden, these are all different manifestations of the same animal and that they can all be referred to by a single name—*Tiddles*, *Bubbles*, *Mog* or whatever. This is an important point since it is worth noting that it takes some time for the young infant to realise that even her mother is a single unitary entity. (An interesting experimental verification of this is provided by Bower 1971: 38.) In general, the development of language is based on certain cognitive prerequisites, a point that will be elaborated in the next chapter.

In addition to the proper nouns, there is a much larger set of words which denote classes of entity rather than a specific object. A word like *dog*, for example, is used by adults to refer to a very wide range of objects—Dalmatians, collies, basset-hounds, poodles and so on. One interesting question (to be discussed in Chapter 2) is: how does the child manage to identify the precise range of objects for which a particular word can properly be used? If a child has a Dalmatian as a pet, for example, and learns to call it a *dog*, how does she learn that *dog* can also properly be applied to poodles and spaniels? One might argue that the answer to this must be that when, at some stage in her young life, she comes across a poodle or a spaniel, she hears adults referring to it as a *dog*. However, this cannot be the case for every possible type of dog—the period of time over which children learn to use the word appropriately is far too short for them to have encountered every possible variety and to have heard them referred to as a *dog*. This point in fact applies to an enormous number of words in the language (*table* is applied to a wide range of objects of all shapes and sizes—also *chair*, *house*, *tree* and any other common noun one may care to name). What must happen, rather, is that at some stage, after exposure to a limited number of dogs, the child formulates some idea of what criteria an animal must meet in order to be properly called a *dog*. That is, the child constructs some abstract concept of 'dogginess'. It is far from obvious how the child succeeds in doing this for so many words in the limited time in which language is acquired.

The point that many words designate conceptual classes rather than specific phenomena applies as much to those words which refer to processes or attributes as it does to those which refer to objects. A man who climbs a ladder performs a very different sequence of actions from a man who climbs a rope, and this in turn differs from the action of a chimpanzee climbing a tree or a spider climbing a wall. Yet we use the word *climb* to denote all these processes. Similarly, the word *yellow* is the name for a variety of hues, and therefore it, too, designates a class of attributes rather than a single attribute. Linguists are fond of making the point that the class of phenomena designated by a particular word in one language often differs from the class designated by the corresponding word in another language. For example, the word which corresponds to *yellow* in French—*jaune*—is applied like the English word to the colour of buttercups and to the colour of autumn leaves (themselves different hues, of course). However, it is also applied to the colour of (light) brown shoes, so that the French for *brown shoes* is not *des chaussures brunes*, as one might expect, but *des chaussures jaunes*.

What all this means is that, to a certain extent at least, to learn a particular language is to learn a particular way of categorising phenomena in the real world. The world itself is far too multifarious and variegated a place for a language to have a name for every different phenomenon.

Language imposes a classificatory scheme on reality. And one language may impose a rather different scheme from another. This highlights the problem facing the child in identifying the precise referential range for words in her language. Somehow she has to build a general concept for each class-referring word on the basis of a restricted range of experience of both language and of the world.

So far I have identified two major types of relationship that may hold between a referring word and its referent. The first type concerns those words such as proper nouns which refer to specific entities. The second type concerns those which refer to conceptual classes—of object, process or attribute. We now consider a third type, exemplified by such words as *I*, *you*, *this*, *that*, *here*, *there* and so on. Although the relationship between a word like *dog* and its referential class is fairly complex, it is one which is constant across speakers. That is, *dog* is used by all adult native speakers to designate essentially the same class of entities. However, in the case of a word like *I*, reference does not remain constant in this way. In the following exchange:

(4) A: I'll get it.
B: No, I'll get it.

I obviously refers to A in the first utterance and to B in the second. In a dialogue the reference of the word *you* changes in a similar way—sometimes designating one participant, sometimes the other, depending on who is speaking. The variable nature of the reference of these words (called 'shifters') often confuses young children. Some solve the problem by avoiding the words altogether, referring to themselves and their addressees by name, rather than as *I* and *you*. Others refer to themselves as *you*, thereby treating the mother's use of *you* as if it were a proper noun or a constant rather than a shifter (see e.g. Halliday 1975: 113). It can be very disconcerting to hear a child say *you want it* meaning 'I want it'. The shifting nature of the reference of such words as *this* and *that* is illustrated by such exchanges as the following:

(5) A: Could I have that?
B: What? This?

A and B may be referring to the same object but because it happens to be nearer to B than to A, we observe a contrast between the use of *this* and *that* across the two speakers. In one way this situation differs from the use of *I* and *you*. *I* is a single form, the reference of which changes across speakers; *this* and *that* are distinct forms used to designate the same entity by different speakers. Little wonder that children experience difficulties with shifters! The category of shifters includes other words such as *come*, *go*, *give*, *take*. For example, in the following exchange, the words *give* and *take* are essentially used to designate the same process—the transfer of an object from A to B:

(6) A: Could you take this from me?
B: Yes, give it to me.

What we are seeing in these examples involving shifters is the way in which reference to a particular object or process can be influenced by the speaker's relationship to that object or process. In a sense, we can say that the expression of reference here is coloured by the speaker's viewpoint.

SEMANTIC RELATIONS

In order to express meanings, we need to be able to do more than refer to conceptual categories such as object, process, attribute. We need to be able to say something about the relationships between different objects, between objects and processes, objects and attributes and so on. For example, if I wish to help my wife find the newspaper, I may say *the paper's under the table*. Here, not only do I refer to the objects 'newspaper' and 'table' but I also specify the spatial relationship between them. Again, there is a close relationship between a traditional word-class and a particular type of meaning. One of the main functions of prepositions such as *under*, *on*, *near*, *behind* (though not their only function) is to express meanings connected with the location of objects. We will call such meanings 'locative meanings'.

Another kind of conceptual relation that may hold between objects—one which is important to children—is that of possession. In the phrase *mummy's shoe* we find three semantic units. There are two referential meanings expressed by the words *mummy* and *shoe* and the relational meaning of 'possession', expressed by a suffix *'s* on the word referring to the possessor. In this case, then, the relational meaning is expressed by a grammatical element rather than by a word.

Grammatical elements may express not only relations between objects but also relations between objects and processes. Consider the following:

(7) The cat chased the dog.
(8) The dog chased the cat.

The meaning of these sentences is not exhaustively expressed by reference to the objects 'dog', 'cat' and the process 'chase'. These referential meanings are common to both sentences, but there is obviously an important difference in meaning between them. The difference is concerned with the relationships holding between the various referents. We can recognise here two important relational concepts which we will call 'agent' and 'patient'. The agent of a process is that 'object' (including a person or an animal) which is responsible for the initiation and continuation of the process. In (7) the agent is the cat; in (8) it is the dog. In (7) the patient is the dog; in (8) it is the cat. The grammatical element which expresses relational concepts such as agent and patient in these examples is word-order. The word that is placed before the verb refers to the entity designated as the agent; the word that follows the verb refers to the entity designated as the patient. We can thus see the meaning of a sentence like (7) as resulting from a combination of referential meanings—'cat', 'dog', 'chase'—with a number of relational meanings 'cat: agent', 'dog: patient'.

One other important relational concept that should be mentioned here involves time. The fusion of referential meanings such as 'dog', 'cat', 'chase' with relational concepts such as 'agent', 'patient', 'locative' creates reference to a particular event or situation. This event is then situated in time with respect to the moment of utterance. In uttering *the dog chased the cat*, the speaker places the designated event in some time prior to the moment of utterance. In *the dog is chasing the cat* it is placed in a time-frame which includes the moment of utterance. This aspect of meaning is expressed in part by marking the verb for tense—*chased* being a past-tense form; *is chasing*, a present-tense form.

There is a good deal more to be said about relational meanings and particularly about the complex ways in which they are expressed in language. We will return to this topic in Chapter 3. For the moment, however, it will suffice to note that referential meanings and relational meanings are complementary. They combine in statements to form what we will call 'propositional meaning'. For example, when we combine reference to the concepts 'the boss', 'Harry', 'sack' with the expression of the relational concepts 'the boss: agent', 'Harry: patient', 'sack: past time', we have a proposition: 'the boss sacked Harry'. One distinguishing characteristic of the propositions expressed by statements is that they can in principle be tested for truth or falsehood. The point of uttering a sentence such as *the boss sacked Harry* is normally to communicate a piece of true information to someone, information which we assume to be 'new' (or, indeed, 'news') to that person. However, two important points now need to be made. The first is that the expression of propositional meaning in statements is often overlaid with other kinds of meaning. The second point is that there are other types of speech act besides statements; that is, the function of certain types of utterance is to express meanings of a different kind from those to which the test of truth or falsehood is applicable. We will take up these two points separately, dealing with the first in the following section and the second in the section after that.

NON-PROPOSITIONAL MEANINGS

Some of the secondary meanings which can combine in statements with the basic referential and relational meanings have an important role to play at various stages in language development. We will begin, however, with one that has a relatively marginal role in that process. Consider the following utterance:

(9) Unfortunately the boss has sacked Harry.

Here the expression of propositional meaning is overlaid with what we will call 'attitudinal meaning'. The speaker expresses the proposition 'the boss has sacked Harry' but at the same time expresses his attitude towards this event. Language makes available many devices for expressing attitudinal meaning. It can be done as in (9) with an adverb such as *unfortunately*, *sadly*, *happily*, *luckily*, *surprisingly* attached as an adjunct to that part of the sentence expressing the proposition. Alternatively, it can be more closely integrated into the structure of the sentence. In *the bloody boss has sacked Harry* the expression of attitude—in this case anger—is incorporated into the phrase *the bloody boss* rather than attached outside it. In some circumstances this may restrict the expression of attitude to one particular aspect of the proposition. Thus, if I say *the bloody woman has just left, thank God*!, the attitude expressed by *bloody* concerns my attitude to 'the woman' rather than to the fact that she has left, since in this example I am obviously not displeased by her departure. In these examples there are specific words or expressions in the utterance whose exclusive role it is to express attitude. There are other cases in which a word may express both referential and attitudinal meaning. Thus, if I express the proposition 'Harry has just bought a car' by saying *Harry has just bought an old bomb*, then the word *bomb* carries both referential meaning (in that it clearly applies to a car rather than to a house or to a television set) and attitudinal meaning. Perhaps the most obvious group of words that carry both referential and attitudinal meanings are those which express racist attitudes—*wop*, *wog*, *frog*, *kike*, *dago* and so on (Bolinger 1980: 79). There are also many terms for referring disparagingly to women—*chick*, *bird*, *dame*, *doll* etc.—a clear manifestation of the long-established existence of sexist attitudes in our society.

A fusion of referential and attitudinal meanings can be found not only in words referring to objects but also in those referring to processes or attributes. In *John has been lolling about in the garden all day* reference to the process 'lying in the garden' is combined with some hint of disapproval. In *Harry is pig-headed* reference to an attribute (which in other circumstances might be referred to as *strong-minded*) is combined with the expression, once again, of disapproval. Attitude, of course, is very often expressed in speech through intonation. There are all kinds of ways of saying *the boss has sacked Harry* to express attitudes ranging from delight through to fury.

The second type of non-propositional meaning to be noted is illustrated by such contrasts as the following:

(10) He is a very strange man.
(11) He's a really weird guy.

On one level these utterances clearly express the same proposition, but they nevertheless differ with respect to what we will call 'stylistic meaning'. One might be quite happy to say (11) in an informal conversation with friends but feel (10) to be more appropriate in more formal contexts. There are all kinds of ways of expressing one's judgement about the relative degree of formality of the situation involved. Sometimes it is by the use of a particular word—*booze* or *grog*, for example, rather than *beer*; *telly* rather than *television*; *ad* rather than *advertisement*. (Speakers of Australian English are particularly fond of using abbreviated forms of words as an expression of informality (Wierzbicka, forthcoming)). More often stylistic meaning is expressed by phonological means; that is, by systematic changes in the pronunciation of certain sound units in words or by the application of processes such as elision (e.g. the realisation of *he is* as *he's*). There is a good deal of evidence to show that by the age of 10 (and perhaps earlier) children are aware of the existence of stylistic meaning and that they adjust their speech to the situation in the same kind of way that adults do (see pp. 176–8).

Stylistic meaning is very closely associated with a third type of non-propositional meaning which can be called 'social meaning'. Often an important determinant of whether we regard a situation as formal or informal is the speaker's perception of his relationship with the addressee. This relationship is sometimes characterised by differences of status or power, sometimes by differences of 'solidarity'—

whether we feel close to or distant from the person we are talking to. One way in which differences of this kind show up in English has to do with the way we address someone; thus a particular individual might be referred to as *Mrs Smith* by a salesman in a shop or by her subordinates at work but as *Marjorie* at home by her husband and friends.

In some languages, such as Javanese, the expression of social meaning is extremely elaborate. Of this situation Geertz (1960: 248) writes:

> In Javanese it is nearly impossible to say anything without indicating the social relationship between the speaker and the listener in terms of status and familiarity . . . . A number of words (and some affixes) are made to carry in addition to their normal linguistic meaning what might be called a 'status meaning'; i.e., when used in actual conversation they convey not only their fixed denotative meaning 'house', 'body', 'eat', 'walk', 'you', 'passive voice' but also a connotative meaning concerning the status of (and/or degree of familiarity between) the speaker and the listener. As a result, several words may denote the same normal linguistic meaning but differ in the status connotation they convey. Thus, for 'house' we have three forms (*omah*, *grija*, and *dalem*), each connoting a progressively higher status of the listener with respect to the speaker. Some normal linguistic meanings are even more finely divided (*kowe*, *sampejan*, *pandjenengan*, *pandjenengan dalem*, for ascending values of 'you'), others less (*di-* and *dipun-*) for the passive voice.

Since the words which vary in this way in Javanese tend to be those which occur frequently in speech, there is evidently considerable variation in the way in which particular propositional meanings can be expressed in the everyday use of language. Clearly, the learning of language by children is an important part of acculturation into a particular society—it is crucial not only to learn how to express propositions but how to express those propositions appropriately—to learn how situations are defined in one's culture and to understand the role played by language in this definitional process.

The fourth and final type of non-propositional meaning I will mention here is one which, as we shall see in Chapter 2, is particularly relevant to the language development process, although this is not entirely obvious at first sight. Here we are concerned with 'thematic meaning' (Huddleston 1984: 16–18, 437–70). Consider the following pairs:

(12) (a) The dog chased the cat.
(b) The cat was chased by the dog.
(13) (a) It was 'War and Peace' that Tom read.
(b) It was Tom who read 'War and Peace'.

Again, propositional meaning remains constant across these pairs—if (12a) is true, then (12b) must also be true. The difference in each case has to do with the question of 'focus'. If I am talking about some of the things which the dog did today, then I am more likely to use (12a) than (12b). In this case we can say that the dog is 'given', since that is the general topic of my discourse, and the 'new' element is that what he did was to chase the cat. If, however, we are talking generally about the things that happened to the cat, then the cat is now 'given' and the fact that the dog chased it is 'new'. In this case I would tend to use (12b). As far as (13a) and (13b) are concerned, (13a) would occur naturally in response to some statement such as *I thought Tom read 'Anna Karenina'*, where it is given that Tom read something and the new information is that this was 'War and Peace', not 'Anna Karenina'. (13b) might occur in response to the question *who read 'War and Peace'*?, where it is now given that someone read 'War and Peace', and the new fact is that the 'someone' was Tom.

Thematic meaning is much more pervasive than one might suspect at first sight. The point is that we structure all our utterances in such a way that they fit in with previous utterances and—more generally—with what we believe about the extent of our addressee's knowledge. If I want to tell my wife that 'Tom kissed Alice at the office party today', this propositional information can be expressed in many ways, depending on whether it is the opening utterance in an exchange or whether we have already been talking about Tom, about Alice, about both of them, about office parties or about things that happened today:

(14) Tom kissed Alice at the office party today.
He kissed Alice at the office party today.
Tom kissed her at the office party today.
He kissed her at the office party today.
Today at the office party Tom kissed Alice.

Very often thematic meaning—like attitudinal meaning—is expressed by rather subtle intonational differences. A sentence such as *Tom likes Harry's dog* can be uttered in different ways, as in the following examples (where capital letters indicate some intonational emphasis on the word in question):

(15) TOM likes Harry's dog (but I don't).
Tom LIKES Harry's dog (you just suggested he didn't).
Tom likes HARRY'S dog (but not Fred's).
Tom likes Harry's DOG (but not his cat).

Since the differences here relate to the question of which element we wish to treat as new, which is in turn determined by how the utterance fits into the discourse as a whole and what the addressee knows just before the sentence is uttered, we can say that they relate to the area of thematic meaning.

We have now distinguished four different types of non-propositional meaning:

— Attitudinal meaning: that aspect of the meaning of an utterance which is concerned with the speaker's attitude to the propositional content, or to some element of it.
— Stylistic meaning: that aspect of meaning which is concerned with the general social context of the speech event along the dimension formality/informality.
— Social meaning: that aspect of meaning which is concerned with the nature of the relationship between speaker and addressee.
— Thematic meaning: that aspect of meaning which is concerned with the speaker's focus on some element (or elements) of the propositional meaning.

Propositional meaning is created by the combination of referential meanings with the expression of relational concepts, but propositional meaning is often overlaid in particular utterances with one or another (sometimes all) of the kinds of meaning above. Attitudinal, social and stylistic meanings may or may not be present in any specific utterance, but as far as thematic meaning is concerned, there is a good case for saying that there is always some kind of focus involved—either on the whole proposition or on some element within it. We have, of course, touched only briefly on each of these topics. It should, however, be clear why the ability to refer is only part of what the child learns in the development of the full semantic range of the adult language.

SPEECH ACTS

The function of utterances which express propositional meaning is to communicate information from one individual to another about the world. This means, as we have noted, that a proposition can in principle be tested against the state of the world for truth or falsehood. However, although the expression of propositional meaning is one of the central functions of language, it is not the only one. Consider an example such as *pass the salt*! This does not express any proposition—we may note that it would be quite inappropriate to respond to it either by saying *that's true*! or *that's false*!. The function of an utterance such as *pass the salt*! is not to update the addressee's knowledge about the world but to cause him to perform a certain action. It will be useful to distinguish terminologically between those utterances which express propositions (we have called them 'statements') and those which are intended to produce action by the addressee. We will call the latter 'directives'.

One point about directives is that the kind of meanings they express can in certain circumstances be expressed other than through language. I might be able to cause someone to pass the salt by nudging him and indicating it. A teacher may make a pupil close a door by pointing to it or by marching him up to it. This link between action and language is an important factor in the child's early communicative development. As we will see in some detail in the following chapter, directive actions constitute one important avenue into language for the child. It should, however, be emphasised that there is only a partial overlap between meanings that can be expressed through action and those that can be expressed through language. The onset of language enables the child to express a far greater and more subtle range of meanings than those that can be expressed through action or gesture (excluding specially designed gestural languages such as those used by the deaf).

It is important to note that referential and relational meanings play as important a part in directives as they do in statements. In expressing such meanings as 'close the door', 'pass the salt', 'put the paper under the table', we clearly refer to objects and processes such as 'door', 'salt', 'paper', 'close', 'pass', 'put' and to relational concepts such as 'patient', 'location' ('door' being 'patient' with respect to 'close' in 'close the door', for example). There is also an implied or understood relational concept of agent obtaining between the addressee and the process denoted by the verb in directives. The difference between utterances such as *the door is closing* (statement) and *close the door* (directive) is the intention of the speaker in making the utterance—whether she intends to inform or direct. This intention is often referred to as the 'force' of the utterance.

The kinds of meaning discussed in the preceding section may also be incorporated into directives as well as into statements. Thus the differences in meaning between *close the door*!, *please close the door*!, *I wonder if I could possibly trouble you to close the door*! do not relate to the force of the utterance. The speaker's intention is to cause the addressee to perform the same action in each case. The differences here concern the relationship between speaker and addressee and therefore belong to the area of social meaning discussed earlier. Oversimplifying somewhat, *close the door*! would typically be used by a high-status speaker addressing a low-status hearer (e.g. teacher to pupil). This relationship is reversed in an example such as *I wonder if I could possibly trouble you to close the door*!. (One general rule is that directives addressed by low-status speakers to high-status hearers tend to be longer and more complex syntactically than those which flow in the opposite direction.) These considerations have led me to use the term 'directive' rather than the more traditional terms 'command' and 'request'. Given the kind of framework developed here, commands and requests do not have different functions—they are both directives. The differences between them relate to the area of social meaning.

The other types of meaning identified in the preceding section can also be incorporated into directives, as they can into statements. In an utterance like *take the damn book*! we find the basic directive meaning 'take the book!' overlaid by the expression of attitudinal meaning, which may be related either to the book or to the speaker or to some other aspect of the situation. *Bring some beer*! and *bring some grog*! specify the same action but involve different stylistic meanings. *Take the book*! can be uttered either with an intonation centre on *take* or on *book*, depending on which aspect of the situation the speaker wishes to place in focus, so that these choices represent thematic meaning.

In addition to statements and directives, we need to recognise a third major functional category: 'questions'. Questions are much more closely related to statements than to directives in that, like statements, they are concerned with propositional information. If I say *is John here*?, I am seeking information from my addressee concerning the truth or falsehood of the proposition 'John is here'. A rather different type of question is exemplified by the example *where did John go*?. In this case I am asking my addressee to express a true proposition providing a specific piece of information. For fairly obvious reasons it is usual to distinguish between two sub-categories of question—Yes/No questions such as *is John here*? and WH-questions such as *where did John go*? One feature which they do share with directives is that they, too, require an addressee to perform a certain action. However, the type of action required is a very specific one—the addressee is expected to produce a linguistic response.

Again, the various types of non-propositional meaning detailed above can all be incorporated into questions. If I ask *why the hell did you do that*?, I am seeking information but I am also expressing anger; that is, attitudinal meaning. Stylistic, social and thematic meanings can all be incorporated into questions as they can into statements, as the following examples show:

(16) (a) Where's the beer?
(b) Where's the grog?
(17) (a) Why did you say that, Tom?
(b) Why did you say that, Mr Smith?
(18) (a) Why did John take the CAR?
(b) Why did JOHN take the car?

Statements, directives and questions constitute the three major functional categories that we need to recognise. There are also, it should be said, a large number of less important functional categories, but I will not attempt to document them fully here. For our purposes it will suffice to mention just one such category, which I will call 'expressives'. Examples are utterances such as *how strange*!, *what an extraordinary thing to say*!, the main function of which is to give the addressee some idea of the speaker's emotional reaction to what she has just been told. One might wonder whether it is necessary to distinguish expressives from statements—should we perhaps regard *how strange*! as expressing the proposition 'that is strange'? This does not in fact seem entirely satisfactory, again because in most circumstances it would be rather odd for the other person to reply with *that's true*! or *that's false*! to one of these expressive utterances. We would normally see them not so much as conveying new information to our addressee as encouraging her to continue or expressing our involvement in the dialogue. It should, however, be noted that there are many cases in which the distinctions between the functional categories under discussion begin to blur. This is true not only of the distinction between expressives and statements—it also affects the distinction between the major categories. It is not unreasonable, for example, to regard an utterance such as *do you have a light*? as both a question and a directive. This 'fuzziness' is typical of many linguistic categories, but it does not undermine the case for making clear distinctions where they exist.

CONCLUSION

In this chapter we have noted that the total meaning of a particular utterance is the sum total of a whole range of components of meaning, which extend across various dimensions. The basic ingredients are undoubtedly the referential and relational meanings. The former tend to be expressed by words which identify such conceptual categories as objects, processes, attributes and so on. The latter are usually expressed by grammatical elements such as word-order or inflection. Superimposed on these are various attitudinal, stylistic, social and thematic meanings, concerned with how the speaker views the content of what she is saying and the context in which she says it. Another ingredient is the force of the utterance, the speaker's intention in producing it—whether she wishes to express a proposition, seek information, produce action, express emotion and so on. The task facing the child is to discover how these various semantic ingredients are expressed in linguistic form in the target language. Clearly the field is so complex that the various elements will appear at different stages of the child's development, and there will inevitably be some intricate interactions between the different strands of meaning. How does the child even get started on the problem? We try to throw some light on this question in the following chapter.

2 The Development of Meaning

THE DEVELOPMENT OF THE DIRECTIVE

Until fairly recently it was thought that semantic development in children began with the appearance of the first words. Somewhere between the ages of 9 months and 15 months most children begin to produce vocalisations that bear a recognisable resemblance to adult words and which appear to have a similar meaning to that of the adult word. A child begins to say *mama* regularly while looking at his mother; he says *dada* while looking at his father; he might even say something like *odi* ('oh dear') when he drops something.

What researchers have begun to realise more and more in recent years, however, is that these early meaningful utterances do not appear out of the blue. A whole sequence of developments occur in the early months of the child's life which establish the foundation for language. (For detailed exemplification of this point, see Lock 1978, 1980.) In an important sense the child begins to 'learn how to mean' (Halliday 1975) some considerable time before the appearance of such words as *mama*, *dada*, *odi* and so on.

In order to illustrate the point that the development into language is a continuum, which can be traced back to the earliest months of the child's life, we will begin by following the emergence of one type of functional meaning—the directive—through a number of stages up to and including the child's early utterances. We will see that the linguistic expression of directive-type meanings—which involves a number of important linguistic skills—is firmly rooted in earlier pre-linguistic developments. It is, of course, the case that other meanings develop in parallel with directives, and from time to time I will refer to them. I will, however, focus on directives in order to present as clear a picture as possible of the way in which some of the basic components of meaning discussed in the previous chapter develop.

The earliest weeks of the infant's life are characterised by a limited range of behaviour patterns. Most babies (if their parents are lucky) spend a large proportion of their time asleep. Otherwise they are likely to be crying or nursing. Only a small proportion of the time is spent in a state of quiet wakefulness. At any particular moment the infant's behaviour can be said to be 'informative' for the mother. If he is asleep, or awake but quiet, the mother will conclude that all is well in his world. If he cries, she will guess that he is hungry, uncomfortable or tired and that some action is called for. However, although the child's behaviour can be characterised as informative, we clearly would not want to call it 'communicative' at this stage. There are various ways in which a communicative act differs from an informative one (Lyons 1977: 32–5). Perhaps the most important point is that a communicative act involves some intention on the part of one person to transmit a particular message to another. An infant clearly does not go to sleep in order to convey the message that all is well. Crying behaviour is more problematic here, but there are a number of factors which should lead us to regard it, too, as informative rather than communicative in the early stages. The infant's cry is clearly an instinctual rather than a volitional reaction to hunger, and he will cry whether or not there is an addressee present. Moreover, in the early days the child can have little idea of what kinds of action are needed to alleviate his hunger, tiredness or discomfort, so that it is difficult to say that there is a particular message which he is trying to convey. The child's cry is like the yell of pain that I emit when I hit my finger with a hammer. If another person is present, this vocalisation of mine will certainly be informative. It should not be regarded as communicative, however, since I will produce it whether or not someone is there, and since my volitional control over it is rather low.

However, as far as the infant's early vocalisations, including crying, are concerned, this situation undergoes a gradual change over the first few months of life. During this period the child becomes much more aware of the world around him—he begins to perceive certain patterns in it and to react to them. He will notice, for example, that in certain situations the mother repeatedly goes through particular sequences of actions which we call nursing in some cases or nappy-changing in others. Adults generally interact playfully with the child in the form of structured routines in which the infant begins to participate. For example, a mother might engage in a raspberry-blowing routine with the infant. She might initiate a tickling game which involves holding the hand at some distance from the child but clearly in his vision, then bringing it quickly towards the infant and tickling his stomach—all to the accompaniment of vocalisations, smiles and other friendly facial signals. Adults often tend to structure these games so that the same action is repeated several times, with a pause between repetitions, allowing the child to produce some response—leg-kicking, arm-waving, body-shaking, vocalisation or whatever. In this way the child learns many of the fundamental rules of interpersonal interaction. He learns that turn-taking is an important aspect of social interaction—that the pause between the adult's actions is designed to allow him, the child, to contribute to the interaction, before the event is repeated. Turn-taking is, of course, a crucial feature of conversational structure and the basis for it is laid in these very early, pre-linguistic interactions.

Furthermore, the infant learns that his own actions can stimulate reactions in others. An adult who does not receive feedback from the child will tend to observe relatively long pauses between the elements in the routine, but if the child responds through facial or body signals, the adult will in turn respond very quickly to the child's contribution. The pace becomes much more rapid and the excitement generated on both sides much more intense. These experiences stimulate the infant's developing awareness of the fact that he can make things happen in the world and, in particular, that he can cause people to act in ways that are pleasurable or beneficial to him. This development is extremely important for many aspects of the child's mental growth, but it clearly bears particularly on the development of directive-type meanings.

As the child's behavioural repertoire expands, so the range of experiences which can cause him pleasure or distress increases. At the same time, the understanding develops that in certain circumstances an adult's help can be enlisted in initiating and continuing pleasurable activities or in alleviating distress. Vocalisation comes to play an increasingly important role here. A mother will talk to the child as the two share in activities and games, and the child will produce vocal signals in response. Interaction may also be initiated by the child's crying. Vocalisations become differentiated—that is, the infant begins to use different vocal signals in different situations. By the time the infant is 4 months old, mothers can usually tell, for example, whether a particular cry 'means' hunger, tiredness, a wet nappy, boredom or frustration. Clearly, we are getting very close to the communicative use of vocal signals.

As vocalisation begins to acquire communicative rather than informative status, an important parallel development is taking place in the use of gesture. In the first year of life children learn to perform a wide variety of operations on all kinds of objects. To use the terminology of the previous chapter, they learn to apply processes to objects—holding them, sucking them, dropping them and so on. They learn how to co-ordinate visual information with motor operations; for example, causing the arms and hands to perform in a particular way in order to reach out for objects and grasp them. If the desired object is not within arm's length, then the reaching out will of course not be followed by grasping. If the infant is unable to move himself closer, then the situation can become frustrating, in which case he may vocalise. The mother's natural reaction is to provide him with the object he is trying to obtain. Repetitions of this kind of situation lead the child to an awareness that reaching out can be used not only for actually obtaining an object within reach but for bringing an adult's attention to an object which is out of reach. That is, the gesture acquires communicative significance in addition to its basic pragmatic function. Other adult–child interactions contribute to this development. An adult might, for example, hold a desired object in the child's gaze, but out of reach, wait for him to reach out for it and then provide it (to the accompaniment of other signals—vocalisations, smiles and so on). In these developments we see the emergence of referential meaning. The child is beginning to be able to share with others a common focus on elements in the environment through the use of gesture and gaze.

When a child indicates his desire for an object by combining a complaining noise with a pointing or reaching gesture, he is combining an expressive meaning with a referential meaning. His communicative action can be seen as combining the expressive meaning 'I am not happy' with the referential meaning 'my unhappiness concerns that object'. In responding to this situation by providing the object in question, the mother is structuring the environment in such a way that a new type of meaning—a directive meaning—can emerge out of the expressive function.

We have now followed the child through to the stage where he can express a meaning which we can gloss as 'please get me that object' by means of vocalisation and gesture. The next important development concerns the nature of the vocal signal. As infants approach their first birthday, they begin to produce meaningful sounds which are much closer to the sounds of the adult language than are their earlier vocalisations. At about the age of 9 or 10 months, many infants begin to produce meaningful vocal signals that are composed of the kind of units out of which adult words are constructed. For example, Michael Halliday's son, Nigel, began to use a vocalisation *na* when requesting an object (Halliday 1975: 148). One reason why the meaning of this signal was clear was that, when it first appeared, it always occurred accompanied by a reaching-out gesture; as we have seen, this typically forms part of a complex signal (vocalisation and gesture) used for drawing attention to, and thereby indirectly requesting, objects. The form *na* was not based on or derived from an adult word; rather, it was invented by this particular child to help express a particular meaning.

The next development—the appearance of words recognisably based on the adult model—takes the child firmly into language. The ability to refer to objects was already present earlier in the use of the pointing gesture, but the infant now develops the ability to refer by naming. He begins to use linguistic labels such as *teddy*, *mummy*, *daddy* and so on for common objects in the environment. The development of the ability to name objects marks a crucial new stage in the child's interaction with the world. Whereas the pointing gesture serves to indicate specific objects in the child's surroundings, most linguistic labels, as we observed in the previous chapter, serve to designate classes of objects. Specific objects are simply individual manifestations of these more general classes. However, we should not assume that when a word first appears in the speech of a child, he is necessarily using it as an adult would. Many words start out for children as the names for specific objects rather than for general classes. A child may use *table* as the name for a particular object in his environment, without realising that it can also be applied to other objects (i.e. other tables). We will discuss some of the implications of the appearance of words in more detail directly.

Many words appear initially in directives; that is, in the expression of the 'want-object' function. Thus a child might use *teddy* first in a context in which he is clearly asking his mother to get his teddy for him; he might use *raf* (or *dap* or *daf*) in reaching out for a toy giraffe, which an adult is holding up. In other words, their appearance is part of a general tendency towards specification of meaning that has been under way for some time. It is a development which gradually frees the expression of meaning from context. Thus, during the period when requests for objects are expressed by complaining noises plus gestures, or even by such relatively arbitrary vocalisations as *na*, meaning is dependent on context in the sense that the object requested must be a salient feature of the environment, shared by speaker and addressee. The appearance of words makes it possible to focus attention on non-salient objects, even to request objects which may be in another location.

Before we follow the directive through to the next stage,

let us note in passing that the one-word directive is in contrast with one other major functional category at this point. Many one-word utterances are used to draw the addressee's attention to a particular object, without necessarily expressing a wish on the child's part to obtain the object. One typical manifestation of this is the infant's naming of pictures in a book which he is looking at with an adult. Generally, the child takes delight in interacting with others in relation to the environment. In other words the 'comment' function also arises out of the expressive function. The difference between the source of the directive function and the comment function is that the former arises principally out of the expression of dissatisfaction, whereas the latter arises principally out of the expression of pleasure. Both arise from the fusion of expressive meaning with referential meaning, as it develops through gesture into vocabulary. The contrast between the two functions may be marked at the one-word stage by intonation. Rising intonation in utterances like *teddy*, *raf* ('giraffe'), *lion*, *train* and so on typically means that the child wants the object in question; falling intonation is usually a comment by the child on the presence of a particular object (or picture of it) in the environment (see e.g. Halliday 1975: 46).

The similarity between the meanings being expressed by children at this stage and those that are expressed by such adult sentences as *I want the lion* and *that's a lion*, have led some observers to ask whether we should attribute to the child the ability to construct sentences (for discussion, see Dore 1975). For the moment we will simply note that the child's utterance can certainly be analysed as having a complex semantic structure and a complex formal structure. Semantically it consists of a referential meaning ('teddy', 'giraffe', 'lion' etc.) and a functional or 'force' meaning (directive). Formally it consists of a vocabulary item—*teddy*, *raf*—and an intonational element. There is a direct relationship between the level of meaning and the level of form in each case, in that the referential meaning is expressed by the vocabulary item and the functional meaning by the intonation. Note, however, that this is also true of earlier stages, where the referential meaning was expressed by gesture and the functional meaning by the character of the child's vocalisation. This observation would lead us to hesitate before attributing to the child the ability to construct sentences at the one-word stage. The point is that we would hardly want to do this at the earlier stage, and yet there is obviously a close similarity between the way in which the meaning is encoded into form at the two stages. The major advance consists in the development of words rather than in the development of sentence-like structures.

The next stage in the development of the directive is the final one which I will deal with here, since it takes us into grammar. In the previous stage the referential component of the meaning became 'lexicalised' (i.e. expressed in the form of a word). Now the functional component does so. The child begins to produce directives such as *have teddy*, *get book*, *want nana*, *more milk* and so on, in which words like *have*, *get*, *want*, *more* express the directive component of the request. The point about these words is that they have a much more restricted use in the child's utterances than they do in the adult language, and they therefore have a rather different meaning from their adult meaning. In adult sentences *have*, *get*, *want*, *more* can occur in statements such as *I have a teddy*, *you can get the teddy* and *he wants his teddy*. Children, however, tend to restrict their early use of these words to directive utterances. What we are seeing here is a manifestation of a very general process in child language, instances of which have occurred in the earlier discussion. There is a strong tendency, when a new form appears in a child's language, for it to express a meaning which was already present at an earlier stage but expressed differently (Werner and Kaplan 1963: 60; Slobin 1973: 185). The directive function, as we noted above, was typically expressed at the earlier stage by the intonation contour. Now it finds expression in such words as *have* and *get*. A similar example of this phenomenon was the appearance of words to take over referential meanings previously expressed by gestures.

This development, however, is not a mere substitution. As in the case of the lexicalisation of reference to objects, the lexicalisation of the reference to functional meanings can give rise to differentiation between meanings which it was not possible to distinguish at an earlier stage. For example, a child might use *have* as a general request for objects but *more* as a request for the continuation of actions which have temporarily ceased. Thus a child might say *have teddy* as a request that an adult give him teddy, but *more nana* or *more tickle* as a request that an adult should feed him with more banana or should continue a tickling game. Rather than seeing this as a differentiation between different kinds of directive, we should perhaps see it as a differentiation in the referential component. That is, a word like *have* combines the basic functional meaning of 'request' with a particular kind of referential meaning ('object'); *more*, on the other hand, combines the same functional meaning with a different kind of referential meaning ('action').

There are two important points here. The first is that the emergence of language is built on a prior semantic foundation—the child learns how to mean before the emergence of language, and language takes over many of the meanings expressed earlier in some other form. The second point is that this process is not, however, merely a take-over operation, since the nature of language is such that it provides for the elaboration and differentiation of meanings that are inexpressible in other forms. In this sense we can see the role of language as not merely that of following cognitive development but of elaborating and refining it.

Let us look back over this section with a brief summary. The infant's earliest behaviours are informative rather than communicative. They begin to become communicative as his understanding of some of the basic aspects of his environment develops, particularly as the kind of signals which he emits become differentiated. The earliest communicative meanings are expressive in character, relating principally to distress or pleasure. Increasing responsiveness to the environment leads to the fusion of these expressive signals with referential components, expressed chiefly through gaze and gesture. Primitive communicative acts that we can call proto-directives arise out of this fusion of expressive and referential elements. Gradually the vocal signals become more closely modelled on the adult language, leading eventually to the appearance of the first words. At this stage we can still clearly see in the character of the one-word utterance the trace of its origins. The functional expressive-directive meaning is expressed by the intonation contour and the referential meaning by the lexical element. These traces become more blurred as development proceeds into the two-word stage, since vocabulary items can now code either referential meaning or directive meaning or—more interestingly—a fusion of the two. By the two-word stage the child is well on the way to combining different kinds of meaning into a single utterance in a way which, as we saw in Chapter 1, is a crucial characteristic of the adult language.

THE DEVELOPMENT OF VOCABULARY

We noted in the preceding section that the appearance of words in the child's speech raises a number of new questions. If we set aside the small number of words which refer to specific objects in the world—the words traditionally called proper nouns—then the important point about words is that, unlike gestures, they refer to classes of objects rather than to specific objects. The word *cup* refers to a wide variety of objects of various shapes, sizes, colours, materials. The same is true of *door*, *tree*, *dog*, *cat*, *chair*, *table* or any other common noun. Now the majority of words which appear first in the infant's vocabulary are object-referring words. This, therefore, raises the following question: what kind of concepts does the infant have for each of these early referring words? Does each word start as the name for a specific object, so that the child is essentially using words in a fundamentally different way from the way in which the adult is using them? Or is the child's word a class-referring word from the outset? If this is the case, what is the relationship between the conceptual class which an adult associates with a particular word and the one which the child associates with it? Given the enormous discrepancy between the adult's experience of the world and of language and that of the child, the two can hardly be identical.

Research on child-language development has shown that both of the situations just described can apply in the vocabulary development of a particular child. Some words may start out as names of specific objects and then undergo a change in character, as the child realises that their semantic range is much broader. Other words, however, start out as class-referring words. This is an important point for two reasons. In the first place it shows that, at a very early stage, children have some concept of classes; they perceive that a certain range of phenomena in the world can be associated with each other because of the fact that they share certain characteristics which differentiate them as a group from other phenomena. That is, children do not perceive the world as a random assortment of kaleidoscopic impressions; rather, they are sensitive to certain patterns or structures in the world around them. The second point is that they already appear to understand that one of the key functions of language is to refer to the world in terms of these rather abstract structural patterns—that is, to group phenomena into classes in terms of shared features of one kind or another.

Having established that young children, like adults, use many of their early words to designate object-classes, one might suppose that the classes in question would tend to be smaller than those for which an adult uses them. For example, one might guess that since the adult clearly has a wider experience of the world (and of language) than the young child, he might associate with the word *dog* a much wider range of animals than does the young child. In one sense, this must be true. How can an 18-month-old child be aware of the range of animals—Alsatians, Dalmatians, collies, poodles, basset-hounds, boxers, and so on—to which adults would apply the word *dog*? Yet, in another sense the reverse is the case. What most children do in the early stages of language use is to apply the word *dog* not only to any particular dogs that they may encounter, including pictures of dogs, but also to cats, horses, cows, zebras and many other four-legged animals (or to pictures of them). In other words, the concept of 'dog' appears to be much broader for many children than it is for adults. This phenomenon, widely noted in the literature on child-language development, is called 'overextension'.

The phenomenon of overextension, although it is a very familiar one in child language, is not particularly easy to understand, and there are a number of ways in which it can be interpreted. The most obvious interpretation is that the child, having understood that words refer to classes of phenomena, has identified the wrong set of defining characteristics for, say, the word *dog*. He has taken something like the feature 'four-legged' to be the sole characteristic which defines the class of 'dogs'. This interpretation of overextension would suggest, then, that children start with very broad category concepts for many of their early words and that these broad categories become more precisely specified or narrowed-down as cognitive development and language development proceed.

Although there are undoubtedly some cases where this view of overextension is valid, there are indications that it does not cover all cases. One such piece of evidence is an observation made by Thomson and Chapman (1977). One of the children they studied used the word *dog* for pictures of a cat, a horse, a zebra as well as for a dog in his book. However, if he was asked to 'find the picture of the dog', he would consistently point to the correct picture—ignoring the cat, horse and zebra. Here we have a discrepancy between comprehension and production. The child appears to make differentiations in his understanding of language which he does not make in his own speech. (We will see in Chapter 6 that this holds true of certain aspects of phonological development.) But this does, of course, indicate that the child's concept of 'dog'—as it shows up in comprehension—is much closer to that of the adult than appeared to be the case at first sight.

One is then led to ask why the child uses *dog* to refer to animals which he knows are not exemplars of that concept. A number of possible explanations suggest themselves. It may be due to vocabulary limitations. Although he may know very well that the horse is not a dog, he may not yet have acquired the word *horse* and therefore uses a word from the same broad semantic area. This will be a familiar stratagem to anyone who has attempted to learn a foreign language—one often finds oneself having to use a word which one knows to be incorrect because of gaps in one's vocabulary. Another possibility is that the child, in applying *dog* to the picture of a horse or zebra, is simply saying that this animal is like a dog, not that it is one.

The question arising out of this discussion is: how is it possible for the young child to construct a concept for a word which appears in many cases to bear a close resemblance to that of the adult, given his restricted experience of the world and his restricted cognitive development? One plausible answer to this question is to be found in a set of ideas known as the theory of Natural Categories, associated with Eleanor Rosch and her colleagues (see e.g. Rosch and Mervis 1975; see also Clark and Clark 1977: 128–30 for general discussion).

In considering this theory, it will be useful to contrast it with some ideas concerning the relationship between language and reality put forward by the Swiss linguist, Ferdinand de Saussure. Saussure ([1916], 1974: 112) has written, 'Without language, thought is a vague, uncharted nebula. There are no pre-existing ideas and nothing is distinct before the existence of language'. Saussure had in mind that the world as we perceive it is essentially unstructured and that the particular language that we learn as our first language leads us to impose a conceptual framework on it. (This idea was developed independently by two American linguists, Benjamin Lee Whorf and Edward Sapir, as a result of their study of Amerindian languages; it is often referred to as the 'Whorf–Sapir hypothesis'—see e.g. Carroll 1971). Part of the evidence for this view has to do with the fact that there is often a discrepancy between the concept associated with a word in one language and that associated with the corresponding word in another language. An example of this would be the fact quoted in Chapter 1 that the range of hues to which we apply the word *yellow* in English does not correspond exactly to the range of hues to which the French apply the word *jaune*. Although there is a large area of overlap, *jaune* includes the colour of light-brown shoes—a hue which speakers of English assign to a different category: 'brown'. It was the existence of many examples of this kind which led Saussure to suggest that the world was essentially unstructured. In the case of the colour spectrum, it was argued that we have a continuum of hues from one end of the spectrum to the other and that language is free to impose its own set of categories on this continuum independently of the way in which other languages structure it. On this view, language is instrumental in shaping perceptual categorisation and thought. (For a different view of the colour spectrum, see Berlin and Kay 1969; the question is also discussed in Clark and Clark 1977: 524–7.)

The first point we should note here is that our description of the emergence of functional meanings such as the directive, as described in the preceding section, is not compatible with the Saussurian view. There it was argued that as language begins to make its appearance in the child, it takes over meanings that were expressed in another form at an earlier stage. Certain functional meanings are well established before the onset of language as such, so that it would be very misleading to say of this area that 'nothing is distinct before the appearance of language'. It is, however, clear from his examples that Saussure was thinking of referential meaning rather than functional meaning. Is the argument more valid in this area? Again we have to note that Saussure's point is not easy to reconcile with the observation made above that children appear to have a rather precise concept for many of the early words. Saussure's view would suggest that the world should begin to resolve itself into clearly identifiable categories only after considerable exposure to language. His position would in fact predict that children should formulate the kind of very broad categories for the early words that characterised our first interpretation of overextension—an interpretation which we then found to be simplistic.

The central question is: is the world as unstructured as Saussure claims? Let us consider this question in relation to the animal kingdom, particularly in relation to the kind of features (both perceptual and behavioural) which animals possess (or exhibit) and which play such an important part in the way that we classify them and label them in everyday language. Some animals are furry, others are feathered; some have wings, some don't; some have two legs, some have four; some bark, some sing; some mew, some growl; some are domesticated, some are wild; some have a beak, others have a snout and so on. Now let us suppose for a moment that we lived in a different world—a much more chaotic one—from the one that we actually inhabit. Let us suppose, in particular, that we lived in a world in which a rich variety of animals was to be found, exhibiting all the possible combinations of features just mentioned. One animal might be furry, have two legs, no wings, a snout, produce a mewing sound and be wild; another might be identical to this, except that it was feathered; another might be the same except that it had wings and barked—and so on. Now imagine how this situation might be reflected in the languages of the world. As we have seen, the referential words of a particular language denote classes rather than specific objects. Since every possible combination of features exists in this world, each language would be free to set up its own classes in its own way. One language might have a name for all the animals that had wings. Another might ignore this feature and set up as a major group all those animals that had snouts. Another might take the behavioural characteristic of growling as the defining feature of a major class. Children learning one of these languages would come to see the animal kingdom in terms of the structure of the language they had to learn and their perception of the world would therefore come to differ radically from that of children learning another language. Saussure's claim that 'there are no pre-existing ideas and nothing is distinct before the appearance of language' would apply very well to this situation.

Now, of course, the world in which we actually live is not at all like this. The crucial difference is that there are correlations between the features identified above. There is a correlation between the feature 'winged' and 'having two legs', in the sense that any creature which has the first property will also have the second (though not, of course, vice versa!). These two features correlate in turn with the feature 'feathered'. Other correlations exist between the behavioural feature 'emits a barking sound' and 'having a snout'—again the first entails the second, but not vice versa. Similarly, there are negative correlations—for example, between 'beaked' and 'emits a mewing sound'. No animal exhibits both characteristics. According to the theory of Natural Categories these positive and negative correlations constitute the structure of our world, and they hold for human perceptions of the animal kingdom in all cultures. This means that languages are not entirely free to structure the world in any way they choose—they are inevitably influenced by our perceptions of the pre-existing structures in the environment. As far as children are concerned, this means that, as their awareness of their environment develops over the first year of life, they are led to formulate conceptual categories based on these environmental structures without recourse to language. Even limited exposure to a restricted range of dogs, for example, will be enough to enable them to see that these animals are characterised by a certain cluster of features—particularly perceptual features concerning their general shape—which differentiate them from other animals. Children's perception of these clusters enables them to establish different categories before they acquire a name for each. This would explain how it is that a child can pick out the picture of a dog from one of a horse, a cow, a zebra and so on in response to the question *where is the dog*? at a stage where he does not distinguish between them in his own speech. It would suggest that the child tends to construct fairly precise categories and in some cases acquires a name for them considerably later.

We should take care not to overestimate the extent of a child's cognitive-linguistic development at a particular stage. Although the world is undoubtedly a less chaotic place than Saussure suggested, the structural relationships that do in fact hold leave a good deal of room for a variety of interpretations. It is for this reason that we get the kind of semantic discrepancies between languages referred to earlier. This means that, although many of the child's early concepts are more precisely categorised than one might suppose at first sight, there are undoubtedly many adjustments, extensions and refinements to be done before the concept comes into alignment with the adult one. Moreover, the nature of the world is such that categories are not discrete—there is often a great deal of fuzziness at the edges, where one category shades into the next. For example, there are many objects in the world which are situated in the borderline area between the concept 'cup' and the concept 'glass'. An experiment performed by Anderson (1975) shows some of the uncertainties that children of various ages experience here. Although there are certain objects which are consistently assigned to the category 'cup' or the category 'glass', even by young children, there are others which are assigned with much less consistency. Again, the theory of Natural Categories offers an explanation of why this is so. Given that our perception of the world indicates to us correlations between features of objects, which we use to establish conceptual classes, it turns out to be the case that not all objects exhibit the full set of correlations. For example, although there is a general (one-way) correlation between the feature 'made of glass' and 'not having a handle', which shows up in many objects, there are objects in the world that are made of glass but which also have a handle. We can therefore distinguish between the prototypical members of a particular category—those which exhibit a large number of the correlating features (in this case those which are both made of glass and don't have a handle)—and the non-prototypical (or peripheral) members of a category, which do not exhibit all the normally correlating features. The child cannot know in advance whether non-prototypical objects will, nevertheless, be assigned to the same class as the prototypical objects, or whether the language will have a different word for them. Given these indeterminacies in the structure of our world, it is inevitable that it will take some years for children to acquire anything like complete mastery over the referential structure of their native language.

THE DEVELOPMENT OF RELATIONAL MEANINGS

We now turn to the second major type of meaning discussed

in Chapter 1. How do relational meanings develop in child language? We noted earlier that the total meaning of most utterances involves both referential and relational meanings, the latter comprising such concepts as agent, patient, possession, location. Relational meanings, by definition, hold between two semantic entities; for example, between two objects or between an object and a process. It is for this reason that the presence of relational meanings in early child language does not become obvious until the two-word stage; that is the stage at which children explicitly express two referential meanings in a single utterance. If a child says *mummy eat*, while observing her mother eating lunch, or *teddy chair*, indicating her teddy sitting in a chair, then it seems reasonably clear that she is expressing not only referential meanings but also relational ones. That is, she seems to be conceptualising the first situation in terms of an agentive relationship holding between the object 'mummy' and the process 'eat' and the second situation in terms of a locative relationship holding between two objects, 'teddy' and 'chair'.

These claims are not in fact unproblematic. One might argue that although the child appears to see that there is some kind of association between the object and the process in *mummy eat* and the two objects in *teddy chair* (simply because she combines reference to them both in a single utterance), it does not necessarily follow that the perceived association is like the one which the adult sees here. There is obviously a possibility that we are foisting our own interpretation of the situation onto what the child says (Howe 1976). In order to clarify this question, we need to ask if there is any independent evidence for the view that the child sees the world in terms of such relational concepts as agent and location by the time that she produces utterances such as these. (Two-word utterances usually appear at about the age of 21 months.)

There is in fact evidence that children develop the concept of agent during the first year of their life. One of the areas in which it shows up is one we have discussed already—the development of directives. We have noted that even before the onset of language the child is able to express communicative meanings aimed at causing the addressee to perform certain actions. It is very difficult to identify precisely the point at which such directive meanings emerge out of the earlier expressive meanings, but the process certainly seems to be well under way by the age of 12 months. The point about directive meanings is that they request the addressee to act as agent with respect to some process. In many cases the clear intention is that this process should also impinge on some object, which suggests that the relational concept of 'patient' is also developing. Thus the child, in expressing directives, appears to demonstrate some understanding of the fact that animate beings are able to initiate processes, to act upon other objects and to bring about changes of state in the world. This is precisely what we mean by the relational concept 'agent'.

Let me consider some other examples of the way in which the child appears to demonstrate an understanding of the agent concept in early utterances. I will take these examples from Greenfield and Smith (1976: 108–10), although my interpretation of some of these utterances differs somewhat from that of the authors. One of the clearest examples they cite is an utterance produced by Matthew Greenfield at the age of 19 months. He had been trying unsuccessfully to cut his meat with a knife. He then handed the knife to his mother and said *mummy*! as a clear request that she should perform the task for him. It appears that he had conceptualised a potential situation in which his mother was cutting the meat, in contrast to the actual situation in which he was doing so (or trying to do so). In both cases there is a perception of an animate being as agent. A similar example occurred when Matthew was 20 months old. Matthew's older sister, Lauren, had said *let me do it*!; Matthew answered *mummy*!

The emergence of the agent concept can be seen in earlier utterances of Matthew. At the age of 13 months he is reported to have said *daddy*! upon hearing his father come in the outside door and start up the steps to the apartment. A similar example is reported for another child, Nicky, who produced the utterance *ma*! (his name for Matthew) on hearing the sound of Matthew crying outside. I interpret these early one-word utterances as being primarily referential in character, rather than relational. However, the point about them is that in order to be able to refer to the individuals concerned in each case, the child must have understood that the sounds in question were produced by these individuals; that is, he must again have conceptualised the whole situation in terms of an agentive relationship holding between an (animate) object and a process. One final example: at the age of 17 months Matthew, while watching a fish eating, produced the utterance (f)*ishy*, closely followed by the utterance *eat*. This is an obvious precursor to the two-word utterances, in which the concept of agent shows up more clearly.

The relational concept of location is also present in a covert rather than an overt way in the child's one-word utterances. Again, I will cite some examples from Greenfield and Smith (1976: 142–3). At the age of 18 months Nicky said *poo*, putting his hand on his bottom, while being changed. The interesting point about this example is that it was not a referential meaning in the ordinary sense, since there was in fact no 'poo' there at the time. What the utterance shows is that the child clearly understands that a particular phenomenon is associated with a particular location. He demonstrated similar understanding on many occasions at 19 months by going to the refrigerator and asking for various items of food: *apple*, *nana* (banana), *mil* (milk). A particularly interesting example was his utterance of the word *hat*, produced when he put a nappy on his head. The point here is that Nicky had a word *bap* for *nappy* (based on *diaper*), so that his choice of the word *hat* was clearly sensitive to the rather unusual location of the nappy on that occasion. Again there seems to be plenty of evidence here that the concept of location is well established at an early stage in the developmental process.

Clearly, one-word utterances are richer semantically than one might suppose at first sight. We have now identified three types of meaning which play a role in the child's one word utterance—functional meanings such as 'directive', 'comment'; referential meanings such as 'mummy', 'daddy', 'teddy', 'eat'; and relational meanings such as 'agent', 'patient', 'location'. We should, however, distinguish between those meanings which are explicitly encoded in the utterance and those which are implicit. The functional and referential meanings are explicitly encoded in such features of the utterance as the intonation contour (e.g. the use of a rising intonation for directives) and the word (which encodes referential meanings). Relational meanings are only rarely encoded explicitly in one-word utterances. (Exceptions include such utterances as *in*, *down*, which encode reference to processes involving strong locative features.) In the second year of life children clearly demonstrate their grasp of these concepts in terms of what they say in specific situations, but they are not yet at the stage of expressing them explicitly in linguistic form.

THE DEVELOPMENT OF THEMATIC MEANING

The idea that certain meanings are expressed only in a covert way in early child language also applies to the last kind of meaning to be discussed here: thematic meaning. This type of meaning, as we noted in the previous chapter, is concerned with the question of which elements of some proposition are 'given' and which are 'new'. Such adult utterances as

(1) It was John who read 'War and Peace'.
(2) It was 'War and Peace' that John read.

express the same propositional meaning, but they differ with respect to thematic meaning. In (1) the speaker assumes that the fact that someone read 'War and Peace' is given, in that it is already assumed by the addressee, and the new information is that this was John. In (2) the given element is that John read something, and the new information imparted by the speaker is the fact that this was 'War and Peace'.

Obviously, infants in the earliest stages of language development do not use such complex syntactic structures as *it was John who . . .* in order to present certain semantic elements as new. Nevertheless, thematic meaning does play a surprisingly important, though implicit, role in the early utterances. Factors of this kind are influential in determining which aspect of a situation a child will encode in language on a specific occasion. Consider, for example, what a child says when requesting an object and what he says when rejecting one that is offered. In the first situation the tendency is for the child to name the object; in the second situation the typical utterance is *no*. Note that these are not the only conceivable choices in each case. A child might indicate that he wants something by saying *want* or *me*. In some ways this is a rather simpler strategy than the one he actually adopts. Conversely, he could reject an object by naming it and turning away from it. The child's actual behaviour here appears to be determined by questions of focus; that is, by a distinction between elements of the situation that are given (and therefore out of focus) and those which are new (in focus). In the first situation the child has to bring the mother's attention to focus on a new object, perhaps to divert her attention from himself or from some other object with which they may have been playing. Therefore the object is named. In the second situation the addressee's attention is already attached to the object being offered and her attention has to be directed to the child's reaction. This is the new element in the situation, which he expresses by saying *no*.

One point that has been noted by a number of researchers is that the kind of utterance cited in the previous pages in which the child names an agent (e.g. Matthew's utterance of *mummy*! as a request that she cut the meat) is in fact relatively rare. This phenomenon can be explained in terms of questions of focus. In general, agents tend to be fairly stable elements in a particular situation. For example, when mother sits down to eat her lunch, she is likely to have been in the same surroundings as the child for some time, perhaps feeding him, changing him, then preparing her own meal. When she begins to eat, it is the process which is the new element in the situation rather than the mother herself. For this reason the child is much more likely to say *eat* than *mummy*. Similarly, if his father kicks the ball in the middle of a game, it is the process which is the new element in the situation, not the person, and the child is therefore much more likely to say *kick* than *daddy*. In some examples cited earlier, in which the child did refer to an agent, these were circumstances in which the child's attention came to be focussed on the agent as a new element in the situation. The noise of a door closing and footsteps on the stairs indicated the imminent arrival on the scene of the father. The same was true of the utterance *ma* in the context of the sound of the new arrival, Matthew, crying outside. And when Matthew handed the knife to his mother, saying *mummy*!, he was envisaging a situation in which his mother, rather than he, would cut up the meat. In this case the process was the given element, the agent new.

Thematic factors can also influence the ordering of the child's one-word utterances in dialogues with adults. For example, if a child sees someone throw a ball to the ground, then the whole event is a new development. The most salient element in the event is the object, so the child's first attention-directing comment is likely to be *ball*. An adult might respond *what happened to the ball*?. The child now says *down*—the object has been established as the given and the child now comments on the remaining new element.

The influence of thematic factors has been noted at later stages of the development process. Jeffrey Gruber has argued that many children organise their early sentences in terms of a topic-comment structure and that only later do such structures develop in English into subject–predicate structures (Gruber 1967). In other words, one element in the child's utterance has the function of referring to some aspect of the situation (often a salient person or object)—thereby identifying it as 'given'—and the other element constitutes a comment on that given element. The elements in question can occur in either order, with the 'topic' (given) either preceding the 'comment' (new), as in the examples in (3), or following it, as in (4):

(3) Mama goes.
Wheel in there.
Other wheel broke.
Motor in the car.

(4) In there wheels.
Break pumpkin.
There's the man.
Go in there train.

As in the case of relational meanings, thematic meaning does not occur overtly in the child's one-word utterances. Its role is a covert one, in that questions of focus play an important part in determining what the child says rather than the way in which he says it (Weisenburger 1976; Greenfield and Zukow 1978). However, by the time that the child is producing the kind of utterances cited by Gruber, it is beginning to be overtly expressed in the way that the child structures the utterance.

As we noted in Chapter 1, one of the main carriers (or 'exponents', to use a more technical term) of thematic meaning is intonation. We tend to place an intonation centre on those elements which we wish to place in focus (e.g. *JOHN did it*). This possibility becomes available to the child as he develops the ability to combine reference to several components of meaning in a single utterance. It is with the emergence of the two-word utterance that the option opens up for the child to place an intonation centre either on the first element or on the second: *MUMMY eat* or *mummy EAT*. However, the important point is that, although this is the first stage at which thematic meaning shows up explicitly in child language, its implicit presence can be discerned at the earlier stage.

CONCLUSION

In this chapter we have looked at the way in which the child begins to learn how to express meanings in the earliest stages of language development. The various kinds of meaning identified in Chapter 1 do not emerge simultaneously. The earliest meanings, perhaps not surprisingly, are expressive ones. The child discovers how to communicate feelings of pleasure, pain and interest to others, and since these feelings are in many cases oriented towards the environment, referential meanings also begin to emerge.

The combination of expressive and referential meanings leads to the emergence of certain primitive functional meanings such as directives. In the earliest stages these meanings have a very general character and are expressed through action and gesture. The emergence of language, however, allows many of them to be elaborated and refined. The child begins to be able to refer to objects and object categories, to direct the actions of others with respect to these objects and thereby to understand how objects and people relate to each other in the world around him. Certain types of meaning—particularly functional and referential meanings—appear explicitly in the language of the young child at the one-word stage. Others are implicit. Relational and thematic meanings clearly play a role in determining what the child says in specific situations, but the linguistic means for expressing these meanings (e.g. word-ordering and contrastive stress) will not become available until the two-word stage or later. In general, the role of cognitive development as a precursor to and foundation for language development is crucial. There are many ways in which an understanding of concepts is present in the child but where such understanding is exhibited only indirectly in the language produced by the child. In subsequent chapters we will see other manifestations of this kind of discrepancy between a rather limited linguistic output at a particular stage and a richer underlying system.

3 Grammar

THE STRUCTURAL APPROACH

We turn now to the task of describing the system which acts as the vehicle for the encoding of meaning: grammar. How are the grammatical systems of individual languages structured, and what is the nature of the connection between grammatical categories and semantic categories?

Traditional approaches to language are based on the idea that there is a rather straightforward connection between grammar and semantics. Those of us who were taught traditional grammar at school were strongly influenced by this idea. It shows up most clearly in such statements as the following, which are typical of many traditional school grammars:

— A noun is the name of a person, place or thing.
— A verb is a doing word.
— A declarative sentence is one which expresses a statement.
— An interrogative sentence is one which expresses a question.

Here we see that various grammatical categories such as 'noun' and 'verb' and 'declarative sentence' and 'interrogative sentence' are defined in terms of their relationship to semantic categories such as 'object' and 'action' (referential categories), or 'statement' and 'question' (functional categories). A major assumption of the traditional framework is that there is a direct relationship between grammar (where concepts like 'noun', 'declarative sentence' belong) and meaning. We will see that there is indeed some truth in this claim. The relationship is, however, more indirect than the traditional approach suggests.

The first point that we should make about grammatical categories is that most speakers of a language have some feeling or intuition for many of them, particularly for word classes. Suppose that we gave the following list of words to some native speakers of English and asked them to group the words into classes:

tree contain idea in admire see
know courage near under on desk

Most native speakers would group them as follows:

class I *tree idea courage desk*
class II *contain admire see know*
class III *in near under on*

If they have studied traditional grammar at school, they will call the first class 'nouns', the second class 'verbs', and the third class 'prepositions', but in a sense the labels are irrelevant. The important point is that native speakers have certain intuitions about how individual words belong together in classes.

Now, as far as the relationship between grammar and semantics is concerned, the interesting point is that these intuitions are not easy to reconcile with the claim that word classes are based on semantic categories. If we consider the four words grouped in class I (*tree*, *idea*, *courage*, *desk*) only two—*tree* and *desk*—belong to the same semantic category, that of physical objects. The other two words—*idea* and *courage*—are much more difficult to describe semantically. An 'idea' is a rather abstract state of affairs or event in the mind; 'courage' is a personal characteristic or attribute. To a school-child who has been taught that nouns are the names of persons, places or things, the suggestion that *idea* and *courage* are nouns may come as something of a surprise.

A similar point can be made about Class II (*contain*, *admire*, *see*, *know*), which also seems to constitute a rather motley collection from the semantic point of view. *Contain* represents a specific kind of spatial relationship, *admire* denotes an aesthetic or emotional attitude, *see* represents a perceptual experience and *know* a cognitive state. Again the child might be surprised to be told that these are all verbs and that verbs are 'doing' words. It is far from obvious that anything is being 'done' in such sentences as *this box contains tobacco* or *I admire Harry*. Class III (*in*, *near*, *under*, *on*) does seem to be the most homogeneous group from the semantic point of view, in that the words are all used to specify the spatial relationship obtaining between two objects in such sentences as:

(1) The cat is in the box.
The cat is near the box.
The cat is under the box.
The cat is on the box.

This apparent semantic homogeneity does not, however, extend to all members of the class. Prepositions such as *of* and *for* do not tend to express spatial relationships and there are sentences, such as those in (2), where even *in*, *near*, *under* and *on* do not obviously do so.

(2) Fred is in a hurry.
Fred is in a good mood.
Mary is near exhaustion.
Mary is near tears.
Sue is under the wrong impression.
Sue is under treatment.
Alice is on the committee.
Alice is on form.

It seems, then, that the intuitions which native speakers have about word-class membership are not based on the criteria that traditional approaches suggest. Everybody is quite confident that *contain*, *admire*, *see*, *know* all belong to the same category, but this confidence cannot be based on some shared characteristics of meaning. How, then, can it be explained?

Some linguists first became explicitly aware of the problems involved in basing grammatical categories on meaning in the early years of this century, when they began work on the description of 'exotic' languages such as Amerindian languages. One of the things they noticed was that in many of these languages the words for such concepts as 'storm', 'lightning', 'thunderbolt' and many other natural phenomena were treated more like words which denoted processes than words which denoted objects. For example, many of these languages have a suffix—a grammatical element attached to the end of words—to express the idea that a particular process is just beginning. It can be attached, typically, to the words for 'run', 'walk', 'sleep', and so on, in order to express such propositions as 'he is beginning to run', 'we began to walk', 'they began to sleep'. Now linguists noticed that this suffix could also be attached to the word for 'storm', for example, to produce a sentence which might be glossed as 'it is beginning to storm' (i.e. 'the storm is just breaking'). This, in fact, was only one of many properties which words denoting concepts like 'storm' and 'lightning' shared with words denoting processes such as 'run' and 'walk', which linguists obviously thought of as verbs. Moreover, these words did not share any features with those which denoted physical objects. In English the word *storm* shares with the word *tree* the property that it can be made plural by adding the suffix *-s*: *two trees*, *two storms*. However, in the Amerindian languages, there were no such parallels with the physical-object words. These observations led to the conclusion that the words denoting concepts such as 'storm', 'lightning' and so on should be assigned to the same word class as those denoting processes such as 'run', 'walk', 'sleep' in these cases. Using the traditional terminology, they were verbs rather than nouns.

In itself this is, of course, a rather small decision. It is, however, just one example of a wide range of observations which have led to a rethinking of our whole approach to grammatical analysis. Within this century we have seen the emergence of a new type of linguistics, known as 'structural linguistics', which has a very different theoretical and methodological basis from traditional grammar. (The term 'structural linguistics' is intended to have a very general sense here—the 'sense in which particular emphasis is given to the internal combinatorial and contrastive relations within a language system' [Lyons 1981: 220]; see Huddleston

1984, Ch. 2, for a detailed exposition of the principles of structural linguistics in this sense.)

The point about the example discussed above is that it raises the general question of what principles should apply to the process of word classification. This is fundamental to any kind of grammatical analysis. The traditional approach, as we have noted, was based on the concept of shared characteristics of meaning. If this is the principle to be adopted, it is very surprising that we should have to assign the word for 'storm' to the noun class in English but to the verb class in some other language, since it denotes the same concept (roughly) in each case. Once this question had been identified, it then became clear that even in English the correspondence between grammar and semantics in this area was highly problematic. That is, linguists became aware of the kind of difficulty mentioned above in the context of such odd semantic groupings as *contain*, *admire*, *see*, *know*. They then realised that, in assigning a word like 'storm' to the verb class in an Amerindian language, they were in fact using a new principle, not explicitly recognised up to that point. They were assigning words to the same class, if they shared not similar semantic features but similar grammatical (or 'formal') properties. That is, two words were put in the same class if they could, for example, take the same kind of inflection. In these languages, the word for 'storm' was assigned to the same class as the words for 'run' and 'walk', because all these words could be inflected with the so-called 'inchoative' suffix (the one which expresses the idea that a process is beginning). In English *storm* is assigned to the same class as *tree*, partly because it can, for example, be inflected with the *-s* suffix, indicating plurality. This observation was only a beginning. In some ways it posed new problems. For example, although it accounts for the fact that native speakers all intuitively assign *storm*, *tree*, *idea* and *desk* to the same class, because they all inflect for plurality (*storms*, *trees*, *ideas*, *desks*), it does not explain why *courage* and *lightning*, neither of which has a plural form (**courages*, **lightnings*), are also felt to belong in that class. (Following general practice we will use the asterisk notation [*] to indicate that the form in question is ungrammatical.) The development of structural linguistics has been concerned with the resolution of this and related problems, and with the elaboration and refinement of its general methodology. The result of this work has been the development of a much more coherent framework for the description of the grammars of languages than was previously available. This in turn has given us a deeper understanding of how language works and has led to the opening up of a whole host of new avenues of enquiry.

Let us now take our preliminary discussion of word classification a step further in order to illustrate the central role of the concept in grammar and its interaction with grammatical processes in general. One of the discoveries which structural linguists made at a relatively early stage in their work strengthened their view concerning the relative independence of grammar from semantics. This was that it was possible to make a certain amount of progress in the analysis of grammatical systems without any recourse to semantics whatsoever. Let us take an illustrative example. We will imagine that, as newly trained linguists, we have been sent into the field in order to carry out a study of some exotic language not so far described by linguistic science. We might begin by recording and transcribing some of the utterances produced by native speakers. Having spent a few days in the field, we decide to begin some analysis. On looking at our materials, we find that the following utterances occur as part of our data:

(3) nogsigdem
(4) nogsigtin
(5) gilsigtin
(6) nogsigob
(7) gilsige
(8) gilsigdem
(9) nogsige
(10) udsigdem

The examples are in fact based on a language called Kharia, spoken in Bihar, India (Lehmann and Pflueger 1976: 76).

Now, without knowing anything about the meaning of these utterances, we can begin to make a few reasonable guesses as to how this language works. The first thing that we notice is that various utterances can be paired with each other in such a way that the members of each pair have certain elements in common but also differ with respect to other elements. The following examples constitute one such pair:

(3) nogsigdem
(4) nogsigtin

Here we have a sequence *nogsig* common to both utterances. It is followed by *dem* in the first example and by *tin* in the second. It would be a reasonable working hypothesis (we will have to modify it slightly in a moment) that each of these utterances is a two-word sentence; that is, that *nogsig*, *dem*, and *tin* are words in this language. When we notice that the utterance *nogsigob* also occurs in our materials, we can tentatively add a third word—*ob*—to our list. Examination of other pairs leads us to revise and elaborate this description. Consider (3) and (8):

(3) nogsigdem
(8) gilsigdem

We have already analysed the first utterance into two components: *nogsig* and *dem*. Now *nogsig* and *gilsig* also contain a common element *sig* which is preceded in (3) by *nog* and in (8) by *gil*. If we follow the same procedure as before, we are led to consider the possibility that, in these examples too, we have two separate units, *nog* and *sig* in one case, *gil* and *sig* in the other. We cannot of course, yet know whether this analysis is correct, but it would certainly make sense. It has led us to the conclusion that the following are words in this language: *nog*, *gil*, *sig*, *dem*, *tin*, *ob*.

An examination of the other forms would lead us to add one or two other words. For instance, the utterance at item (9)—*nogsige*—looks like a concatenation of the words *nog*, *sig* and a new word *e*. Example (10)—*udsigdem*—suggests a new word, *ud*, followed here by the now familiar items *sig* and *dem*. (Some of these 'words' may, of course, turn out to be other kinds of grammatical element such as prefixes or suffixes, but this does not affect the general argument.)

This is clearly as much as we can do here with this restricted range of data, as far as the identification of potential word-like units is concerned. We can, however, pursue the grammatical analysis a little further. Having identified the 'words' *nog*, *gil*, *ud*, *sig*, *dem*, *tin*, *ob*, *e*, we can now say something about their position in sentences in Kharia. The words *nog*, *gil*, *ud*, for example, always appear to occur in the position preceding the word *sig* rather than in the position following it. This latter position is occupied by the words *dem*, *tin*, *ob*, *e*. These observations would suggest a description of these sentences in the following terms:

(11) (a) The words *nog*, *gil*, *ud* all belong in one class: (class I).
(b) The word *sig* belongs in a different class: (class II).
(c) The words *dem*, *tin*, *ob*, *e* all belong together in a third class: (class III).
(d) Some sentences in this language consist of a class I word, followed by a class II word, followed by a class III word.

This particular description may, of course, turn out to be wrong in one or more respects, when we see more of the language. Let us assume for the moment, however, that it is correct. We have taken a considerable step forward here. We have moved from a collection of particular sentences to the formulation of a general scheme for constructing sentences in this language. We will call this set of rules a preliminary 'grammar' of the language.

There are now a number of important points to be made about this grammar. The first is that we have adopted here what looks at first sight to be a rather different principle of word classification from the one indicated earlier. The discussion of the word for 'storm' in some Amerindian languages led to the conclusion that words should be assigned to the same class, if they take the same inflections (e.g. the inchoative suffix in these languages or the plural *-s* suffix in English). Here, however, we have assigned words to the same class if they occupy the same position in sentences. The words *nog*, *gil*, *ud* have all been assigned to the same class because they all occur in the position preceding the word *sig* in the data and because this makes it possible to formulate statements like (11), which describe how sentences are constructed. Do we now, therefore, have two different principles of word classification in structural linguistics?

In fact, we do not. The apparent conflict here disappears once we realise that one important property of grammatical systems in general is that words which occur in the same positions in sentences tend to take the same set of inflections. Consider, for example, the words *tree*, *idea*, *table*, which we earlier allocated to the same class on the basis of the fact that they can all be inflected with *-s* for plurality. If we now consider a sentence frame such as:

(12) The ------- was good.

we may note that any of these words can be inserted into this frame in order to give a well-formed sentence of English. Again they differ from a word like *contain* in this respect, since there is no well-formed sentence in English: **the contain was good*.

As far as word classification is concerned, then, we can say that the general principle operating in structural linguistics is that words are assigned to the same class if they share a number of formal properties, including their position in sentence frames. Words which occupy the same position in such frames are said to have the same 'distribution'. The principle of assigning words to the same class, if they have the same distribution, is known as the 'distributional principle'. It is obviously a very different principle from the one which operates in traditional grammar, where words are generally classified according to their meaning.

The contrast between the two principles was made very clear to me recently, when I received a telephone call from an irate mother concerning the way in which one of her son's grammar exercises had been marked at school. The sentence in question was *the fighting was fierce*. The boy had classified *fighting* as a noun in this sentence and *fierce* as an adjective. The teacher had marked these answers as wrong. For him *fighting* was a verb and *fierce* an adverb (since it described the 'verb' *fighting*). What we have here is a clash between the two principles of word classification discussed above. The teacher, in claiming that *fighting* is a verb, is applying rigorously the key principle of traditional grammar—that words are assigned to classes on the basis of their meaning. *Fighting* is clearly a 'doing' word here, hence it must be a verb. The interesting point is that the boy and his mother were quite convinced that the teacher was wrong, although they could not say why. They are in fact intuitively applying the distributional principle of structural linguistics. Thus, if we consider the sentence frame:

(13) The ------ was fierce.

the kind of words that can be inserted into this slot are words like *lion*, *tiger*, *animal*, *dog* and so on; that is, words that everybody agrees to call nouns. Verbs such as *like*, *see*, *know*, *contain* do not occur in this slot. The distributional principle therefore assigns *fighting* to the noun class here. This incident suggests that the formal approach adopted by structural linguists provides a much more satisfactory explanation for the intuitions of native speakers concerning word-class membership than does the 'notional' approach of traditional grammar. As it happens, there are indications that even traditional grammarians implicitly used formal criteria. Most would unhesitatingly have assigned *fighting* to the noun class in this example, without realising that it was a counter-example to the general principle which they claimed to be using. For school-children struggling to master grammar, these inconsistencies in the traditional approach must be extremely confusing. They have no doubt contributed to the decline in the teaching of grammar in schools.

There is in fact one area in which semantics still has a part to play in word classification. Let us return for a moment to our data from Kharia, in order to illustrate this point. In our analysis we were able to go a long way without any reference to semantics whatsoever. We still do not know what sentences (3) to (10) mean, but we have nevertheless managed to set up three word classes and construct a description of how these word classes are combined in well-formed sentences. Note, however, that we have not yet been able to apply names such as 'noun', 'verb', 'adjective' to any of these classes in our statements at (11) above.

This is where semantics has a contribution to make. The general situation that we find, when applying the structural principle of word classification, is that many of the members of a particular formal category also share important semantic properties. In English, for example, we find that among the words *tree*, *idea*, *table*, *train*, *shed*, *thought*, *wall*, and many others that have to be assigned to the same class because of shared formal properties, there is a large subset of words denoting physical objects. This subset includes the words *tree*, *table*, *train*, *shed*, *wall* but excludes the words *idea* and *thought*. The same is true of other languages. When we come to look at the meanings of the words in the class to which *nog*, *gil* and *ud* belong in Kharia, we may find that many of them refer to physical objects. In that case we would wish to capture the fact that there is a relationship between the formal class *tree*, *idea*, *table*, and so on, in English and the formal class *nog*, *sig*, *ud*, and so on, in Kharia, in that both classes contain a large number of words denoting physical objects. The obvious way to do this is to give the same name to both classes, and the most obvious name which suggests itself is 'noun'. In other words, in structural linguistics nouns are a class of words in a particular language, established on the basis of shared distributional and inflectional characteristics in that language and containing a large number of object-denoting words. This is quite different from the principle in traditional grammar that a word has to name a person, place or thing in order to be a noun. In traditional approaches, semantics was thought to play the key role in determining whether such and such a word was a noun. In structural linguistics its contribution is limited to the question of which name is to be allocated to a particular formally defined class in some language (for discussion, see Huddleston 1984: 74–6).

The kind of considerations relevant to the question of which class of words is to be called the noun class also apply to the verb class. Again we will find that one important formal class of words will contain a large subset of members denoting processes. In English, words like *walk*, *run*, *sing*, *contain*, *kick*, *hope* share important formal characteristics. They can all be inflected for tense, for example, and they all take an *-ing* suffix. Many of them, though not all, also share the semantic property of denoting actions or processes. It therefore makes sense to call this class the 'verb' class. Thus in structural linguistics a word need not possess any particular semantic characteristic to be a verb and, in particular, it does not have to denote an action. On the other hand, it does have to possess the important formal properties of the class which contains a large number of words denoting actions or processes.

There is one final point to be made here about word-class membership, since it connects with the discussion of grammatical development in the next chapter. We have noted that word classes are set up on the basis of shared formal characteristics. Thus some typical properties of nouns in English are that they can occur in a plural form with a *-s* inflection, they can take a possessive suffix (represented by *'s* in the written language, e.g. *the tree's trunk*), they combine with words such as *the* and *a* to form a 'noun phrase' (a concept to be illustrated in the following section) and so on. Many of them also have the semantic property of denoting physical objects. Now, we have already noted that not all nouns possess this last characteristic. It also turns out to be the case that not all nouns possess all of the formal characteristics either. The word *lightning*, for example, does not take a plural suffix (**the lightnings were terrible*). It does, however, possess the other formal properties mentioned above—it takes a possessive suffix (*the lightning's effect was devastating*), and it does combine with *the* to form a noun phrase (*the lightning*). The word *courage* does not naturally take a plural suffix, nor does it take a possessive suffix (**her courage's effect was remarkable*), but the fact that it combines with *the* to form a noun phrase is sufficient to make it a noun. What these observations mean is that we have to distinguish between central (or 'prototypical') members of the noun class, and non-central (or 'peripheral') members. Thus a word like *tree* is a central member, since it possesses all the formal and semantic characteristics of nouns. It takes plural and possessive inflections, combines with *the* in a noun phrase and denotes a physical object. *Idea* is a less central member, since it does not possess the last characteristic. *Courage* is a peripheral member (but still a noun), since it possesses only one of the defining characteristics discussed. (For a more complete description of the properties of nouns see Huddleston 1984, Ch. 6.) One further criticism that can be levelled against traditional grammar (and incidentally also against early work in structural linguistics) is that it did not recognise that word-class membership is a 'gradient' phenomenon; that is, whereas all nouns are nouns, some are more 'nouny' than others.

GENERATIVE GRAMMAR

One important outgrowth of structural linguistics has been a theory of language called generative grammar, associated primarily with the name of Noam Chomsky, Professor of Linguistics at the Massachussetts Institute of Technology. In 1957 Chomsky published a book called *Syntactic Structures*, which established the foundations of this new approach to the analysis of language. The theory has had an enormous influence in the last few decades on many areas of academic enquiry, particularly philosophy and psychology. It is highly relevant to our concerns here firstly because of its central importance in linguistics in general and secondly because of the role it has played in the development of studies in child language.

Chomsky's work is founded on the achievements of structural linguistics in developing a systematic methodology for the description of the grammatical systems of languages. In order to illustrate some of the central characteristics of Chomsky's work, we will begin by referring back to the fragmentary grammar of Kharia (see p. 53). There we noted that it was possible to arrive at grammatical descriptions such as the following, purely on the basis of an examination of the forms of a particular language, without reference to meaning.

(14) The words *nog*, *gil* and *ud* all belong in one class: class I.
(15) The word *sig* belongs in a different class: class II.
(16) The words *dem*, *tin*, *ob* and *e* all belong together in a third class: class III.
(17) Some sentences in this language consist of a class I word, followed by a class II word, followed by a class III word.

The Chomskyan approach begins by noting that fragmentary grammars of this kind can be more elegantly expressed by using a more formal notation. For example, statement (17) can be expressed in the form of a 'rule', as follows:

(18) S → I + II + III

Here the symbol S stands for 'sentence'; the arrow, →, means 'consists of'; the symbols I, II, III represent the word classes; + represents sequential ordering. This rule, therefore, is simply a slightly different way of expressing (17) above. Statements (14), (15) and (16) can be recast as follows:

(19) I → {*nog*, *gil*, *ud*}
(20) II → *sig*
(21) III → {*dem*, *tin*, *ob*, *e*}

(The symbol { } encloses the members of a particular word class.) We have a distinction here between two rather different types of rule—a grammatical or syntactic rule at (18), which describes how word classes combine to form sentences, and a set of lexical rules at (19), (20) and (21), which specify the members of each class. It is conventional to state the syntactic rules before the lexical rules.

The first thing we note when we express grammatical rules in this formal way, is that grammars of this kind are 'generative'. This technical term needs some explanation. One way of looking at rule (18) is to note that it 'specifies' or 'generates' the following structure:

(22)

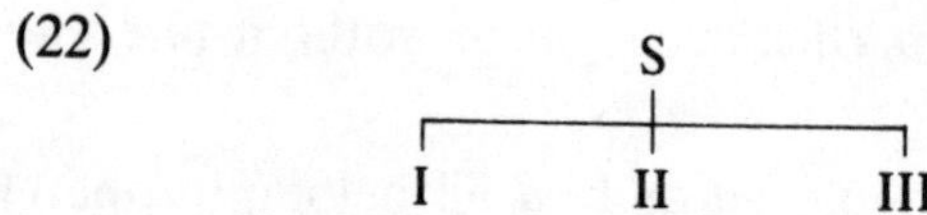

This in fact is the only structure which it does generate. There are other conceivable structures such as (23) and (24), which it does not generate:

(23) (24)

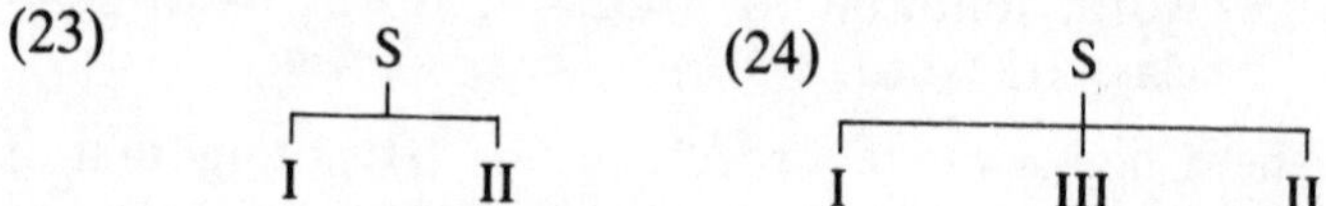

It does not generate (23) since, as it stands at the moment, the rule states that a class-I element is always followed by a class-II element and that this in turn is always followed by a class-III element. All of these items are essential or obligatory elements of a sentence, according to (18). It does not generate (24), because the elements are not in the order specified by the rule.

Now the lexical rules allow the structure (22) to be elaborated in a number of ways. Rule (19), for example, is interpreted to mean that either *nog*, *gil* or *ud* can be inserted in the structure under the 'node' I. One possible elaboration, therefore, is:

(25)

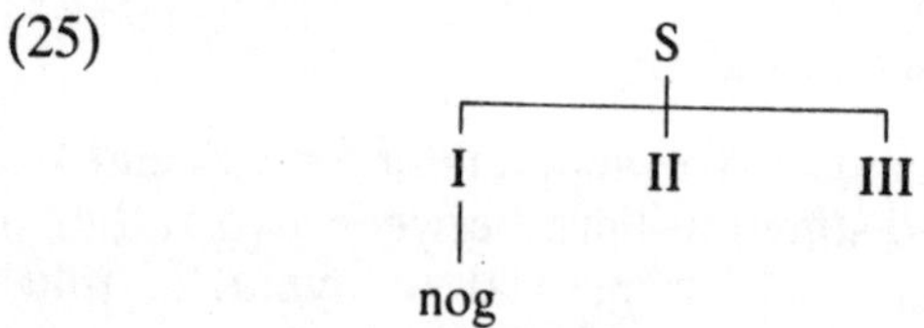

Rule (20) further elaborates this structure, allowing only one possible choice under II:

(26)

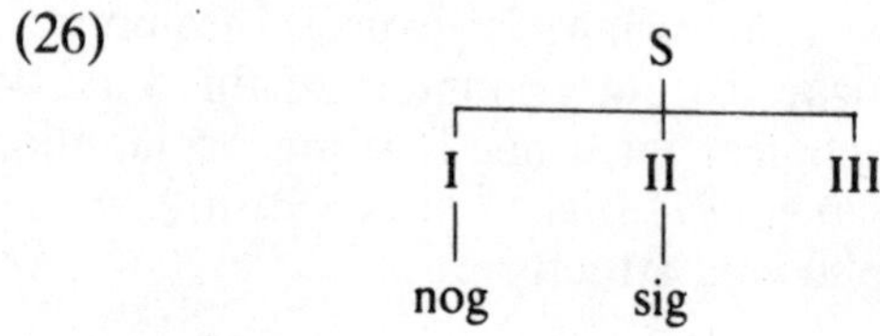

Finally rule (21) allows any of *dem*, *tin*, *ob* or *e* to be inserted under III, giving (27) as one possibility:

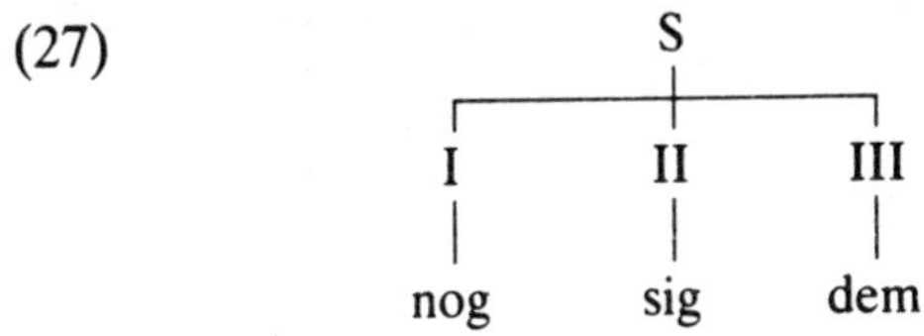

Thus a grammar which consists of rules (18), (19), (20), (21) can be said to generate the sentence *nog-sig-dem*, amongst others.

We can discover the full set of sentences generated by a particular grammar by making a number of 'passes' through the rules, until all the various combinatorial possibilities have been exhausted. Thus, if we choose the word *tin* on a second pass through the rules instead of *dem* in rule (21), we will end up with structure (28):

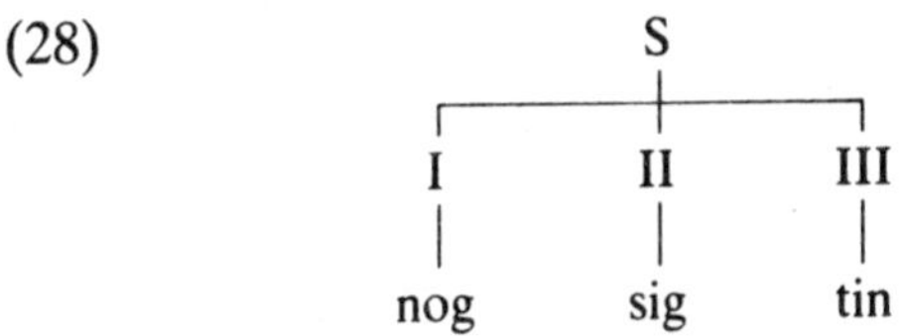

Other sentences in our original data such as *gil-sig-tin*, *nog-sig-ob*, *gil-sig-e* are also generated by the rules—a point which can easily be verified by making further passes through them.

In performing this exercise, however, we may also note that sentences are generated which are not in our original sample. For example, if on one pass we choose *ud* in rule (19) and *ob* in rule (21), then we obtain the following structure:

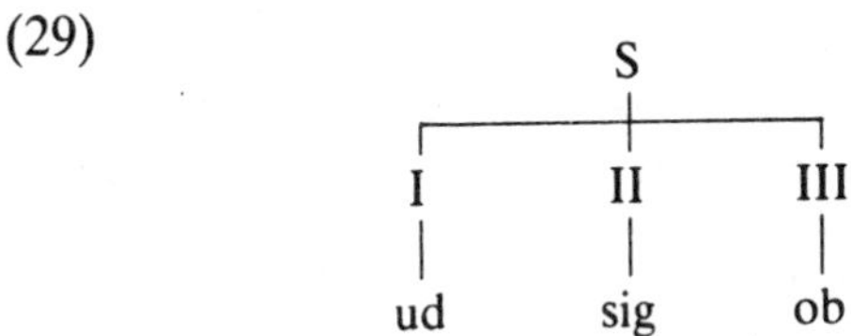

What this means is that our grammar makes a prediction: namely, that *ud-sig-ob* is a grammatical sentence in the language, even though it did not appear in our original list of utterances, (3) to (10). This prediction can now be tested by referring back to native speakers. They will either accept it as a well-formed sentence, in which case our grammar is confirmed, or they will reject it. If this happens, the grammar needs to be revised.

One of the attractions of the Chomskyan approach for many was that it brought into linguistics the same kind of methodology that is used generally in other scientific disciplines. The procedure we have just followed involves the following stages, all of which are familiar to scientists:

1. Observation of phenomena—in this case collecting well-formed sentences such as (3) to (10).
2. Setting up a hypothesis to explain these phenomena in the form of a law or set of laws (a theory) which generates them—in this case the grammar consisting of rules (18), (19), (20), (21).
3. Testing the validity of the theory beyond the data for which it was originally set up.

This concept of verifiability was not a characteristic of traditional grammars.

There is, however, a more important reason why Chomsky's approach to linguistic analysis was of considerable interest to many working outside the field of linguistics as such. The point here is that there is an important psychological dimension to his work. In adopting the concept of a generative grammar, Chomsky has moved away from the traditional approach in which grammar is used as a tool for the analysis of sentences. In that approach one takes a sentence such as *I saw the cat in the garden* and one breaks it down into its constituent units: subject, predicate, object, pronoun, verb, article, noun, preposition and so on. The exercise is simply a descriptive or analytic one, and it remains within the confines of linguistic analysis. The introduction of the concept of generative grammar, however, opens up new horizons. In this approach the linguist is concerned not so much with the process of analysing sentences but in discovering the grammatical rules according to which sentences are constructed in the language. Moreover, when we talk about the 'rules of the language', we are in fact talking about a psychological entity. We are referring to a system which must in some sense be in the mind of the native speaker. It is the concept of a grammar as a psychological phenomenon which in recent years has made linguistics an important focus of interest for psychologists, educationalists, anthropologists, sociologists, philosophers and others working in related disciplines.

Let me pursue this idea a little further. The system of rules in our minds, which enables us to produce (and understand) sentences in our native language, is a system which we construct during the process of language development. Most of this system takes shape over the first few years of life. Children construct it on the basis of exposure to language, without any explicit instruction as to how to do it and without being told anything about the nature of the system. The extraordinary complexity of the system, the relatively short time in which most of it is laid down and the apparent ease with which very young children realise this achievement suggested to Chomsky that the task of grammar construction is facilitated by some innate 'knowledge' of how grammatical systems of languages work. Although this is still a controversial claim, it is one that has had a major impact in recent years in a number of fields.

A good deal of Chomsky's argument rests on the claim that grammatical systems are complex in nature, and I will try to give some indication in the rest of this chapter of the nature of this complexity. The first question which needs to be answered is: how can we go about the task of identifying the rules which constitute the native speaker's mental grammar? How are we to describe this system? Chomsky proposed that the way to do this was to attempt to construct an explicit system of rules which, ideally, would generate all and only the sentences of the language; that is, one which would generate every grammatically well-formed combination of words but which would not generate any grammatically ill-formed combinations.

Let us take an example from English to illustrate this

point. If we consider the words *man*, *the*, *bus*, *a*, *cat*, *stopped*, there are only a small number of ways in which words from this set can be combined to constitute a well-formed sentence of English. We can combine *the* or *a* with *man* or *bus* and then combine that sequence with *stopped* to give sentences such as:

(30) The man stopped.
(31) The bus stopped.
(32) A man stopped.
(33) A bus stopped.

We cannot, however, combine *man* with *bus* and then with *the* as follows:

(34) *Man bus the.

(34) is not a well-formed sentence of English, and there are, of course, many other ill-formed combinations; for example:

(35) *Man the stopped.
(36) *A stopped the.
(37) *Bus the a.

A system of rules which would generate all the well-formed combinations here but not generate any ill-formed combinations might look somewhat as follows:

(38) S → Art + N + V
Art → {a, the}
N → {man, bus}
V → stopped

In order to check the validity of this grammar, we can make a number of passes through the system to see what kind of sequences it generates. The first rule generates the following structure:

(39)

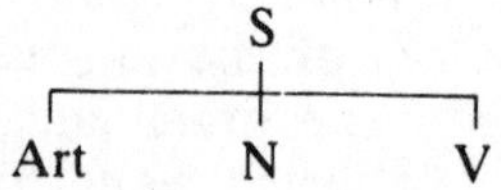

S
Art N V

The second rule allows us to insert either *a* or *the* under Art (an abbreviation for 'article'). Thus for example:

(40)

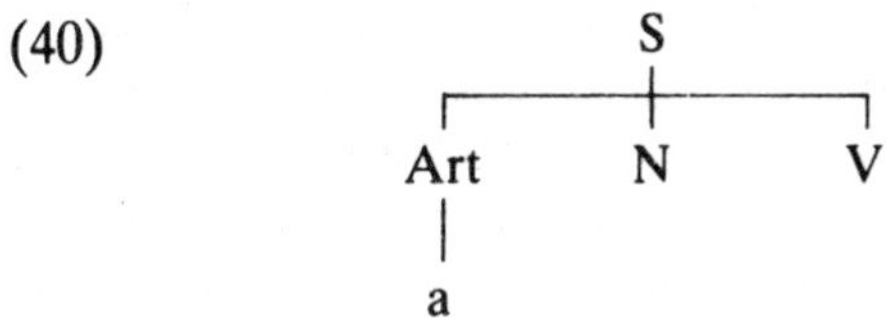

The third rule allows for either *man* or *bus* under N; for example:

(41)

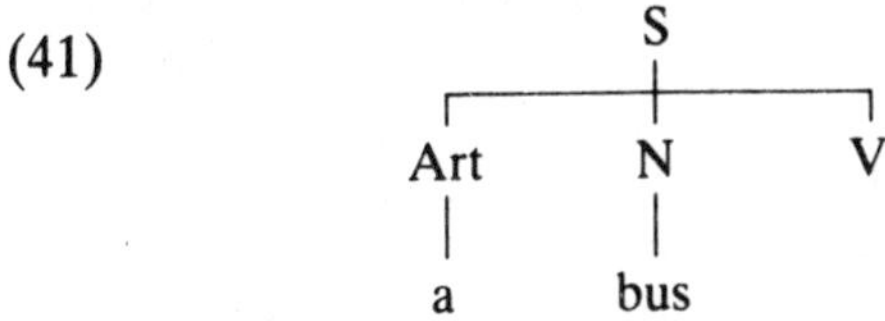

and the fourth rule specifies that *stopped* is to be inserted under V:

(42)

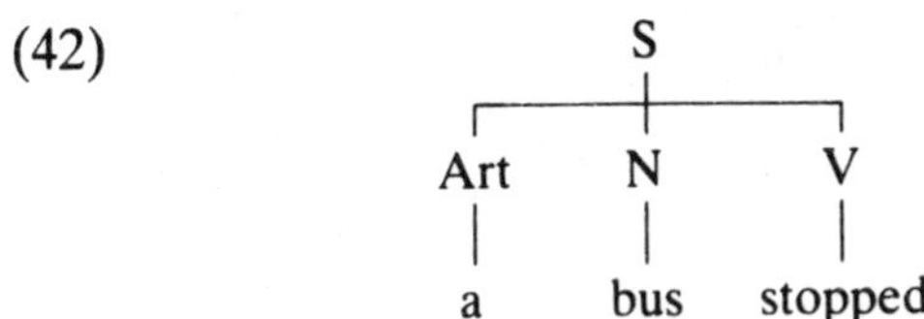

This completes a 'pass' through the system, so that we can say that the grammar generates the sentence *a bus stopped*. Other passes will give us sentences such as *the bus stopped*, *the man stopped*, *a man stopped* but there is no way in which we can get **man bus the*, **man the stopped* or any of the other ill-formed combinations. To the extent that the grammar corresponds to the judgements which native speakers make here, it can be said to be a reasonably satisfactory grammar for this tiny area of English.

One interesting feature of the generative approach to linguistic analysis is that it establishes a certain parallel between the linguist and the child, which was not true of earlier approaches. Just as the child, during the first few years of life, constructs a grammar on the basis of exposure to his or her language, so the linguist adopting the generative approach has to construct a grammar which will match with the observed patterns in the language. The difference between the two situations is that, whereas the child's grammar is not directly observable, the linguist's system is formulated explicitly. This, of course, is the whole point of the exercise. The linguist's grammar is intended as an explicit description or 'model' of the grammar which the child ultimately constructs; that is, the adult native speaker's grammar of the language. For Chomsky, the only way in which we can describe the latter is to construct a generative system. In doing this we are in fact discovering how the native speaker's internal, mental system is structured.

Let us turn now to a more detailed description of what a generative system of a natural language such as English would look like, in order to throw a little more light on the claim that it is of considerable complexity. The first, very basic, point is that such a system contains a list of words. We refer to this component of the grammar as the 'lexicon'. In order to describe how the words can be combined with each other to construct well-formed sentences, we will need to organise them into various classes. We have already seen this in operation in the simple grammars illustrated above. In the fragmentary grammar for English at (38), for example, *a* and *the* were grouped together in the second rule and called 'articles', *dog* and *cat* were grouped together as 'nouns', and we could of course add other items such as *left*, *disappeared*, *moved*, *came* to the category 'verb'.

In a sense, the lexical component of a generative grammar corresponds to the 'parts of speech' component in traditional grammar, which was also concerned with word classification, and it may have struck the reader that much of the traditional nomenclature has been carried over into generative grammar. There are important differences, however. The main one is that in generative grammar the structural principle of word classification discussed in the first section of this chapter is adopted explicitly. Indeed, the very nature of generative grammar requires that words be classified according to their distribution in sentences. Thus suppose that we adopt a rule like the first rule in (38), above, which states that one type of English sentence consists of the sequence Article + Noun + Verb, so that the grammar generates such sentences as *the man stopped*, *the bus stopped*. Now, *the fighting stopped* is also a well-formed English sentence, apparently conforming to the same pattern; we should obviously want to assign *fighting* to the class of nouns (i.e. N → {*man, bus, fighting* . . .}) in order to be able to account for this sentence. The fact that *fighting* refers not to a 'thing' or 'object' but to an event or activity is irrelevant. The crucial factors which determine how our rules are to be organised have to do simply with what word combinations constitute well-formed sentences. We express this property of generative grammar by saying that the approach is based on 'formal' patterns in the language, not on semantic or 'notional' considerations. Therefore, although generative grammar uses much of the terminology familiar to us from traditional grammar, the concepts are not equivalent in the two approaches. On a practical level particular words may not necessarily be assigned to the same class in both systems, and there is not, in fact, a direct correspondence between many of the categories in the two approaches. (For detailed discussion of the traditional classification, see Huddleston 1984: 90–9.)

In addition to lexical rules which assign individual words to classes such as article, adjective, noun, verb, adverb and so on, the grammar also contains syntactic rules which specify how word classes combine to form higher-level units which we call phrase-units. The point here is that, if we look at even a relatively simple English sentence such as *the brown fox was chasing the lazy dog*, it is not a sufficient description of the syntactic structure of this sentence to say that it consists simply of a sequence of words—*the*, *brown*, *fox*, *was* and so on—each belonging to a particular class. Rather, we can identify a number of units in this sentence which are intermediate between the level of the word and that of the sentence as a whole. We would wish to identify at least three main units of this kind: *the brown fox*, *was chasing*, *the lazy dog*. There are also reasons for treating *was chasing the lazy dog* as a unit intermediate between the lower-level units *was chasing*, *the lazy dog* and the whole sentence. That is, we can represent what is usually called the 'constituent structure' of this sentence as follows:

(43)

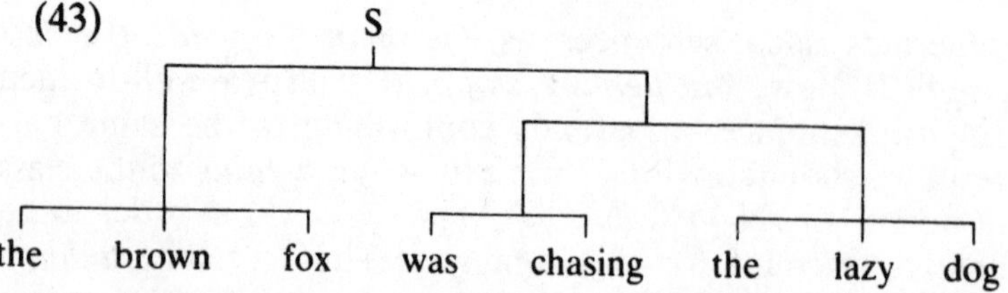

It is useful to have names for the various phrase-level units (or 'constituents) in this diagram. We call *the brown fox* and *the lazy dog* 'noun phrases' (NP) and *was chasing* a 'verb phrase' (VP). I will use the term 'predicate' (Pred) for the unit *was chasing the lazy dog*. (Many books use 'verb phrase' for what I have called the 'predicate', and 'verb group' for my 'verb phrase'; the advantage of the nomenclature adopted here is that it captures more clearly the relationship between verb phrases and other phrase-level units.)

Incorporating these details, we can represent the constituent structure of the sentence as follows:

(44)

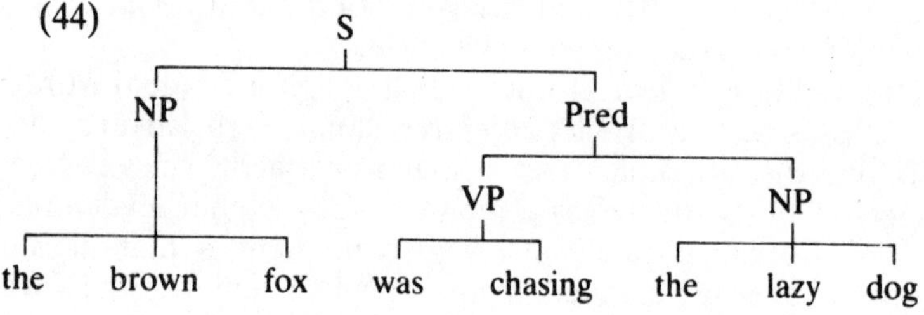

We now wish to describe in our generative grammar how word classes combine to form units such as noun phrases, verb phrases and so on, and how these units then combine with each other at the higher level. In order to generate *the brown fox was chasing the lazy dog* in such a way as to take account of these points, we might set up a system of rules of the following kind:

(45) S → NP + Pred
NP → Art + Adj + N
Pred → VP + NP
VP → Aux + V

The first rule states that a sentence consists of a noun phrase, followed by a predicate. The second rule specifies a noun phrase as being made up of an article, adjective and noun in that order. The third rule states that a predicate consists of a verb phrase followed by a noun phrase. The fourth rule specifies a verb phrase as being made up of an 'auxiliary verb' (Aux) and a 'main verb' (V). A pass through these rules will generate the following structure:

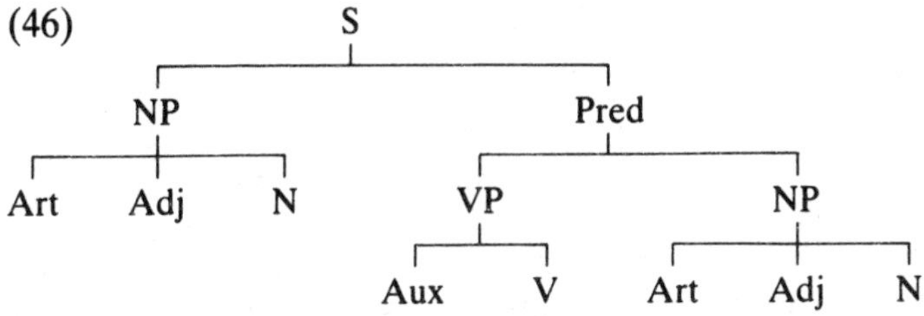

When these rules are supplemented by lexical rules such as:

(47) Art → the
Adj → {brown, lazy}
N → {fox, dog}
Aux → was
V → chasing

then the system as a whole generates the sentence *the brown fox was chasing the lazy dog*, assigning the following structure to it.

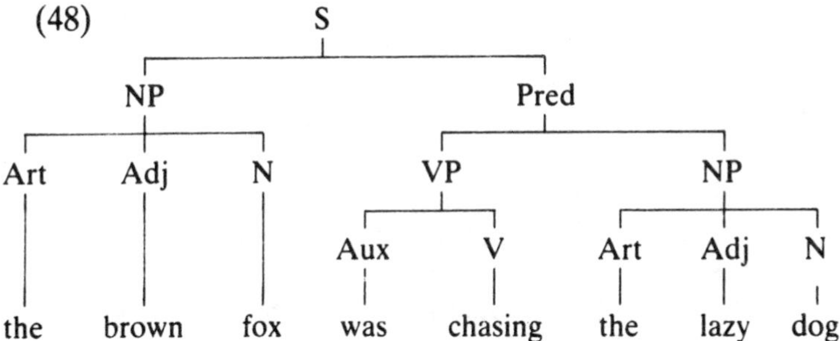

We can say, then, that one important component of a generative grammar of English—and therefore, presumably, of the mental grammars of native-speakers of English—consists of a set of hierarchically organised rules, specifying which words belong to which classes, how these classes combine with each other to form higher-level syntactic units such as noun phrase, verb phrase, adjective phrase and so on, and ultimately how these higher-level units combine to form sentences. The rules which describe these patterns are called 'phrase-structure rules'.

TRANSFORMATIONS

Although phrase-structure rules play an important part in generative grammar, the main thrust of Chomsky's early work in this field was to argue that there are other important components in the grammatical system in addition to the phrase-structure rules. He was particularly concerned to argue that a crucial component consisted of a set of rules of a different kind, which he called 'transformations'. (For this reason his approach is called 'transformational generative grammar', usually abbreviated to 'transformational grammar' or simply 'TG'.) It was largely the recognition of this kind of rule which led linguists to the realisation that the system as a whole was one of enormous complexity. This, in turn, led to the argument for some kind of innate knowledge in the human infant concerning the principles of grammatical organisation, which I have mentioned above. Given the restricted scope of this book, I can give here only some very simple examples in illustration of the concept of transformational grammar. Those interested in pursuing the question in greater detail are referred to one of the standard textbooks on TG (e.g. Langacker 1972; Akmajian and Heny 1975; Soames and Perlmutter 1979).

Let us take first an example of a simple transformation and the kind of argument which can be used to justify it. Consider again the sentence (49a) and the related sentence (49b).

(49) (a) The brown fox was chasing the lazy dog
(b) Was the brown fox chasing the lazy dog?

We have seen that a simple system of rules such as those at (45) and (47) generates (49a). These rules do not, however, generate (49b), since this sentence does not begin with a noun phrase. The question arises as to how they can best be modified so that they do so. The crucial rules here are the following:

(50) S → NP + Pred
Pred → VP + NP
VP → Aux + V
Aux → was
V → chasing

These generate the following structure:

(51)

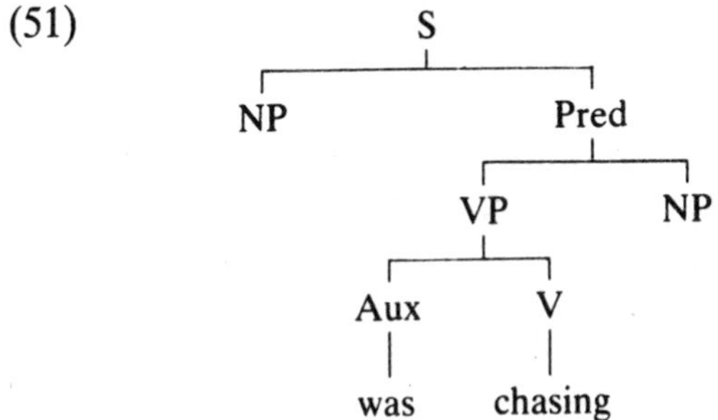

We could modify the first rule in (50) in such a way as to allow the auxiliary verb *was* to occur before the initial noun phrase. We might do this by recasting this rule as (52):

(52) S → (Aux) NP + Pred

In effect, (52) stipulates that on a particular pass through the rules, the item Aux may be selected in the position preceding the first noun phrase, thus generating the structure:

(53) S
Aux NP Pred

There are, however, a number of reasons why this solution is unsatisfactory. The main one is that the Pred rule which we have built into the system also introduces the item Aux, so that structure (53) would be elaborated by later rules as follows:

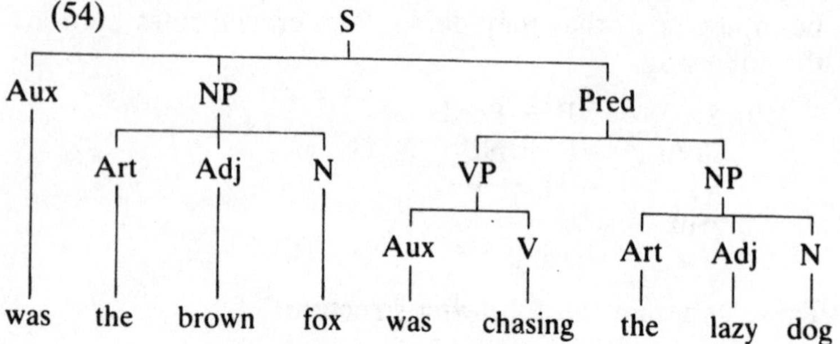

This is not a well-formed sentence of English. Nor is there any easy way of modifying the system in order to prevent such a grammar from generating this sentence.

A much more appealing way of handling this situation is to revert to the simple rule for S from which we started:

(55) S → NP + Pred

We make a pass through the system in the normal way in order to arrive at the structure:

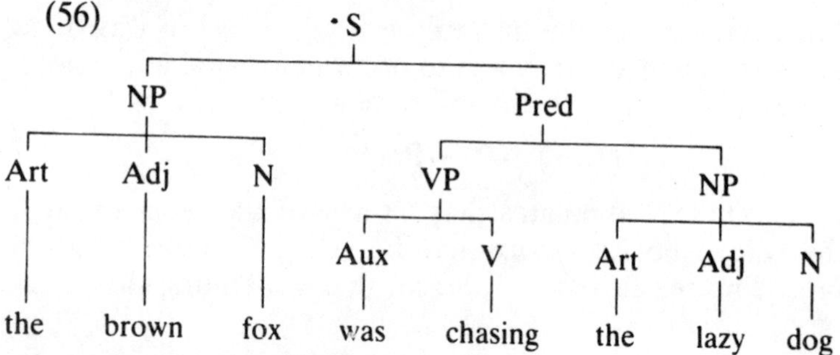

We now introduce a new type of rule into the grammar which applies to the 'output' of the phrase-structure rules; that is, to structures such as (56). In this case a rule is needed which MOVES the item Aux from its position in the VP to initial position in the structure, converting (56) to (57).

(57)

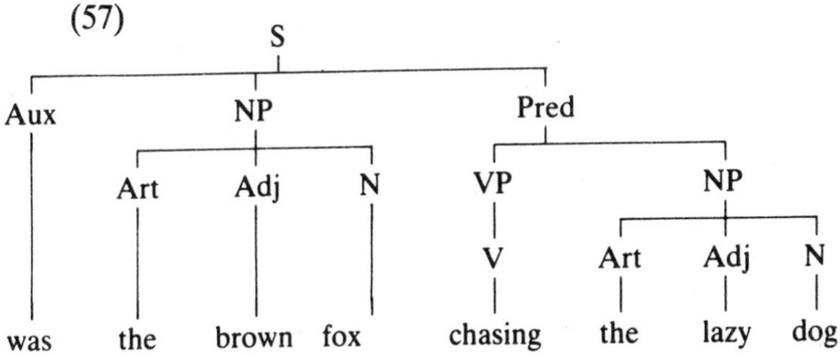

This clearly avoids the situation which arose before, where we had two occurrences of Aux in the structure. We would wish to say that this particular rule (it is usually called 'Inversion') is an optional rule; that is, on any given pass through the system it may or may not be applied. In this way we ensure that both the declarative and interrogative sentences (49a) and (49b) are generated.

Transformational rules clearly have to be formulated in a quite different way from phrase-structure rules. The latter, as we have seen, generally take the form:

A → B + C + . . .

where a symbol such as NP, VP, Art and so on, on the left-hand side of the arrow, is developed as one or more symbols on the right. A pass through a set of rules of this kind leads to the development of a tree structure (or 'phrase marker'). Transformations are quite different in that they do not DEVELOP the phrase marker of a sentence; rather, they CHANGE it in some way. Informally, and at a first approximation, the transformational rule of Inversion can be expressed as follows:

An auxiliary verb is (optionally) moved out of the predicate into the position preceding the first noun phrase.

Transformational rules in general are very powerful rules. Inversion, for example, creates interrogative structures from a wide variety of declarative structures. Thus, if we set up the phrase-structure rules in such a way that they generate structures (58), (59) and (60):

(58)

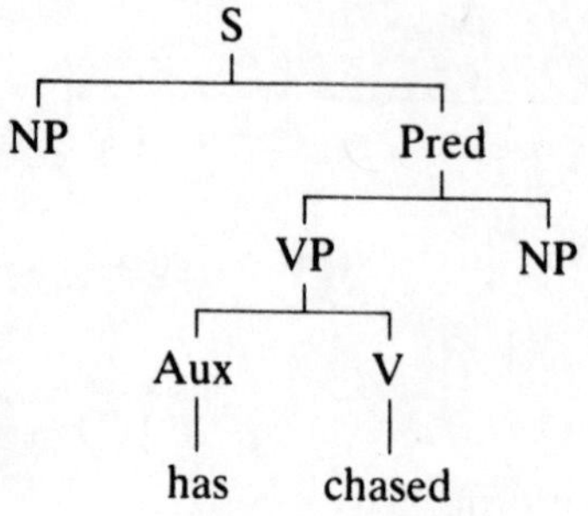

S
NP
Pred
VP
NP
Aux
V
has
chased

(59)

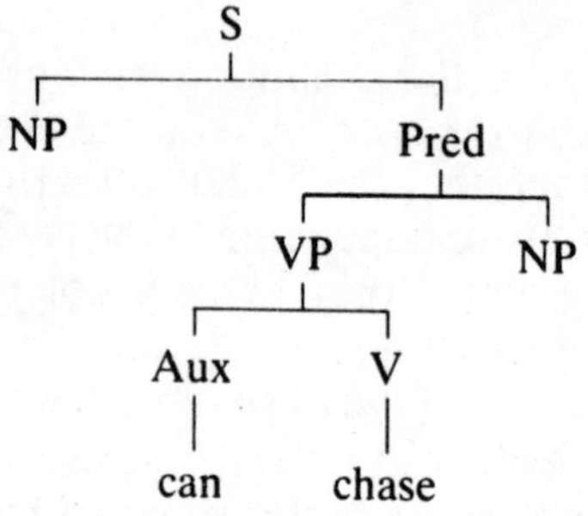

S
NP
Pred
VP
NP
Aux
V
can
chase

(60)

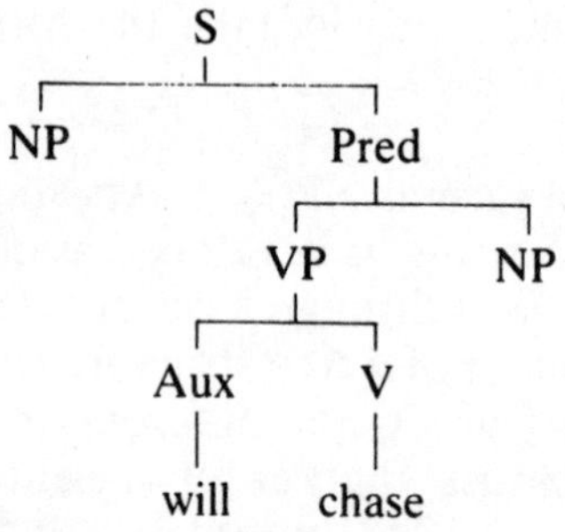

S
NP
Pred
VP
NP
Aux
V
will
chase

then Inversion can apply to each of these to give the corresponding interrogative structures:

(61)

S
Aux
NP
Pred
VP
NP
V
has
chased

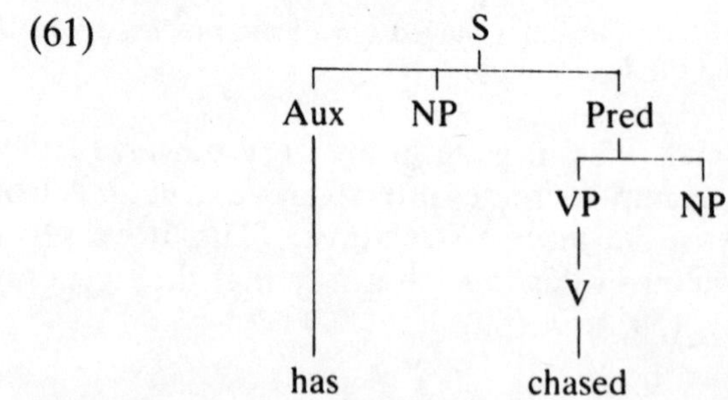

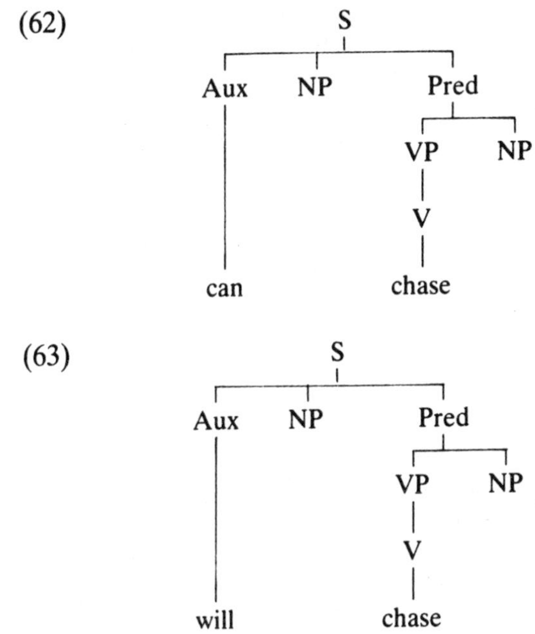

so that sentences such as *has the fox chased the dog*?, *can the cat chase the rabbit*?, *will the fox chase the rabbit*? are generated.

The concept of transformation was not unknown in traditional grammar, and the particular example I have cited here is one that is not entirely unfamiliar to those schooled in that approach. Chomsky showed, however, that the concept is more pervasive and far more crucial to linguistic analysis than had been suspected before. (Moreover, like most concepts in generative grammar, it is in many ways very different in nature from the corresponding concept in the traditional approach.) For our purposes here there were two key points to emerge from early work in TG. The first was that the transformations interacted with each other in complex and intricate ways to generate the full range of English sentence patterns. (How do children cope so easily with this kind of complexity at such an early stage in their life?) The second point was that, as more and more transformations were identified, our view of the role of the phrase-structure rules in the system began to change. Instead of seeing them as directly generating basic sentences in the way that has been illustrated above, linguists began to see them as generating rather abstract structures, which the transformations then converted into sentences. This added another level of complexity to the system and brought into even sharper focus the magnitude of the child's achievement in constructing a grammar.

I will conclude this chapter by attempting to give two illustrations of this point. As a relatively simple example consider a pair of sentences such as:

(64) He made up the story.
(65) He made the story up.

These are typical of a large number of pairs where a class of words called 'particles', represented by *up* in this example, may occur either in the position preceding the object or the one following it; for example:

(66) (a) He picked up the match.
(b) He picked the match up.
(67) (a) They cut down the tree.
(b) They cut the tree down.

The standard way of dealing with pairs of this kind in TG is to set up the phrase-structure rules in such a way that they generate the first member of each pair, and then to incorporate into the system a transformational rule ('Particle-Movement') which 'derives' the second example from the first. Thus the phrase structure rules are organised so that they generate (68):

(68)

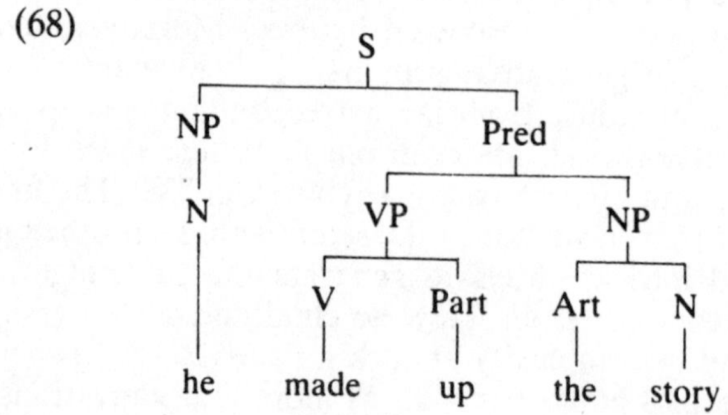

The transformational rule of Particle-Movement is then expressed somewhat as follows:

Any particle preceding a NP may (optionally) be moved to the position following the NP.

When this rule is incorporated, the grammar generates both (68) and (69).

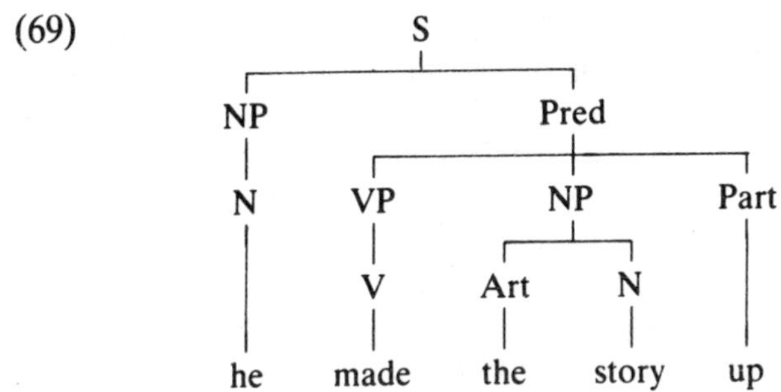

Now, the point here is that although Particle-Movement is normally optional, there is one situation in which it must apply. This is when a pronoun, rather than a full noun phrase, is selected in the object NP position, as in the following example:

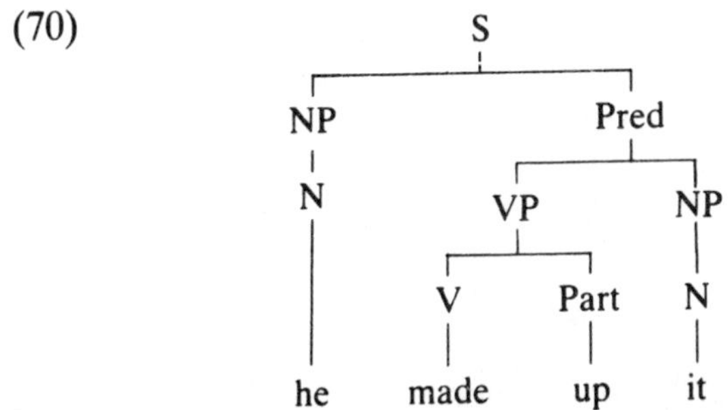

Since the phrase-structure rules are designed to generate (68), they must also, inevitably, generate (70). However, *he made up it* is not a well-formed sentence of English; it requires the obligatory application of Particle-Movement in order to be converted into one—*he made it up*. We see here, then, a small example of how the phrase-structure rules are designed so that they generate a rather abstract structure such as (70), which does not occur as a sentence in English. Only if the grammar is organised in this way can we construct a system which will work as economically as possible.

In transformational grammar the structures generated by the phrase-structure rules only are called 'deep structures'. The role of the transformations, then, is to convert these deep structures into 'surface structures'—the structures associated directly with particular sentences.

Another example of the relatively abstract nature of deep structures is provided by so-called 'extraposed' sentences, such as *it is obvious that George is rich*. We do not need here to go into the details of how the grammar is designed so that it generates sentences of this kind. The main point is that there are compelling reasons why the phrase-structure rules need to be organised in such a way that they generate a structure like (71):

(71)

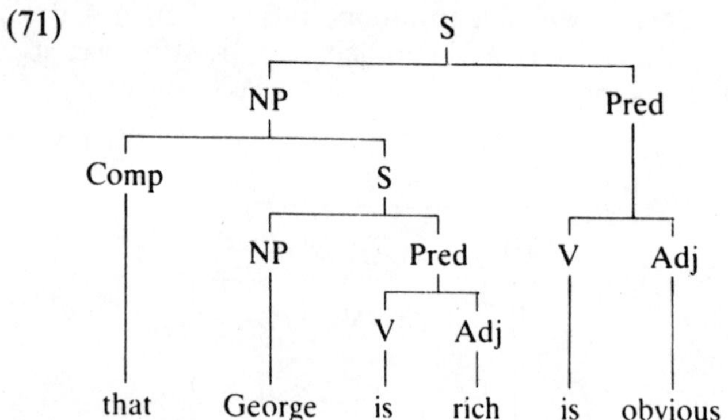

(Here the term 'Comp' stands for a small class of words, including *that*, called 'complementizers'.) That is, the phrase-structure rules generate a structure corresponding to the sentence:

(72) That George is rich is obvious.

and this is then changed by the transformational rule of 'Extraposition' into:

(73) It is obvious that George is rich.

Essentially, what Extraposition does is to move all the material under the initial noun phrase in this kind of situation to the right of the predicate and to introduce a pronoun—*it*—into the initial position.

Now, the adoption of an Extraposition rule of this kind has particularly interesting consequences for sentences such as *it seems that George is rich*. We have just noted that *it is obvious that George is rich* is derived from *that George is rich is obvious*. This means that *it seems that George is rich* must be derived from *that George is rich seems*, since it has a structure which is parallel to *it is obvious that George is rich*. The deep structure in this case, then, is (74):

(74)

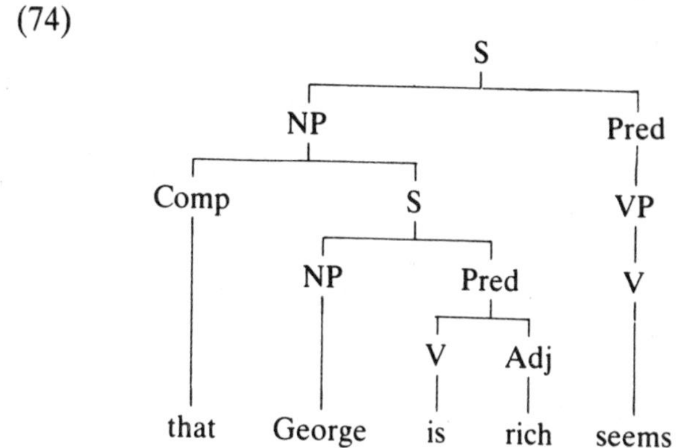

Again, the argument leads us to organise the phrase-structure rules of the grammar in such a way that they generate a somewhat abstract structure, which is converted into an actually-occurring sentence of English by a transformation.

As I noted above, these two examples can give only a rather sketchy idea of the way in which the discovery of the importance of transformational rules in the grammatical system led to an understanding of the abstractness of the structures generated by the phrase-structure rules. Most deep structures allow a considerable range of sentences to be derived from them. From a deep structure such as (75), for example, (which I will not attempt to justify here), all the sentences in (76) can be generated by a small number of transformations interacting with each other in intricate ways on different passes through the rules:

(75)

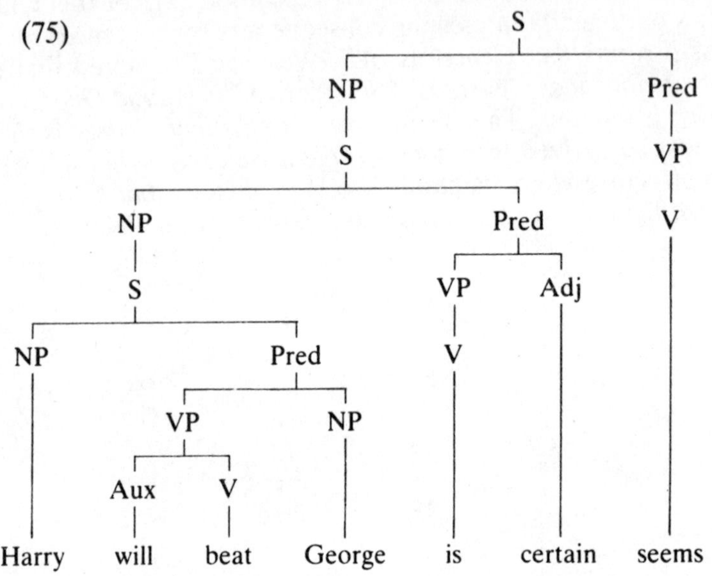

(76) It seems to be certain that Harry will beat George.
It seems to be certain that George will be beaten by Harry.
It seems that Harry is certain to beat George.
It seems that George is certain to be beaten by Harry.
Harry seems to be certain to beat George.
George seems to be certain to be beaten by Harry.
Harry seems certain to beat George.
George seems certain to be beaten by Harry.

Since the concept of deep structure was first established in transformational grammar, the theory has developed in a number of different directions and the concept has been modified accordingly. At the present time there are different views about the precise status of deep structure. There is, nevertheless, general agreement that some concept of the kind has an important role to play in grammatical organisation. There is certainly widespread agreement among linguists that the system which children construct is a remarkably complex and abstract one.

CONCLUSION

The argument in this chapter has led us to the conclusion that grammatical systems consist of a number of different components. In one component, usually called the lexicon, the words of the language in question are assigned to syntactic classes, such as noun, verb, adjective and so on. Many of the words which belong to a particular class tend to share certain semantic properties (many nouns in English, for example, refer to physical objects), but these properties do not characterise all members of the class and they do not therefore constitute a defining property of the class. Rather, the class is defined by shared distributional and inflectional properties. Some words possess the full set of properties concerned and are, therefore, central members of the class; other words possess only some of these properties and are, therefore, peripheral members.

A second component of the grammar consists of a set of rules which define how the various word classes combine to form higher-level units such as noun phrases, verb phrases, adjective phrases and so on, and also how these higher-level units combine to form sentences. These rules are called phrase-structure rules. Linguists who adopted the generative approach to linguistic description set out to construct explicit rule systems for generating sentences, comprising both a lexicon and phrase-structure rules. The main advantage of such grammars is that they are testable. To the extent that they are confirmed (by generating all and only the sentences of a particular language), they can be regarded as descriptions of the mental grammars of the people who use the language.

The generative approach has led to a recognition of the fact that a third component needs to be added to those mentioned above—a transformational component. This finding has led to a reappraisal of the nature of the phrase-structure rules. Instead of seeing them as generating sentences directly, we now see them as generating rather abstract structures, which are converted into sentence forms by the transformations.

One important question arising out of this view of grammar has to do with the process of child-language development. How do children succeed in constructing a system of this kind in such a relatively short time at such an early stage in their development? Linguists are still far from having succeeded in creating a comprehensive generative grammar for any natural language, although considerable progress has been made in recent years, and they are still a long way from identifying the full range of principles which govern the organisation of grammars of natural languages. Yet, in most cases, children succeed in constructing their own mental grammar in the first few years of life with consummate ease, at a stage in their life when they do not show any other obvious signs of mental prowess of exactly this kind, involving, as it does, complex skills of analysis and rule construction. In the next chapter we look at this mystery in a little more detail.

4 Syntactic Development

AN EARLY DESCRIPTION: PIVOT GRAMMAR

One of the reasons for discussing transformational grammar in the previous chapter was that it was largely as a result of Chomsky's pioneering work in that area in the 1950s and 1960s that scholars first began to study seriously the process of language development in children. The point about Chomsky's theory was that it was 'mentalistic' in character. That is to say, Chomsky, in constructing a transformational grammar, claimed to be describing a psychological entity—the internalised system which enables a person to produce and understand sentences in his native language. Chomsky's findings concerning the abstract nature of this system, briefly outlined in the previous chapter, were so startling that scholars began to ask themselves how children went about constructing a system of this kind. This was the beginning of a veritable explosion in work on child-language development, which continues unabated up to the present time. In this chapter we will attempt to trace the main developments in the study of the child's acquisition of syntax from the early 1960s.

Although there was marked enthusiasm for the task at hand in the early 1960s, there were considerable problems in setting about it. The first problem was the very strong emphasis in grammatical analysis on the formal aspects of language as opposed to the semantic aspects. There are very good reasons why form and meaning should be kept apart in the study of adult language. As we saw in Chapter 3, grammatical categories in adult language need to be defined in formal terms rather than semantic ones. It simply will not do, for example, to define nouns in the adult language as words that denote persons, places or things. In the early stages of child language, however, there are no formal features of the kind that characterise the adult language. An infant who is in the one-word utterance stage does not use inflections such as *-s* (as in *toys*), *-ing* (as in *playing*) and so on, nor are her utterances characterised by any word-order patterns. So, although the child is clearly using language at this stage, there was very little that could be said about it by a linguist who was familiar with the structural approach. It was not just that form and meaning were separated from each other in this approach. As we noted in Chapter 1, the clear importance of formal considerations in adult language had meant that very little attention had been devoted to semantics up to this time—a situation which the advent of transformational grammar did little to remedy in the early stages of its development.

Yet, as we have seen, the child's semantic system is already quite rich by the time that she starts to produce one-word utterances. Since most of the material covered in the first two chapters was not available to linguists at the time, they were not in a position to appreciate the importance for future language development of the communicative basis already established by children at about the age of 18 months.

Much of the work being done in transformational grammar also seemed to be irrelevant to the task of tracing the child's initial steps in language. Clearly, operations like Inversion, Extraposition, Particle-Movement, and indeed most of the other transformational processes that were being identified, were well beyond the horizon of the 2-year-old child. There was just one aspect of TG that could be applied to early language—the generative aspect. This was where work started.

In the previous chapter we saw how a linguist setting out to describe a language might begin by constructing a simple grammar, designed to generate some of the very basic sentence types in the language. Thus the following grammar, together with a few lexical rules, generates very basic structures for such sentences in English as *the dog chased the cat*, *the cat ate the meat* and so on.

(1) S → NP + Pred
NP → Art + N
Pred → VP + NP

The obvious approach to child language seemed to be to try to set up an explicit grammar of this kind which would generate all the sentences that children produce in the early stages and then follow their development through into the later stages, constructing further generative grammars for each step along the way. Thus it was hoped to use the generative methodology in order to trace the developmental path. Linguists did not realise immediately, however, that the differences between the adult-language situation and the child-language situation are so great that the task of constructing generative grammars for children poses special problems.

As we have noted, there is very little that can be said in this approach about the one-word stage. All that we can do is to write a rule such as:

(2) S → W

Here the symbol W stands for 'word'. If this rule is supplemented by a lexical rule specifying the words which a particular child uses, such as:

(3) W → {mummy, daddy, teddy . . .}

then we have a (rather uninteresting) generative grammar which generates all the sentences produced by one particular child.

The situation becomes a little more interesting when the child begins to produce two-word utterances. The first overt signs of grammatical organisation start to appear here, and the system begins to acquire characteristics with which the generative grammarian can get to grips. It was here at the two-word stage, then, that the early exponents of the application of generative grammar to child language were forced by their methodology to begin.

We have seen that in the structural approach as a whole, word classification (which is fundamental to syntactic description) is based on the inflectional properties of words and on their distribution in sentences. At the two-word stage, children are not producing inflectional forms (such as suffixes), but there do appear to be certain distributional patterns in their sentences. The first thing which struck generative linguists about the two-word stage was that certain words showed a strong tendency to appear only in initial position in these utterances. Examples were words like *more* and *my*. Children often said things like *more milk*, *more nana*, *my teddy*, *my daddy* but very rarely produced sentences with *more* and *my* in final position. There were other words, however, which appeared conversely to occur only in final position. This set included words like *off* and *down*. Children often said things like *shoe off*, *teddy off*, *that down*, *me down* but they very rarely put these words in first position. There was a third set of words which occurred in either initial or final position. These were words such as *mummy*, *teddy*, *see*. Children said things like *mummy eat* and *want mummy*; *teddy down* and *my teddy*; *mummy see* and *see shoe*. In other words, there appeared to be two major word classes: those words which were restricted to a particular position, and those which occurred freely in either position. They named the first class the 'pivot' (P) class and the second set the 'open' (O) class. (See e.g. Braine 1963; Brown and Fraser 1964; Miller and Ervin 1964; for general discussions of pivot grammar, see Aitchison 1976: 109–15; Brown 1973: 116–38.) The pivots were divided into two sub-categories: those which were restricted to initial position and those which were restricted to final position. The former were called the pivot$_1$ (P_1) class; the latter were called the pivot$_2$ (P_2) class. This scheme led linguists to set up a generative grammar of the following kind for a particular child in the two-word stage:

(4) syntactic rule:

$$S \rightarrow \begin{Bmatrix} P_1 + 0 \\ 0 + P_2 \end{Bmatrix}$$

(5) lexical rules:

$P_1 \rightarrow$ {more, my}
O $\rightarrow$ {mummy, teddy, see, milk, nana}
$P_2 \rightarrow$ {off, down}

The syntactic rule states that a two-word sentence is composed either of a P_1 word followed by an O word or by an O word followed by a P_2 word. The sequences O + P_1, P_2 + O are not generated by the grammar. The fact that children do not produce sentences such as **nana more*, **teddy my*, **my more* is therefore accounted for, by attributing to the child a grammar consisting of rules like those at (4) and (5).

It was thought that most children in the two-word stage would have a syntatic rule like (4) but that they might differ from each other slightly in so far as the lexical rules were concerned. Thus one child might use the word *see* in initial position only, in which case it would be for her a P_1 word rather than an O word. In the later part of the two-word stage it was thought that the grammar underwent a minor development in that the child began to produce O + O sequences. Some of the examples cited above (e.g. *mummy see*) belong in this category. This can be seen as an example of the kind of grammatical development in children which parallels the way in which linguists need to progressively elaborate their grammatical descriptions in order to extend the range of their grammars.

It was not long, however, before a number of problems concerning this particular application of generative grammar to child language became apparent. The first problem concerned the nature of the generative approach itself. We have already noted that one of the most important (and attractive) features of the approach is that it makes testable predictions. A grammar is initially set up to account for a particular set of sentences. By its very nature, however, it generates new sentences not in the original sample. The validity of the grammar is confirmed if these new sentences are judged to be well-formed by native speakers. The problem, however, is that this methodology works only for adult speakers. Certainly, one can examine a grammar like that comprising rules (4) and (5) and note that it generates new sentences. We established it here on the basis of the observation that such sentences as *more milk*, *more nana*, *my mummy*, *teddy down* and a number of others were typical two-word utterances. However, it also generates examples which were not cited, such as *more mummy*, *more see*, *my see*, *my nana*, *mummy off*, *see off*, *see down*, *nana down*. The major difficulty here is that we cannot check the well-formedness of these sentences with a 2-year-old child. (Roger Brown and Ursula Bellugi tried it once, asking their informant, 'Which is right, Adam—*two shoe* or *two shoes*?'; the answer they received was 'Pop goes the weasel!'.) Now, this undermines the whole point of the generative approach, since it means that the grammar is not verifiable. If we cannot check its ouput against the judgement of the people whose internal system it is supposed to represent, then we have no means of knowing whether it constitutes a valid description of that system or not.

In point of fact, some of the predictions made by the grammar do not appear to be at all plausible. Utterances like *more mummy*, *more see*, *my see*, *see off* are not examples that 2-year-olds tend to produce. It could, of course, be that the specific situation which might be expected to produce one of these utterances does not often occur, so that their absence from the data may be due to this accidental circumstance rather than to the nature of their internal grammar. The point is that there is no means of knowing for certain which of these factors is the relevant one in a particular case. In other words, a cloud of vagueness or indeterminacy hangs over the application of the generative approach to early child language, which makes its application to this domain more problematic than its application to adult language.

One point which this discussion shows is that there are clearly considerable difficulties for any description of this early stage of the child's language development which does not take semantics into account. Utterances such as *more mummy*, *more see*, *my see* probably do not occur at this stage, because they do not express the kind of meanings which children want to express. (In some cases it is difficult to see any meaning that they could express.) This seems a much more plausible explanation than one based on a purely formal description. It was this kind of consideration that was soon to lead linguists to adopt a more semantically based approach to early child language.

There were other features of the two-word stage which created unease about the pivot-grammar approach. Paradoxically, some of these considerations had to do with distributional phenomena, which the pivot grammarians were taking to be the main focus of their description. Consider, for example, words like *hi* and *bye-bye*. Utterances such as *hi mummy*, *hi daddy*, *bye-bye mummy*, *bye-bye office* were common. *Hi* and *bye-bye* showed a strong tendency to occur in initial position, and they were therefore confidently put in the pivot$_1$ category, along with *more*, *my* and others. However, it was then realised that there were more subtle distributional factors at work here than those recognised by the grammar. *Hi* and *bye-bye* showed a strong tendency to occur with animate object words (and more rarely with a restricted set of non-animates such as *office*). On the other hand, *more* tended to occur with inanimates such as *biccy* ('biscuit'), *nana* ('banana') or with process words such as *tickle*. (As we noted in Ch. 2, *more* is typically used to request objects or services.) The kind of pivot grammar illustrated above was therefore failing in two ways. It was not recognising, much less explaining, these distributional differences between *hi* and *bye-bye*, on the one hand, and *more* (or *my*), on the other, in that it assigned them all to the same class. Even more interestingly, it was not distinguishing between such categories as 'words referring to animate objects', 'words referring to inanimate objects', 'words referring to processes'. It simply put most of these in the category of O words. Yet such distinctions appeared to be necessary in order to achieve the very limited goal which the pivot grammarians had set themselves—of describing distributional differences between words at the two-word stage.

More subtle distributional factors than those that could be handled by the pivot-grammar approach were also illustrated by such words as *fall* and *get*. *Fall* tends to occur in final position in such utterances as *teddy fall*, *that fall*, whereas *get* can turn up either in initial position (*get it*, *get teddy*) or in final position (*mummy get*). The obvious way of handling this in pivot grammar is to assign *fall* to the P_2 category and *get* to the O category. This, however, does not provide an EXPLANATION for the observed distributional contrast here. If we ask WHY these patterns should occur, it seems reasonable to surmise that children are distinguishing here between those processes which involve action by one entity on another (e.g. 'get') and those which affect only one entity ('fall'). When the child uses one of the first set in a two-word utterance, the other word will refer either to the agent of the action (e.g. *mummy get*) or to the patient (e.g. *get teddy*). Children tend to put the agent before the process and the patient after (Angiolillo and Goldin-Meadow 1982). When the child uses one of the second set of process words (e.g. *fall*) in a two-word utterance, the other word will normally refer to the object affected by the process, and it will tend to be placed before the process word. We can therefore explain the distributional patterns here, if we invoke the semantic relational concepts of 'agent' and 'patient' discussed in Chapter 1. This explanation is not, however, available within the purely formal framework of pivot grammar.

A SEMANTICALLY BASED APPROACH

The considerations outlined above led linguists to take a fresh look at the two-word stage and to argue that a satisfactory description of it would need to pay much more attention to meaning. This development was reinforced by the fact that semantics was beginning to play a much larger part in the study of adult language, as the realisation grew that there were also problems in the application of purely formal models to that area. However, this move towards semantics does not necessarily solve all the problems. Grammatical knowledge certainly develops during the first few years of the child's life in parallel with semantic development, and we need to find some satisfactory way of charting it.

Let us come back to the question of word classification in this context. It is clear that already during the one-word stage the child develops a varied vocabulary. She acquires words for referring to objects, processes and attributes, and she acquires words for expressing various functional meanings such as directives (e.g. *more*), greetings and farewells. How are we to describe this vocabulary in grammatical terms? We have now rejected the grammatical labels 'pivot' and 'open' on the grounds that the child's word classes are rather more sophisticated than these categories suggest. Does this mean that we can now use such concepts as 'noun', 'verb', 'adjective' and so on for the words that the child is producing?

In order to answer this question, we need to recap on what these terms mean within the framework of general linguistic theory. In Chapter 3 we noted that word classes are established primarily on formal grounds rather than on semantic grounds. In English nouns typically take a plural *-s* suffix or a possessive *'s* suffix, and they combine with the articles *the* and *a* to form noun phrases. We also noted, however, that the category as a whole has certain semantic characteristics; namely, that many of its members denote physical objects (animate or inanimate). This is particularly true of its prototypical members—a very high percentage of those words which have the formal features of nouns are object-referring words. This is an important point about the structure of languages in general. It is perfectly possible to conceive of a language in which the prototypical members of a formally defined class did not share any significant semantic properties. In this situation it would be very difficult to know which class of words should be called 'nouns', which class should be called 'verbs' and so on. The fact that this situation does not tend to occur means that grammatical organisation—although it is far from being entirely consonant with semantic structure—is nevertheless not totally independent of meaning. We could say that semantics pervades grammatical structure.

With this perspective in mind it does not seem unreasonable to suggest that, even at the one-word stage, the young child has at least some 'emergent' grammatical categories such as 'noun' and 'verb'. The concept 'emergent categories' means that the child's words are already characterised by one of the features which plays a part—albeit a relatively small one—in the identification of adult categories. The child certainly does not have nouns in the sense in which the adult has them, since there are as yet no clear formal patterns in her speech. But she does have nouns in the sense that a significant number of her early words are used to denote physical objects, which obviously constitute an important conceptual category for her. We could say that in adult language, word classification is determined by formal characteristics, with semantic factors making a smaller contribution. In child language the converse is true—semantic factors are predominant, with formal properties playing a minor role. As the child's mastery of the formal aspects of language increases, so the nature of her system comes increasingly into line with that of the adult.

A good example of the emergent nature of the child's grammatical categories is provided by the concept of 'subject'. There has been a good deal of debate in the literature on child language as to whether the first element of utterances such as *mummy eat*, *daddy kick*, *teddy fall* should be regarded as the 'subject' of the child's sentence. Much of this debate has been vitiated by the failure to define exactly what we mean by the concept 'subject' in grammar. Concepts like 'noun', 'verb', 'adjective' are class concepts. A particular word in a language may be a member of one of these classes. 'Subject', however, is a relational concept. In a sense, it is like such previously discussed relational concepts as 'agent', 'patient', 'locative', except that these are relational concepts in semantics. 'Subject' is a relational concept in grammar. When we say that *the doctor* is the subject of a sentence such as *the doctor has examined the child*, we are saying that a particular relationship holds between the noun phrase *the doctor* and the rest of the sentence—that this relationship is different from that holding between the noun phrase *the child* and the rest of the sentence.

As with other grammatical concepts in structural linguistics, the subject relationship is defined primarily in terms of its formal characteristics. For example, if the noun phrase *the doctor* is made plural, then this causes a change in the verb phrase. *The doctor has examined the child* becomes *the doctors have examined the child*, where *has examined* changes its form to *have examined*. On the other hand, if we make the second noun phrase plural, no corresponding change takes place in the form of the verb phrase:

(6) The doctor has examined the child.
The doctor has examined the children.

In other words, one important property of the subject of a sentence is that the verb phrase 'agrees' with it.

A second formal property of the subject is that in basic sentence patterns it precedes the verb phrase. If we change the example above to *the child has examined the doctor*, it is now the noun phrase *the child* which is the subject of the sentence. It is this NP which determines the form of the verb—if it becomes plural, then the verb phrase also changes its form:

(7) The child has examined the doctor.
The children have examined the doctor.

Changes in the second NP here—*the doctor*—do not affect the form of the verb.

A third formal property of the subject is that in the interrogative form of a particular sentence it changes position with the first member of the verb phrase. This (transformational) process is known as 'Inversion' (see p. 73). For example, the interrogative form of (8) is (9):

(8) The doctor has examined the child.
(9) Has the doctor examined the child?

where the NP *the doctor* has changed places (or 'inverted') with the first element of the verb phrase—*has*. Similarly, the interrogative form of (10) is (11):

(10) The child has examined the doctor.
(11) Has the child examined the doctor?

where the same Inversion process has applied.

In the context of structural linguistics as a whole, then, the subject of a sentence is the NP (a) with which the verb phrase agrees, (b) which precedes the verb phrase in basic sentence patterns and (c) which inverts with the first element in the verb phrase in interrogatives. (There are other formal properties, but these will suffice for our purposes here; for more detailed discussion see Huddleston 1984: 58–72.) As far as semantics is concerned, the relationship between the syntactic category of subject and semantics is similar to the relationship between the grammatical category of noun and the semantic class of physical objects. Just as many nouns denote objects, so does the subject relationship in many cases express the agent relationship. This situation accounts for the fact that many traditional grammars define the subject of a sentence as the agent or the 'performer of the action'. However, there are many sentences in which the subject does not correlate with the agent, as the following examples (based on those of Fillmore 1968: 25) show:

(12) This door opens easily.
(13) This knife cuts well.
(14) Chicago is windy.

In (12), although *this door* is the subject of the sentence (cf. *these doors open easily*, where the verb form changes from *opens* to *open*), it is not the agent of any action. The semantic relationship between *the door* and *open*, rather, is one of 'patient'. In (13) *this knife* is syntactically subject but semantically 'instrument'. In (14) *Chicago* is subject but stands in a locative relationship to the process of 'being windy'. In other words, the subject relationship can be said to express a variety of semantic relationships. In any given sentence the semantic interpretation assigned to the subject depends largely on the character of the verb. If the verb is one which denotes an action, the subject will in most cases be an agent—examples like (12) and (13) are minor exceptions to this rule. If the verb denotes some other semantic category, however, the subject will tend to express some other kind of semantic relation. Thus the strong correlation between subject and agent, which was noted by traditional grammarians, is a consequence of the fact that many verbs denote actions. On the other hand, the lack of a semantic homogeneity in verbs also results in a lack of complete correlation between grammar and semantics in the case of the subject concept.

The answer to the question of whether the concept 'subject' should be attributed to children in the early stages of language development is now reasonably clear. Since grammatical processes like verb agreement and inverted word-order are still some considerable way over the child's horizon at the two-word stage, and since these processes play a crucial role in defining the concept of subject in the adult language, there is no sense in which the child's grammatical system can be equated in this respect with that of the adult at this stage. On the other hand, certain properties of the subject concept are beginning to emerge. We have noted above that children show a strong tendency to place the agent before the process word in two-word utterances. Since the semantic concept of agent and the formal property of pre-verb position both have a part to play in the definition of subject in adult language, it does not seem unreasonable to say that the grammatical concept of subject has at least begun to appear at the two-word stage. This conclusion is in fact reinforced by the observation that not all pre-verbal nouns are agents in the child's speech at this stage. Utterances such as *teddy fall* are attested, where the pre-verbal position is occupied by a semantic role which is closer to that of patient than agent. This means that it would be unsatisfactory to describe the child's speech purely in semantic terms. The child's syntax is beginning to gain a certain autonomy with respect to semantics, and this should be recognised by attributing the concept of an emergent subject to the child.

THE DEVELOPMENT OF CONSTITUENT STRUCTURE

We have now followed the child through to the stage where we can legitimately ascribe a minimal amount of grammatical apparatus to her, providing that we bear in mind the difference between the emergent nature of this apparatus and the nature of the corresponding apparatus in the adult's language. At the one-word stage the most salient grammatical feature of her speech is the appearance of nouns. At the two-word stage the number of nouns continues to increase, but verbs also begin to feature prominently. Concepts such as subject and object also begin to make their appearance, albeit in a rather primitive form. Some functional meanings, such as directives and greetings, begin to be lexicalised at this stage into words like *want*, *get*, *more*, *hi*, and grammatical structure also affects these items in that they tend to occur in first position in the utterance. (It is no doubt the emergence of word-order preferences in many children such as pre-verbal position for agent, pre-nounal or pre-verbal position for directive words, pre-nounal position for greetings and post-verbal position for patients which gave rise to the early recognition in pivot grammars that word-order patterns did occur in the two-word utterance.)

One very important development in the two-word stage is the emergence of two types of grammatical structure. These have been characterised by Crystal *et al.* 1976: 67–70 as phrase-structure patterns and clause-structure patterns. Examples of phrase-structure patterns are utterances such as *my teddy*, *red train*, *in box*. Examples of clause-structure patterns are *daddy kick*, *find boat*, *where mummy*?. In terms of the adult language the reasons for distinguishing between these two types of structure are fairly clear. In Chapter 3 we noted that adult sentences do not consist of sequences of isolated words. The words in a particular sentence can be grouped together as units. In *the dog chased the black cat*, *the* and *dog* combine to form a noun phrase, as do *the*, *black* and *cat*. The same is true of *has* and *examined* in sentences like *the doctor has examined the child—has examined* constitutes a verb phrase here. Examples of more complex verb phrases are *has been examining*, *may examine*, *may have examined*, *may have been examining* and so on. Other types of unit that have to be recognised are adjective phrases (AdjP) (e.g. *very big*, *rather small*, *quite interesting*), adverb phrases (AdvP) (e.g. *very quickly*, *rather slowly*, *quite happily*) and prepositional phrases (PP) (e.g. *in the box*, *under the table*, *outside the bank*). In other words, the adult's sentences are made up of combinations of units such as NP, VP, AdjP, AdvP, PP and so on, rather than of sequences of words, and each of these units has its own internal structure. In the kind of generative grammar discussed in the previous chapter this is recognised by writing such rules as:

(15) S → NP + Pred
(16) NP → (Art) (AdjP) N
(17) Pred → VP (NP) (PP) (AdjP)

An example of a NP consisting of an article, an adjective phrase and a noun might be *the very big cat.*

(18) Art: the
AdjP: very big
N: cat

An example of a predicate consisting of a verb phrase, noun phrase, prepositional phrase and adverb phrase might be *had put the money on the table rather carefully.*

(19) VP: had put
NP: the money
PP: on the table
AdvP: rather carefully

The internal structure of the various 'high level' units featuring in rules (15), (16) and (17) is then specified in lower-level rules such as:

(20) AdjP → (Int) Adj
(21) AdvP → (Int) Adv
(22) PP → P + NP

(The symbol Int here stands for the class of intensifiers such as *very, rather, quite*; the symbol P stands for 'preposition'—*in*, *on*, *outside* etc.)

With this in mind it is relatively clear why two-word utterances such as *my teddy*, *red train* and *in box* should be placed in a different category from *daddy kick* and *find boat*. In the latter the child is combining two high-level units to form a clause or sentence. *Daddy* occupies the kind of position filled by a full noun phrase in adult English and *kick* occupies the position filled by a full predicate. In such utterances as *my teddy, red train*, *in box*, on the other hand, the child is building up the internal structure of units such as NP, PP and so on; that is, in *daddy kick* the child is constructing a high-level unit, a sentence, while in *my teddy* she is constructing a lower-level unit, a NP.

Now, although there is a clear justification for this distinction in the adult language, one should obviously ask whether there is any justification for it in the child's language? How do we know that the child subconsciously assigns a different grammatical status to *my teddy* from the one she assigns to *daddy kick*? There is no absolutely hard-and-fast evidence for this distinction, but a number of points are suggestive. In the first place, many of the phrase-level structures differ semantically from the clause-level structures. The phrase-level structures are often utterances intended to comment on or draw attention to objects—*my teddy*, *red train*. The clause-level structures, on the other hand, tend to be comments on events in which semantic relationships such as agent, patient, locative are involved—*daddy kick*, *find teddy*, *teddy chair*. The second point is that there is a tendency for phrase-level structures to appear as units at the three-word stage. Thus *my teddy* may appear in such three-word utterances as *see my teddy*, *my teddy fall*. In other words, a group of words such as *my teddy* is beginning to exhibit some of the important semantic and syntactic characteristics of noun phrases, in that it typically refers to an object (a semantic property) and is beginning to take on subject-like and object-like functions. In this respect it differs markedly from such two-word utterances as *daddy kick* which (a) refers to an event rather than to an object and (b) does not appear in both pre-verbal and post-verbal positions in three-word utterances. *Daddy kick* develops into such structures as *daddy kick ball* at the three-word stage and, in this respect, therefore, behaves like a subject-verb structure rather than a noun-phrase structure.

The three-word stage (usually starting at about the age of 2 years) is an important one in that it is at this point that constituent structure begins to emerge overtly in the child's language. If it is correct, as has just been argued, that sequences such as *my teddy* constitute a unit in utterances such as *see my teddy*, *my teddy fall*, then these utterances have the structures diagrammed at (24) rather than those at (23):

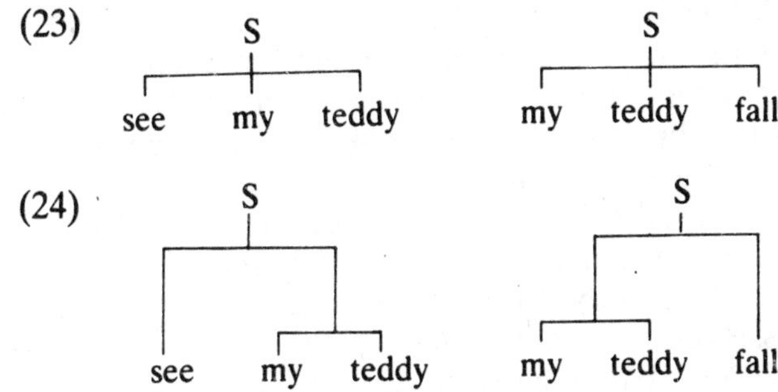

The development from the two-word stage to the three-word stage can in fact be seen to involve a much more complex set of processes than that of simply adding an extra word. There are at least three separate strands that are developing simultaneously. The structures illustrated at (24) constitute the first of these strands. Here the phrase-level structures of the two-word stage are combined with another word to form a dual-layered structure. The most typical examples—though not the only ones—involve the combining of a noun phrase with a verb. Such structures are called 'blends' by Crystal *et al.* (1976: 70). A second developmental strand involves elaboration of the kind of high-level structure exemplified by *daddy kick*. When this is developed into an utterance such as *daddy kick ball*, we see the addition of a new major unit to the basic subject-verb pattern. There is no strong evidence for postulating two layers of structure for these sentences, so that a structural contrast emerges between *see my teddy* (for example) and *daddy kick ball*:

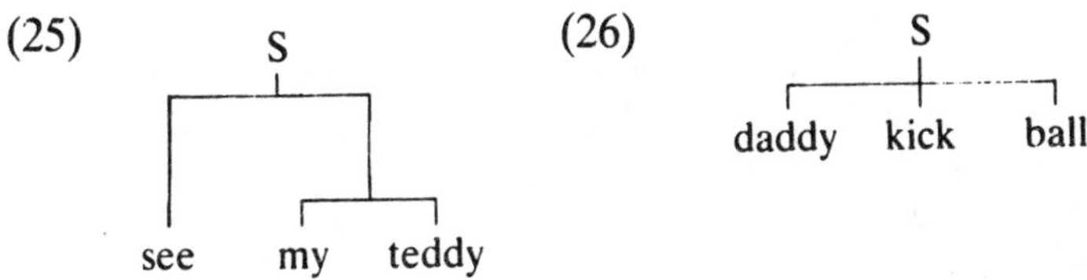

The third strand involves development at the relatively low level of the phrase rather than at the high level of the clause. We have noted that there is evidence for taking the view that the noun phrase is an emergent category at the two-word stage in such examples as *my teddy* and *that train*. At the three-word stage we see development of these structures into such examples as *my nice teddy*, *that red train*. At first sight these look like counter-examples to the earlier claim that units such as *my teddy*, *that train* preserve their integrity into the three-word stage. Their problematic status dissolves, however, if we see them as developments within the NP itself. That is, we can analyse these examples as follows:

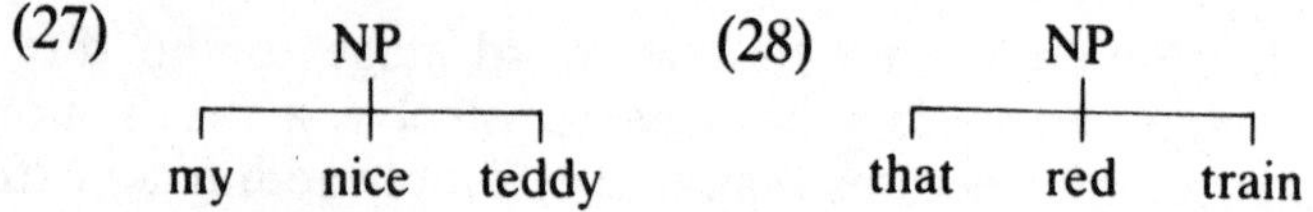

Furthermore, children appear to exhibit word-order preferences in these examples—*my nice teddy* and *that red train* are much more typical utterances than **nice my teddy* and **red that train*. This would suggest that a distinction between two further word classes is emerging. On the one hand, we have a class which includes *my* and *that*, typically occupying first position in the noun phrase. *Nice* and *red*, on the other hand, belong to a separate class, which typically follows any member of the first class. This situation could be expressed by a grammar consisting of the following rules:

(29) NP → (Art) (Adj) N
Art → {my, that . . .}
Adj → {nice, red . . .}
N → {teddy, train . . .}

Such a set of rules generates sentences like *my teddy*, *that train* (Art + N); *nice teddy, red train* (Adj + N); *my nice teddy, that red train* (Art + Adj + N); but they do not generate such implausible examples as **nice my teddy*, **red my train*.

The three-word stage, then, is a good deal more complex than might appear at first sight. A description in these terms is, however, justified by the fact that it provides a natural explanation for the rapid development of the system, once it has reached this point. The blends, illustrated by such examples as *see* [*my teddy*] and [*my teddy*] *fall* can become more complex in a number of ways. One possibility is for a third clause-level unit to be added—*you see my teddy*, *my teddy fall there*:

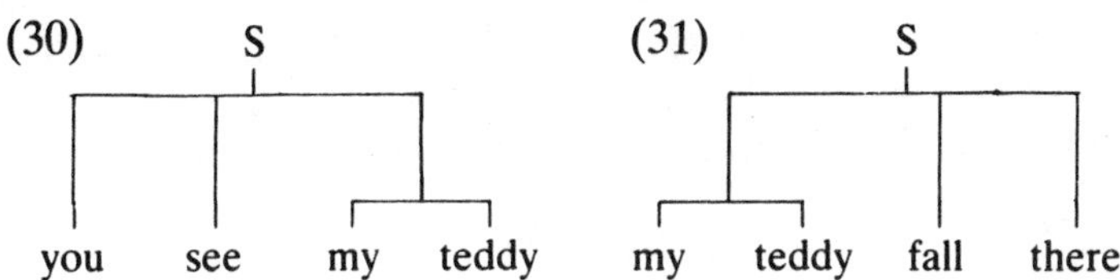

A second possibility is for one of the units to be made more complex—*see my nice teddy*, *my teddy be falling*.

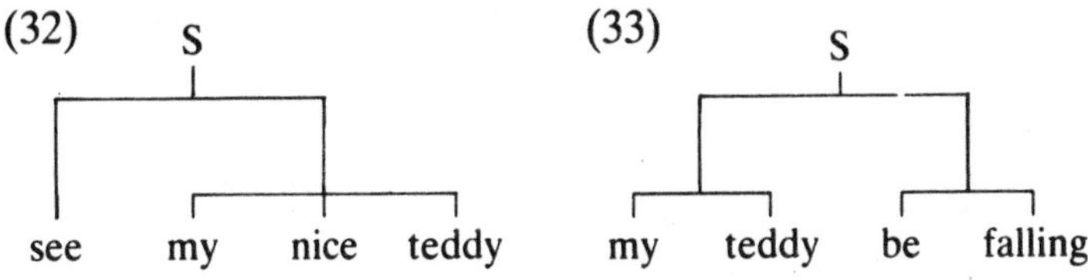

The three-element clause-level structures such as *daddy kick ball* can be elaborated by the addition of a fourth element: *daddy kick ball here*. The three-element phrase-level structures such as *my nice teddy* may be elaborated by the addition of a fourth element—*my nice big teddy*. As the grammatical units of the child's system at their various levels undergo simultaneous development, the combinatorial possibilities expand exponentially. By the age of 3½ most children are producing sentences that sound remarkably adult-like.

Perhaps the most important stage in the development of the phrase-structure rules is when the child begins to produce subordinate clauses. In utterances such as *I know he wants the chocolate*, the structure *he wants the chocolate* is in fact a sentence within a sentence. Like many other sentences, it consists of a subject noun-phrase and a predicate:

(34)

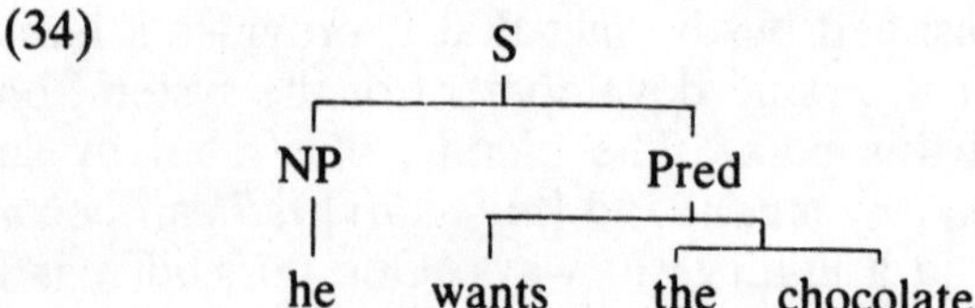

One way of accounting for the fact that children can produce sentences containing other sentence structures is to attribute to them a grammar of the following kind, in which the symbol S, as well as occuring on the left-hand side of the first rule, also occurs on the right-hand side of another rule:

(35)

$$\begin{aligned} S &\rightarrow NP + Pred \\ Pred &\rightarrow VP \begin{Bmatrix} NP \\ S \end{Bmatrix} \end{aligned}$$

The rule for Pred here allows for VP to be followed either by a NP or by a sentence, thus generating (36) as one possibility.

(36)

S
NP Pred
VP S

This can then be expanded by reapplication of the first rule into:

(37)

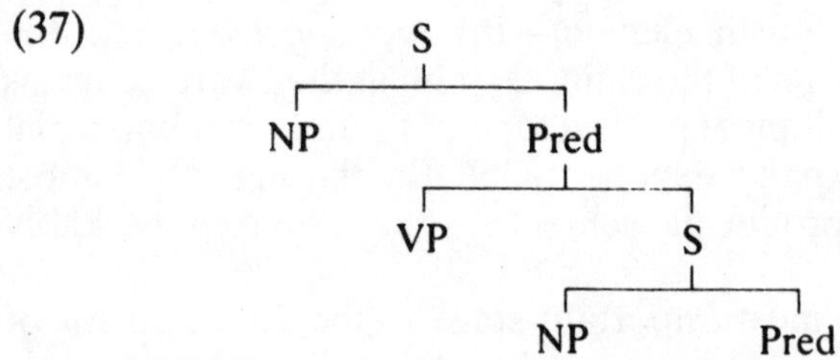

and finally into (38) by reapplication of the second rule (and lexical rules).

(38)

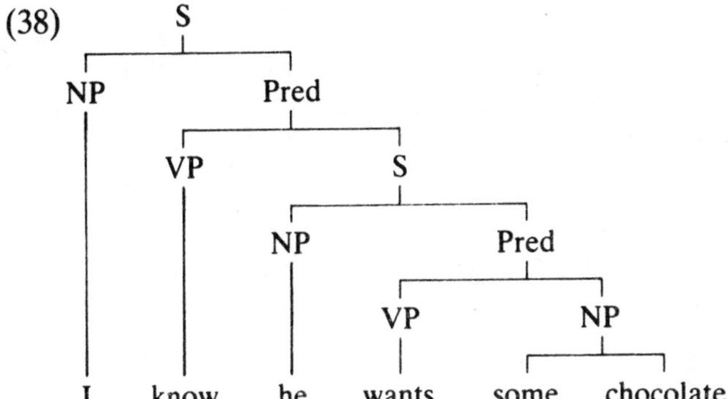

(In referring to a subordinate 'sentence' such as *he wants the chocolate* in this example as a 'subordinate clause', I am following traditional practice.)

A grammar consisting of a rule like (35) is a very powerful device since it allows for very complex structures, in which there are several layers of subordinate clauses, as in the following example:

(39)

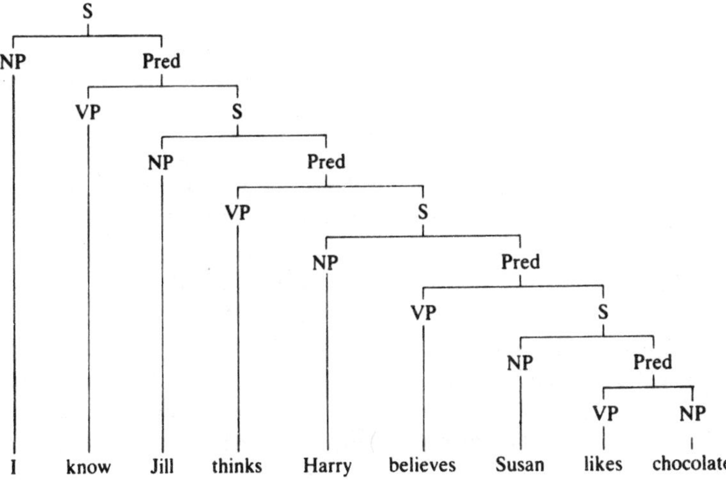

Therefore, in attributing to the child a grammar containing a rule like (35), we can provide some explanation for her developing ability to construct the kind of complex sentence patterns that characterise adult English.

THE DEVELOPMENT OF TRANSFORMATIONS

In the previous chapter we noted that linguists adopting a generative approach have argued that there are two important syntactic components in the grammatical system of a language. In addition to the phrase-structure rules, there are rules called 'transformations' which change the structures generated by the phrase-structure rules in precisely specifiable ways in order to generate the surface structures of the language.

The question arising now is whether there is any evidence in the child-language development process that children are constructing grammars consisting of both types of rule. If the grammar produced by the linguist is intended to be a description of the native speaker's mental grammar, then we might expect there to be evidence of this kind.

There are a number of forms which such evidence might take. One might, for example, expect some transformations to appear at a relatively late stage in the acquisition process. The point here is that, since transformations apply to the structures generated by the phrase-structure rules, there is a sense in which the latter are logically prior to the former and need to be constructed first. This expectation is complicated, however, by the fact that children hear sentence patterns that result from the application of both sets of rules. Since in many cases the structures generated by the phrase structure rules only are relatively abstract (see p. 76), these are not structures to which children are directly exposed. I will return to this point directly.

A second expectation which follows from the idea that children are 'little linguists' is that, when they do begin to construct transformations, then these rules might differ in certain ways from those which constitute the adult's grammar. The point here is that, even if one has noted that a particular set of sentences can be accounted for by means of some transformational rule, this does not mean that it is entirely obvious exactly how the rule works. There have been and continue to be many disagreements between linguists concerning the precise formulation of individual rules. It would be surprising if differences of this kind did not arise in the process of grammar construction by children.

Let us consider each of these points in more detail, beginning with the question of the opposition between phrase-structure and transformational rules. Do children realise that the sentences which they hear are the output of two different kinds of rule, and do they give any indications of separating out these two components from each other? Such indications would emerge most clearly from situations where children used a structure which was closer to the deep structure than to the surface structure. Since the former is generated by the phrase-structure rules only, whereas the latter is generated by the phrase-structure rules plus transformations, this would constitute strong evidence for the view that they had identified the distinction between the two separate rule systems. It would mean that they were simplifying their own task of grammar construction by filtering out the adult's transformation(s), using instead a structure generated by a rather simpler system than the adult's grammar.

An example of such a situation is provided by the transformational rule called 'Particle-Movement' (see pp. 76–8). Consider the following sentences:

(40) (a) She picked up the pen.
     (b) She picked the pen up.
(41) (a) He cut down the tree.
     (b) He cut the tree down.

As we noted in Chapter 3, transformational linguists take the (a) sentence in each case to be closer to the deep-structure pattern than the (b) sentence. For both (40a) and (40b) the deep structure is somewhat as follows:

(42)

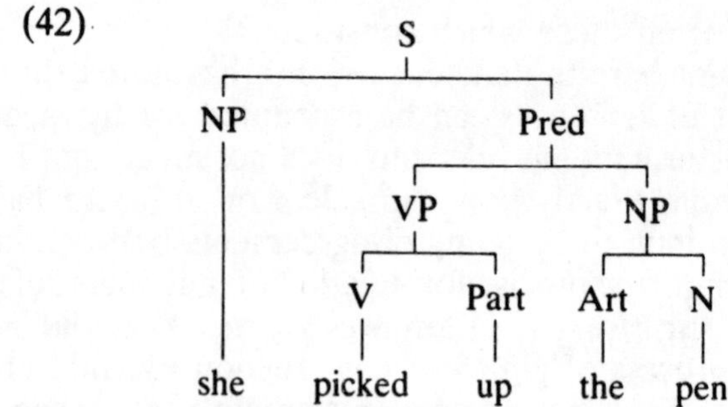

The rule of Particle-Movement optionally moves the particle *up* to the right of the object NP here, giving (40b). There is one situation, however, where the rule is obligatory. If the object NP is a pronoun, as in deep structure (43), then Particle-Movement must apply, given that *she picked up it* is not a well-formed English sentence.

(43)

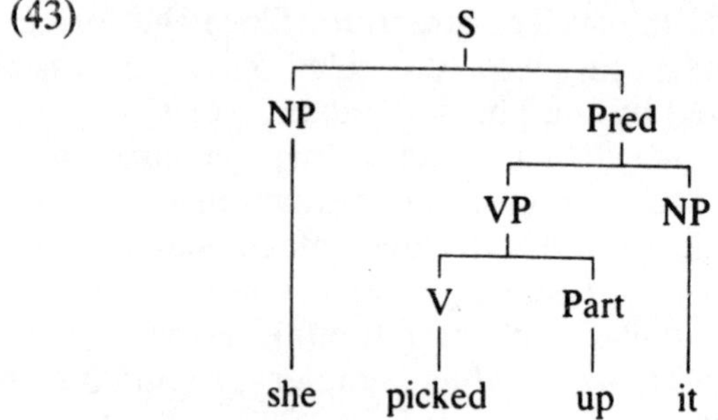

Now sentences such as *she picked up it* and *she put down it* are very frequent in children's speech. They must therefore be regarded as one piece of evidence in favour of the view that children in some sense 'know' that the adult's sentences are the output of two different sets of rules and that the system can be simplified by filtering out the transformational rules. Moreover, there is a further point here. Since children who produce sentences such as *she picked up it* often have no difficulty in understanding adults when they say *she picked it up* or *pick it up*!, even though they never use this structure themselves, it would be misleading to say that they did not possess the transformational rule of Particle-Movement at all. Only if we attribute such a rule to them, can we account for the fact that they appear to be aware of the relationship between the two types of structure and to understand them both. The point is, however, that, as far as their productive abilities are concerned, the system containing the transformational rule appears to be too complex to handle. At this stage the rule is available only to the processes used in comprehension.

A similar illustration of this point is provided by some of the early interrogative forms used by children, such as *what that is*?, *why he went*?. Children don't, of course, hear these forms from adults, who produce structures characterised by the transformational rule of Inversion—*what is that*?, *why did he go*?. It is interesting that here too children not only use a structure that is much closer to deep structure than the one used by adults but also that they have no difficulty in understanding the adults' forms. Again the point is that children appear to operate comfortably with two parallel systems—one for production which lacks a particular transformation, the other for comprehension which includes it. There does seem to be evidence here that, although transformations constitute a hurdle to be overcome, they are not of a totally unexpected kind from the child's point of view. (This general issue concerning children's readiness to abstract away from the adult's surface-structure patterns in the direction of deep structure is discussed in more detail in Lee 1982.)

A cautionary note needs to be sounded with respect to the point made above. The examples do not show that children always produce deep-structure patterns before surface-structure patterns, that they construct the phrase-structure rules before the transformations. Given the fact that the phrase-structure rules generate rather abstract structures and that the adult's utterances are the output of the system as a whole, there is no sense in which such an expectation could be seriously entertained. On the other hand, it does seem reasonable to suggest that certain transformations will cause children problems, particularly if the transformations involved are complex ones, in which case their own forms may be closer to deep structure. The hypothesis that certain transformations are acquired at a relatively late stage has been explored in an interesting series of experiments on comprehension (Chomsky 1969; Cromer 1970; Warden 1981; Chomsky 1982).

Let us now turn to the question of how transformations show up in the language produced by children and how the rules which they construct relate to those of adults. It will again be necessary to confine ourselves to just one example of what is in effect a very general phenomenon. Consider the following 'errors' produced by children acquiring English:

(44) What did you bought?
(45) What did you saw?

(The following discussion is based on Mayer *et al.* 1978; Erreich *et al.* 1980.) In designing a transformational grammar to generate sentences such as *what did you buy*?, *what did you see*?, a linguist would set up a system of phrase-structure rules somewhat along the following lines:

(46) S → NP + Pred
NP → N
Pred → VP(NP)
VP → Aux + V
Aux → {pres, past}

(where *pres* and *past* stand for 'present tense' and 'past tense' respectively). When supplemented by such lexical rules as:

(47) N → {you, they, what}
V → {see, buy}

these rules generate the following deep structures:

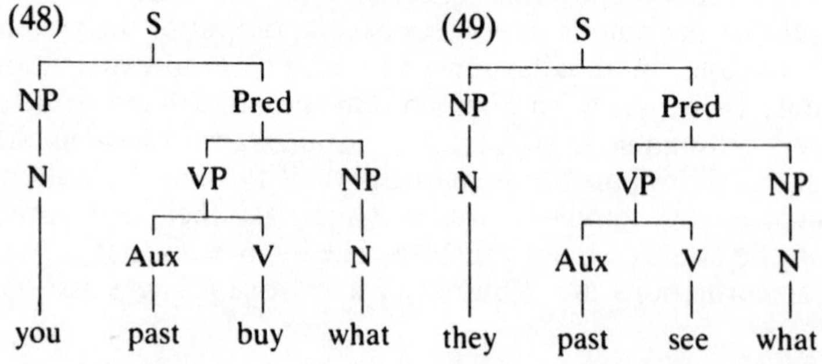

These structures are then converted into the appropriate surface structures by the following transformations—(48) is taken as an illustration:

1. A rule called 'WH-Movement' moves the interrogative word *what* to initial position:

(50)

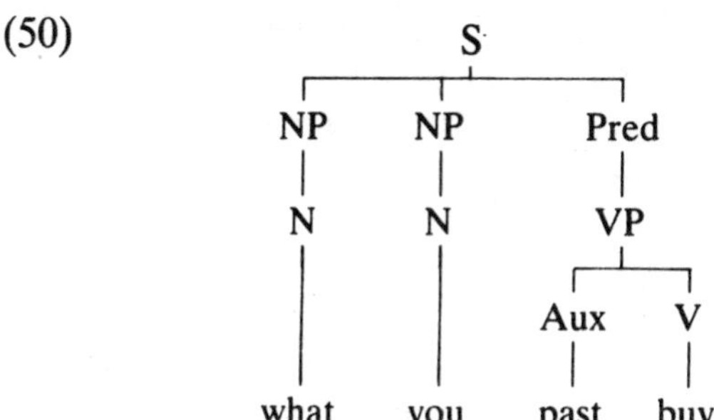

2. 'Inversion' moves the Aux element to the position preceding the subject NP:

(51)

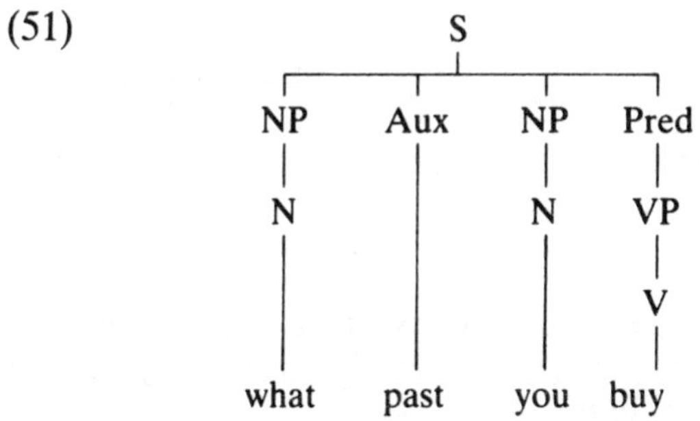

3. A rule called 'Do-Support' introduces the auxiliary verb *do* under the Aux node, since the tense element has been separated from the verb:

(52)

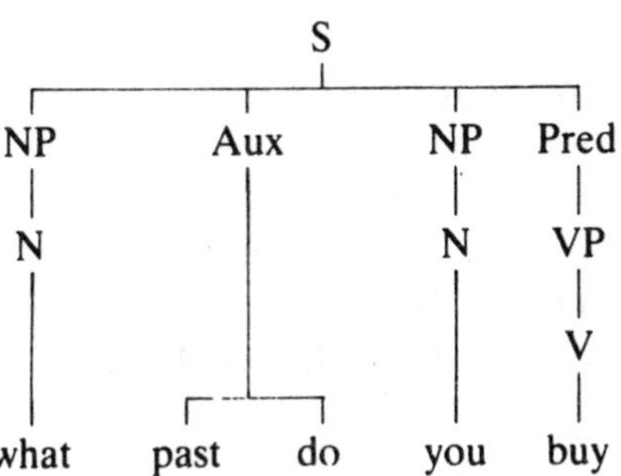

A 'realisation rule' then converts the sequence *past* + *do* to *did*, giving the surface structure *what did you buy*?

Children who produce utterances such as *what did you bought*?, *what did you saw*? seem to have identified the three transformational rules in question very successfully. There is, however, one respect in which their formulation of the Inversion rule differs from that of adults. They appear to have a version of the rule which, when it applies to structure (48), COPIES the Aux element into pre-subject position, rather than simply moving it there. Instead of giving structure (50), this gives structure (53), in which there are two Aux elements:

(53)

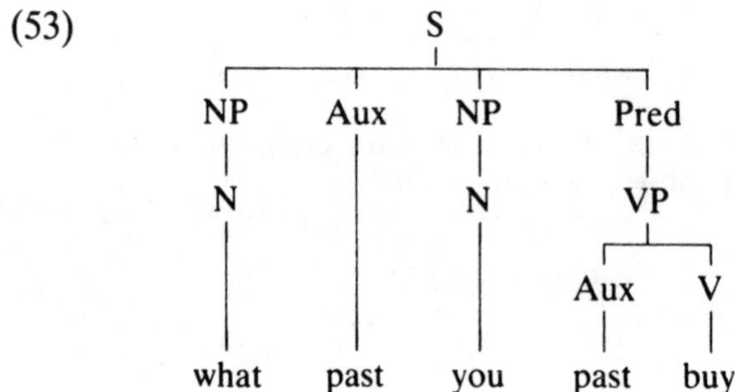

Two realisation rules then convert *past* + *do* and *past* + *buy* into *did* and *bought* respectively, giving the sentence *what did you bought*?.

The interesting point about this situation is that there are some sentences in adult English which are not inconsistent with the child's version of the Inversion rule apparently used here. Consider the following examples:

(54) What do you like?
(55) What do they know?
(56) What do we see?

A transformational linguist would give a similar description for these sentences to that given above for *what did you buy*?. The deep structure for (54), for example, is:

(57)

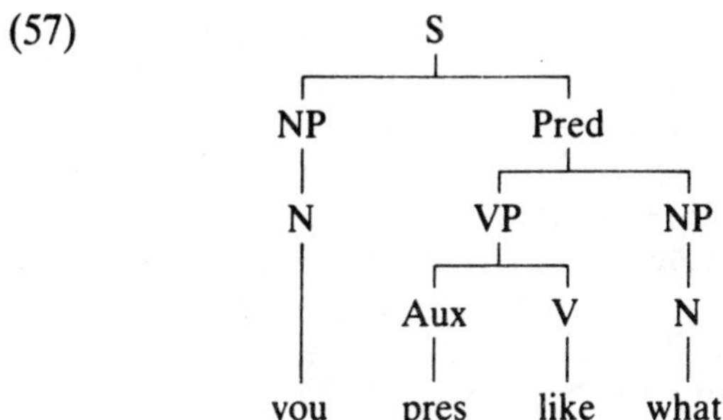

The transformational rules of WH-Movement, Inversion (adult version) and Do-Support convert this to the following surface structure:

(58)

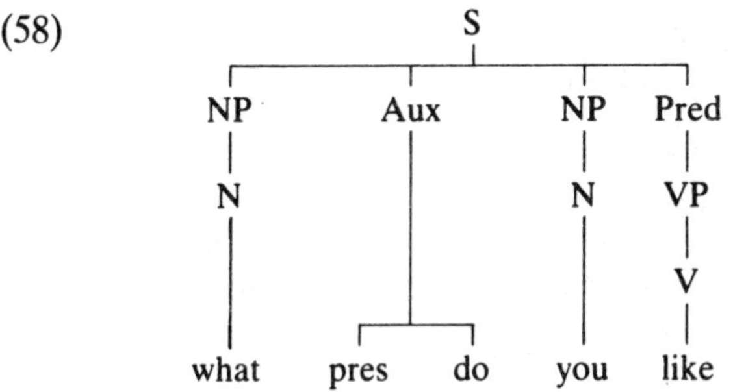

i.e. *what do you like*?. Now the child's version of the Inversion rule gives a rather different structure, when the three rules are applied:

(59)

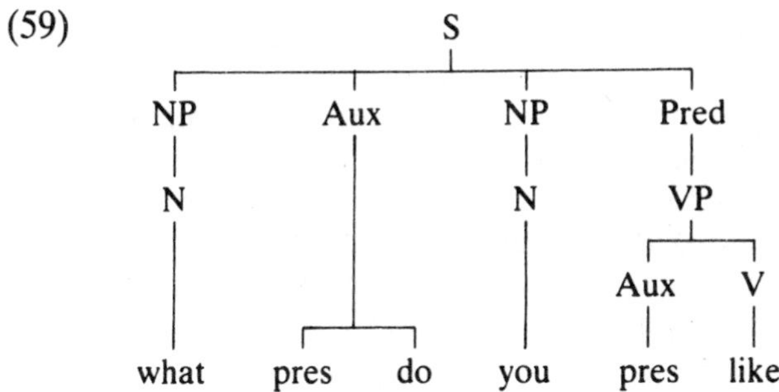

However, if the child has a normal set of realisation rules, such that *pres* + *do* and *pres* + *like* are realised as *do* and *like*, respectively (when the subject of the sentence is *you*), then this structure too will give the sentence *what do you like*?. What all this means is that there are a large number of sentences in English which do not make it clear whether Inversion is a rule which MOVES the Aux element into subject position or whether it COPIES it into that position. There are, of course, some sentences (e.g. *what did you buy*?) which do make it clear that it is a movement rule. We cannot, however, expect that all children will necessarily identify these crucial sentences when they make their early attempts to construct the rule. It is not surprising, therefore, that they might be misled into an incorrect (though not a totally implausible) formulation of it. Again, there is evidence here for the view that children are constructing transformational grammars.

One final point should be made about the relationship between grammar construction by the linguist and grammar construction by the child. We noted in the previous chapter that in the generative approach in general and in the transformational approach in particular, linguists go through a number of steps characteristic of scientific enquiry as a whole. The first step involves collecting data, which in this case means observing sentences and sentence patterns in the language under investigation. The second step involves formulating a hypothesis (in this case constructing a generative grammar) which is compatible with the observed data. The third step involves testing the hypothesis. Any generative grammar will inevitably predict that certain combinations of words which were not part of the set originally observed are also well-formed sentences, and these predictions can be checked, either by looking for such sentences in actual usage or, as a short cut, by simply asking native speakers whether they are indeed grammatical. Similarly, there will be actually-occurring sentences not generated by the grammar, which therefore suggest that the grammar needs to be modified in some ways. The material discussed here suggests that children adopt a very similar strategy, with the proviso that for them it operates on a subconscious rather than a conscious level. The indications are that children construct a series of evolving hypotheses, or grammars, which they constantly test against the observed data. Such grammars appear to consist, from a relatively early stage, of both phrase-structure and transformational rules and are constantly under review and elaboration in the light of observed utterances. This parallel between the child and the linguist (and at a more general level between the child and the scientist) is an intriguing one, which goes some way towards explaining the upsurge of interest in child-language development in recent years. The child's grammar is clearly a complex and abstract system, and yet it takes shape within a remarkably short time span. These points constitute part of the case for the view advocated by Chomsky that the child is innately equipped with a powerful mental instrument for formulating and testing hypotheses concerning grammatical structure.

One point which we will not be able to develop here but which nevertheless deserves to be made, however briefly, has to do with the contribution of mothers (and of other caretakers) to language development. In his early arguments for the so-called 'innateness hypothesis' Chomsky suggested that the language to which children were exposed during the crucial early years of grammatical development differed little in character from the language addressed by adults to each other. He took this to be an additional argument for the innateness hypothesis. If it were so, it would mean that children received virtually no assistance from the surrounding linguistic environment in identifying the basic units and structures of their language. We could therefore only assume, Chomsky suggested, that the child has a particularly rich innate endowment for linguistic analysis. This alone could account for the extraordinary progress made between the ages of 18 months and 3 years.

However, this particular argument has lost some of its force as a result of a series of investigations into the language addressed by caretakers to children, pioneered by Catherine Snow. (For a review of this work, see Snow 1979.) Snow and others have shown that the language to which children are exposed is not by any means as unhelpful or as unstructured as Chomsky had suggested. There are many ways in which mothers and others talking to children simplify their language, often subconsciously, in such a way that it helps the child to identify certain basic units and structures. One interesting point about this research is that in some ways children themselves appear to play some part in structuring the linguistic 'input'. There is evidence to show that if adults use structures which are in some sense too advanced for the child, then he is apt to respond less positively. Most mothers are sensitive to this reaction and tend to modify their language accordingly.

Snow has taken care to point out that these findings do not in any sense make the process of grammatical development any less remarkable. They certainly do not in her view seriously undermine Chomsky's general position on innateness. What they do show is that the factors involved are complex. There is an intricate interaction between the environment and the mental structures innate in the child. In Chapter 2 we saw that this was quite clearly true of semantic development; it is no less true as far as the acquisition of grammar is concerned.

CONCLUSION

In this chapter we have noted that the description of syntactic development in the child poses a number of complex problems. Although the concept of generative grammar opened up a new range of questions concerning child-language development, it was designed principally for the description of already-formed adult grammars and was not easily adaptable to the question of how such grammars are constructed. We can nevertheless trace the general development of phrase-structure rules, as the child gradually learns how to combine words into syntactic units such as noun phrases, verb phrases, adjective phrases, out of which sentences are built. The grammatical constructs which characterise adult speech do not come into being ready-made in the child's speech—rather, they emerge over time, as the child gradually constructs the rules for expressing meanings in grammatical form. The transformational approach suggests that children do not simply analyse syntactic structure at the surface level but look for rather abstract underlying patterns, which are mapped onto the sentences of the language by a variety of transformational rules, interacting with each other in complex ways. The approach provides some explanation for the fact that children do not appear to acquire grammar by simply copying structures produced by adults. Their role in syntactic development is a creative one, involving the subconscious construction and testing of hypotheses concerning grammatical structure.

5 The Phonological System

THE PRIMACY OF SPEECH

For the linguist, as for the young child, language is predominantly a spoken phenomenon. In this respect the approach of modern linguistics differs from that of traditional approaches, in which there was a strong tendency to think of language mainly in its written form. Indeed, the forms which characterised the written language were often thought to be the 'correct' or 'proper' forms of the language. Where spoken language differed from the written, the spoken forms were often thought to be inferior, less regular, less 'grammatical' than the written ones. One of the main contributions of twentieth-century linguistics has been to point out the richness and complexity of the spoken language in its own right.

There are several reasons for taking spoken language to be the primary focus of interest in linguistics. Historically, spoken languages evolved before writing and existed for many thousands of years without any written record. Today, spoken language is still very much a defining characteristic of our species—all members of the species use it—whereas written language is not universal in this sense. Even in our society in which the written form of the language is well established, each individual encounters it first in its spoken form. The process of language development is grounded in speech.

Speech is produced by an extremely complex and intricate mechanism. The fundamental process involves the controlled expulsion of air from the lungs, with various delicately-tuned operations being performed on the airflow to provide a variety of acoustic signals, which we recognise as different sounds. The sounds of speech can be divided into two major categories: vowels and consonants. We will look at each in turn.

VOWELS

The main organs involved in the production of vowel sounds are the vocal cords and the tongue, with other articulators such as the lips playing a secondary role. We can set the vocal cords in such a way that they vibrate rapidly as air is expelled from the lungs through the larynx. This vibration produces a basic acoustic signal which is amplified and modified by the oral cavity (i.e. the cavity inside the mouth). A useful analogy can be drawn here with a stringed instrument such as a violin. The function of the vocal cords is analogous to the string. When a string is plucked or bowed, it vibrates and produces an acoustic signal. The vocal cords are caused to vibrate by a rather different mechanism—air flow from the lungs sets them in motion when they are drawn lightly together by the muscles of the larynx—but the overall acoustic effect is similar. In the case of the vibrating string, the actual nature of the sound perceived by the hearer is determined by the sound-box of the instrument—the same string will produce a different acoustic signal, if it is plucked on the sound-box of a violin, from the one which it produces on a sound-box of a different size and shape, such as a viola. In the case of speech it is largely the oral cavity which plays the role of the sound-box. The difference between the two situations is that the shape of the oral cavity can be changed from one moment to the next—a facility which is obviously not afforded by a violin. It is this constant changing of shape of the vocal tract which produces the various sounds of speech.

One way in which a human being can change the shape of the vocal tract is by moving the tongue to different positions in the mouth. If the tongue is placed in a very high, forward position, and if the lips are spread, then vibration of the vocal cords causes a sound like the vowel of the words *peat*, *meat* to be produced. If the tongue body and the jaw are lowered, then the vowel of the words *part* and *guard* is produced. If the back (dorsum) of the tongue is raised (and if the lips are placed in a rounded configuration), then the vowel of the words *pool*, *shoe* is produced. These three vowel positions are particularly important, since they constitute the extremes of the system. Other vowels are produced with the tongue in some intermediate position between the extremes of high front position (*peat*, *meat*), low back position (*part*, *guard*) and high back (*pool*, *shoe*).

One important point about the phonological structure of English is that there are many more vowels in the language than the written system would suggest. In the written language there are just five symbols that we think of as vowels: *a*, *e*, *i*, *o*, *u* —or six, if we include the *y* of such words as *my* and *by*. In the spoken language, however, there are twenty-one vowel units. (This figure varies slightly from one variety of English to another).

The vowels can usefully be divided, from the articulatory point of view, into two subsets: simple vowels and diphthongs. Simple vowels are produced with the tongue in a relatively stationary position. (I use the word 'relatively' here, since the tongue is never really still during speech.) In the diphthongs, however, the tongue moves significantly during the articulation of the vowel.

Let us consider first the simple vowels. These can be divided in turn into three subsets—front vowels, central vowels and back vowels. The four front vowels are those which occur in the words *peat*, *pit*, *pet*, *pat*. These vowels are all pronounced with the tongue well forward in the mouth. The vowel of *peat*, as we have noted, is pronounced with the tongue very high as well as forward. The others are pronounced with the tongue in progressively lower positions, so that the last in the series—the vowel of *pat*—is produced with the tongue in a low front position. There are, it should be noted, one or two secondary differences between some of these vowels. The vowels of *peat* and *pit*, for example, are differentiated by length as well as by tongue position; the first is a long vowel, the second short.

It is useful to have a single symbol for each simple vowel.

We will adopt the following widespread conventions:

/i/ for the vowel of *peat*, *seal*, *keen*, *meet* etc.
/ɪ/ for the vowel of *pit*, *pill*, *tin*, *sip* etc.
/ɛ/ for the vowel of *pet*, *bell*, *ten*, *web* etc.
/æ/ for the vowel of *pat*, *pal*, *can*, *cap* etc.

(I adopt here the usual convention of enclosing symbols which represent the sound units of speech within obliques: / /.) Thus in the spoken language the words *peat*, *pit*, *pet* and *pat* all consist of three sound units (or 'phonemes')—two consonants, /p/ and /t/, and an intervening vowel. The words are represented phonemically as /pit/, /pɪt/, /pɛt/ and /pæt/, respectively.

The five back vowels are those which occur in the words *pool*, *pull*, *port*, *pot*, *part*. They constitute a similar series to the front vowels, in that they are also differentiated by relative tongue height. The vowel of *pool* is pronounced with the tongue in a high back position in the mouth and the others with the tongue in progressively lower positions. Again, there are secondary differences. *Pool* has a long vowel, *pull* a short one; the vowels of *pool*, *pull* and *pot* are pronounced with significant rounding of the lips, whereas that of *part* is 'unrounded'. The phonemic symbols used are:

/u/ for the vowel of *pool*, *boot*, *soon*, *troupe* etc.
/ʊ/ for the vowel of *pull*, *put*, *look* etc.
/ɔ/ for the vowel of *call*, *port*, *dawn* etc.
/ɒ/ for the vowel of *doll*, *pot*, *gone* etc.
/ɑ/ for the vowel of *snarl*, *part*, *barn*, *calf* etc.

The central vowels are pronounced with the tongue in an intermediate position between that for the articulation of the front vowels and that for the back vowels. They occur in the words *but* and *pert* and in the initial (unstressed) syllable of *above*. The vowel of *but* is pronounced with the tongue in a low central position. Its phonemic symbol is /ʌ/, so that this word is represented phonemically as /bʌt/. It also occurs in such words as *cut, pun, cup, tug* (phonemically /kʌt/, /pʌn/, /kʌp/, /tʌg/, respectively). The vowel of *pert* is produced with the tongue in a rather higher (mid) central position. It is represented phonemically as /ɜ/. It is a long vowel, occurring in such words as *bird*, *word*, *fern* (phonemically /bɜd/, /wɜd/, /fɜn/). There is a shorter counterpart to this vowel, which occurs very widely in unstressed syllables in English. This vowel is known as 'schwa' and is represented phonemically by the symbol /ə/. Schwa occurs, for example, in the initial syllables of *above*, *aloof*, *akin* (phonemically /əbʌv/, /əluf/, /əkɪn/) and in the final syllables of *butter, killer, Peter* (/bʌtə/, /kɪlə/, /pitə/). The simple vowels are given in Table 5.1.

Table 5.1: Simple vowels

	Front	Central	Back
High	i (p*ea*t)		u (p*oo*l)
	ɪ (p*i*t)		ʊ (p*u*ll)
	ɛ (p*e*t)	ɜ/ə (p*er*t/*a*bove)	ɔ (d*aw*n)
	æ (p*a*t)	ʌ (b*u*t)	ɒ (p*o*t)
Low			ɑ (p*ar*t)

Two important points need to be made at this stage. The first is that the standard orthographic system exhibits widespread inconsistency, in that it often uses different symbols, or different combinations of symbols, for the same vowel. Thus the words *seat*, *meet*, *Pete* all contain the same vowel in the spoken language but have different symbols in the written language: *ea* in *seat*, *ee* in *meet*, *e-e* in *Pete*. The second (more important) point is that the foregoing description is orientated towards one particular variety of English, that type of British pronunciation often referred to as 'Received Pronunciation' (RP), sometimes said to be the kind of English used by BBC news readers. The description also works reasonably well for some American and Australian varieties. If we were to describe other varieties, however, various modifications would have to be made. Many northern speakers of British English, for example, use the same vowel in *but* that they use in *put* (/ʊ/ in both cases). In other words, these speakers have two central vowels—/ɜ/ and /ə/—rather than three. There are also differences in the distribution of the various vowel sounds. The words *put* and *look* were cited above as containing the same vowel, /ʊ/, and *pool* as containing a different vowel, /u/. Again, this does not hold for many northern speakers, who use the same vowel in *pool* and *look*, pronouncing the latter /luk/ (as in *Luke*). Another illustration of this point is provided by a word such as *bird*. We noted above that it consisted of just three units, the consonants /b/ and /d/ and the vowel /ɜ/. However, this would not be an accurate description of the speech of many American or Scottish speakers, who have a /r/ sound following the vowel. For these speakers words such as *bird*, *part* and *corn* should be transcribed as /bɜrd/, /pɑrt/, /kɔrn/, by contrast with RP speakers, who pronounce them /bɜd/, /pɑt/, /kɔn/.

All this highlights a rather different kind of inconsistency in the standard orthographic system from the one mentioned earlier. The *r* that is found in the spelling of such words as *bird*, *part* and *corn* goes back to a period when a /r/ sound was present in the pronunciation of these words in all varieties of English. In some varieties, including RP, it disappeared from these words after the spelling had been standardised. We now, therefore, have a spelling which represents the pronunciation of some varieties better than that of others. As far as those varieties are concerned where /r/ has disappeared, the spelling is somewhat abstract in character, in that the *r* symbol following a vowel represents a long vowel rather than a /r/ sound. Given that the spelling system has to serve speakers with a wide variety of accents, it is in fact advantageous to have a system which is abstract or indirect in this sense. Anyone seeking to impose a 'phonetic' spelling on English would either have to accept that each accent should have its own orthography or would have to select one variety, somewhat arbitrarily, as the basis for the whole system. A range of issues arising out of the question of 'underlying' phonemic representations (to be discussed in Ch. 6) and the whole question of sociolinguistic variation (to be discussed in Ch. 7) add further complexities to this question.

We will deal with the second major class of vowels—the diphthongs—very briefly. It has been noted that the main characteristic of these vowel units is that they involve significant tongue movement. Consider, for example, the word *bait*. There are arguments for regarding this word too as consisting of just three phonemic units—the consonants /b/ and /t/ and an intervening vowel. For speakers of RP (and for many American and Australian speakers) the pronunciation of this vowel starts with the tongue in the mid front area associated with the simple vowel /ɛ/ of *bet*. In the case of *bait*, however, the tongue moves rapidly upwards from the /ɛ/ to the /ɪ/ area (/ɪ/ being the vowel of *bit*), before moving to the alveolar ridge for the /t/. We can therefore represent this vowel phonemically as /ɛɪ/. Words such as *bait*, *plane* and *tray* are transcribed phonemically as /bɛɪt/, /plɛɪn/, /trɛɪ/.

The vowel /ɛɪ/ is classified as a 'fronting' diphthong, because the tongue movement involved is into the (high) front area associated with /ɪ/. There are two other fronting diphthongs in most varieties of English. One is the vowel of such words as *bite*, *tile*, *mine*, for which the tongue starts in the low back area associated with /ɑ/ (the vowel of *part*) but then moves rapidly upwards and forwards towards the /ɪ/ area. This vowel is represented as /ɑɪ/ and the words *bite*, *tile* and *mine* as /bɑɪt/, /tɑɪl/, /mɑɪn/, respectively. The third fronting diphthong is the vowel of such words as *coil*, *loin*, *toy*. This starts in the /ɔ/ area (the vowel of *port*), again moving upwards and forwards into the /ɪ/ area. The vowel is represented as /ɔɪ/ and the words *coil, loin, toy* as /kɔɪl/, /lɔɪn/, /tɔɪ/, respectively.

There are two further sets of diphthongs: centring and backing. The centring diphthongs all involve tongue movement into the mid central position associated with /ə/ (the vowel schwa occurring in the unstressed syllables of *above*, *aloof* etc.) The vowel of *beer*, *here*, *fear*, for example, starts in the /ɪ/ area (*bit*), then moves towards /ə/. These words are transcribed /bɪə/, /hɪə/, /fɪə/. The vowel of *pear*, *where* and so on starts in the /ɛ/ area, then for many speakers moves towards /ə/. The vowel of *tour* and *poor* is usually described as involving tongue movement from /ʊ/ to /ə/.

For some speakers there is a fourth centring diphthong starting in the /ɔ/ area (*port*) and moving towards /ə/. This occurs in such words as *soar* and *four*. Even within RP, however, there is a good deal of variation in these phonemes. Many speakers use long vowels rather than diphthongs in the words cited—particularly in words such as *pear* and *where*, in which a long /ɛ/ vowel is often heard and in *soar* and *pour* a long /ɔ/ rather than a diphthong is common (Gimson 1970: 115, 144).

The two backing diphthongs involve movement into the area associated with the vowel /ʊ/ (*pull*, *put* etc.). The first is the vowel of *house*, *cow* etc., in which there is movement from the low back /ɑ/ area (*part*) towards the higher back /ʊ/ area. *House* and *cow* are transcribed /hɑʊs/, /kɑʊ/. The second backing diphthong is the vowel of *stone*, *go* and so on. This vowel has a particularly wide range of pronunciations across the gamut of English varieties. For most speakers of RP it starts in the /ə/ area, with the tongue then moving upwards and backwards towards /ʊ/ – /stəʊn/, /həʊm/ and so on. Table 5.2 lists the various diphthongs.

Table 5.2: Diphthongs

Fronting	Centring	Backing
ɛɪ (b*ai*t)	ɪə (f*ear*)	ɑʊ (h*ou*se)
ɑɪ (t*ie*)	ɛə (p*ear*)	əʊ (g*o*)
ɔɪ (c*oi*l)	ʊə (t*our*)	
	ɔə (s*oar*)	

The main point I would like to bring out of this brief discussion of the vowels of English is the extraordinary fineness of control involved in the production of speech. The differences between the tongue positions of such vowels as /i/ and /ɪ/, /ɪ/ and /ɛ/, /ɛ/ and /æ/ are minimal, and yet speakers make these extremely subtle differentiations consistently and at high speed in the production of speech.

We also recognise these differentiations very accurately in listening to speech. That is, although the articulatory (and acoustic) differences between *peat*, *pit*, *pet* and *pat* are very small indeed, we seldom have any difficulty in deciding which word a speaker has produced. This is one area where there surely can be no disagreement about the intricacy and delicacy of the human being's biological endowment for the production and perception of language. No other species is as well equipped as we are to deal with these articulatory and perceptual nuances.

CONSONANTS

Let us now look at the consonants of English, where the same general point concerning the delicacy of the system is illustrated even more clearly. The consonants are particularly relevant to the language-development process.

From the articulatory point of view the main difference between consonants and vowels is that, whereas vowels are produced with a relatively 'open' vocal tract, some degree of 'closure' is involved in the production of consonants. This means that for vowels the air flow from the lungs through the mouth is relatively unrestricted, and the main function of the oral cavity, as we have seen, is to act as a sounding box or resonator with respect to the vibrating vocal cords. In the production of consonants, on the other hand, the role of the tongue and the lips is quite different. We use them to restrict the air flow in a variety of ways at various places in the mouth.

There are two major consonant classes and three minor ones. We will concentrate on the major ones here, since these are most relevant to early child language. Sounds known as 'stops' constitute the first major class. Stops are produced when the air flow is blocked completely for a few milliseconds, either by the lips or the tongue. When this happens, air pressure builds up behind the constriction and there is a sudden release of this pressure when the constriction is removed. This sudden burst of air escaping at a particular point of the oral tract creates a particular sound which we hear as one of the stop consonants. (Stops are sometimes called 'plosives' because of the role of the sudden release of air pressure in their articulation.)

There are six stop consonants in English:

/p/ the initial sound of *pat*
/b/ the initial sound of *bat*
/t/ the initial sound of *tin*
/d/ the initial sound of *din*
/k/ the initial sound of *cot*
/g/ the initial sound of *got*

These consonants can be usefully grouped into pairs. The first pair, /p/ and /b/, are called labial stops, because it is the lips which cause the blockage of the air flow in the articulation of these sounds. The lips are brought together, air pressure builds up behind them and is then suddenly released. We hear the sound as /p/ if the vocal cords are not vibrating just after the release of air; if the speaker sets the vocal cords to vibrate as the air is released, we hear the sound as /b/. In the articulation of all the other stops it is the tongue rather than the lips which produce the closure, and these four stops are all therefore 'lingual' stops. They can be further subdivided into two pairs: 'alveolar' (/t/ and /d/) and 'velar' (/k/ and /g/). In the case of /t/ and /d/ the tongue is raised to the alveolar ridge, just behind the upper row of teeth, in such a way as to effect a complete closure of the air flow. Again, air pressure builds up at this point and is released when the tongue is quickly drawn away. If the vocal cords are 'switched off' during this operation, the sound is heard as /t/; if they are set to vibrate immediately, a /d/ is produced. The velar sounds /k/ and /g/ are produced by raising the back of the tongue to make contact with the rear section of the roof of the mouth, known as the 'velum'. Again the tongue effects complete closure here, followed by sudden release. The acoustic effect is /k/ if the vocal cords are 'off', /g/ if they are 'on'.

Any sound in which vocal-cord vibration is a necessary ingredient is known as a 'voiced' sound. All the vowels are voiced and so are the consonants /b/, /d/, /g/. Sounds in which the absence of vocal-cord vibration is a necessary ingredient such as /p/, /t/, /k/ are 'voiceless'.

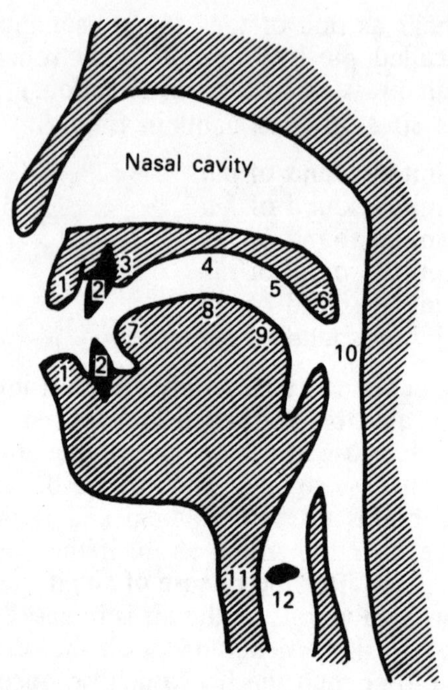

Figure 5.1: The organs of speech

1. Lips	5. Velum (soft palate)	9. Back of tongue
2. Teeth	6. Uvula	10. Pharynx
3. Alveolar ridge	7. Tip of tongue	11. Larynx
4. Hard palate	8. Blade of tongue	12. Vocal cords

We can now give a reasonably full articulatory description of the six stop consonants of English:

/p/ a voiceless labial stop
/b/ a voiced labial stop
/t/ a voiceless (lingual) alveolar stop
/d/ a voiced (lingual) alveolar stop
/k/ a voiceless (lingual) velar stop
/g/ a voiced (lingual) velar stop

We will see that such features as voiceless, voiced, labial, lingual, alveolar and velar are not simply technical descrip-

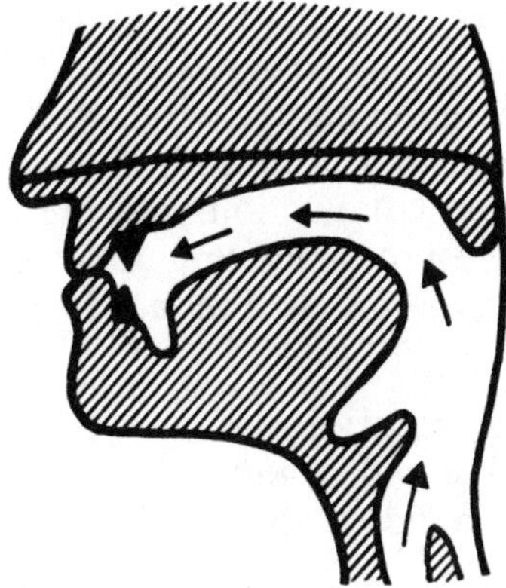

/p,b/ Note the closure at the lips and the raised uvula

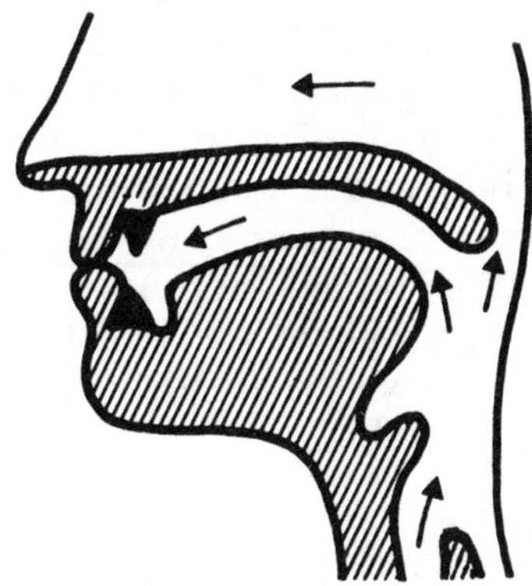

/m/ Note the open nasal cavity with lowered uvula

Figure 5.2: Articulatory diagrams for p, b and m

tive categories. They are very relevant to an understanding of early child language.

The stops listed above are all produced with the uvula (i.e. the rear section of the velum) in a raised position. In this position the uvula makes contact with the back of the throat (the pharyngeal wall), thereby closing off the nasal cavity and directing the air flow fully into the mouth. The uvula can, however, be lowered. The effect of this is to direct some air into the nasal cavity and thus to add a nasal resonance to the sound produced. For example, when the uvula is lowered in conjunction with the basic articulatory gesture for /b/ (closure of the lips, followed by release and voicing), the 'nasal' /m/ is produced. English has three nasals:

/m/ the initial sound of *mat*
/n/ the initial sound of *nest*
/ŋ/ the final sound of *sing*

The second nasal, /n/, bears the same relationship to /d/ as /m/ does to /b/. It is produced by lowering the uvula as the tongue effects closure (followed by release) at the alveolar ridge. The third nasal, /ŋ/, is related to /g/ in the same way: it results from the superimposition of nasal resonance on the basic articulatory gesture for /g/ (closure at the velum). /ŋ/ differs from /m/ and /n/ in its 'distribution' in English, in that it occurs only in the middle or at the end of words. There are no words such as *nga*, *ngu* and so on in English. (Interestingly, some infants appear to enjoy producing sounds such as *nga*, *ngu* at the babbling stage; the significance of this point will be discussed in Ch.6.) The nasals can be described as follows:

/m/ a labial nasal
/n/ an alveolar nasal
/ŋ/ a velar nasal

We come now to the second major class of consonants: the 'fricatives'. For our purposes the interesting point about

Table 5.3: Stops and nasals

		Labial	Alveolar	Velar
Stops	voiceless	p (*p*at)	t (*t*in)	k (*c*ot)
	voiced	b (*b*at)	d (*d*in)	g (*g*ot)
Nasals	(voiced)	m (*m*at)	n (*n*est)	ŋ (si*ng*)

fricatives is that they do not appear in the early language of many children, although this does not mean that children do not produce adult words containing them. What children often do is to substitute a stop for a fricative in these words. (We will look at this process in more detail in the next chapter.) Both stops and fricatives are produced by imposing some restriction on air flow through the mouth. The difference between them is that, whereas the restriction is complete for stops, it is only partial for fricatives. Let us take /f/—the intitial sound of *fat*—as an example. In order to produce /f/, the speaker brings the lower lip very close indeed to the upper row of teeth. (Since lip and teeth are involved, /f/ is a 'labiodental' fricative.) The effect of this is to squeeze the air flow through a very narrow gap. This produces turbulence, which creates an acoustic signal that we perceive as /f/. The main difference between /f/ and /p/, then, apart from the fact that it is the upper row of teeth rather than the upper lip that is involved, is that the air flow is continuous for /f/ but interrupted for /p/. For this reason fricatives are often called 'continuants'.

The nine fricatives of English are as follows:

/f/ the initial sound of *fat*
/v/ the initial sound of *vat*
/θ/ the initial sound of *thatch*
/ð/ the initial sound of *that*
/s/ the initial sound of *sip*
/z/ the initial sound of *zip*
/ʃ/ the initial sound of *ship*
/ʒ/ the middle consonant sound of *leisure*
/h/ the initial sound of *hat*

Again, this series can be divided into pairs (except for the last item), with the second member of each pair being the voiced counterpart of the first member. So /v/, for example, is produced like /f/, with the lower lip close to the top teeth, but with the additional element of vocal-cord vibration. The fricative /θ/ (the initial sound of *thatch*, *think*, *thistle* etc.) is produced with the tongue close to the top teeth. Air is thus squeezed through a narrow gap at the same point as /f/, but in this case the use of the tongue produces a different acoustic effect, which we perceive as /θ/. (Since the tongue moves to a position between the two rows of teeth, /θ/ is termed 'interdental'.) This is another case where a single sound is represented in the written language by two letters because of the limited resources of the orthographic system. The complexity of the relationship between the spoken and the written languages is further highlighted by the fricative /ð/. This is the voiced counterpart of /θ/ and occurs at the beginning of such words as *that*, *this* and *those*. The written language uses the same symbol, *th*, for both of these sounds, which is perhaps why beginning students of linguistics often have some difficulty in deciding which one occurs in a particular word. In their use of the language, however, native speakers do distinguish quite clearly between them. Contrast, for example, the pronunciation of *thistle* with *this'll* (as in *this'll work*). Here the only difference is between the initial consonants—/θ/ in *thistle*, /ð/ in *this'll*. (Note also that *bath* ends in /θ/, *bathe* in /ð/.)

The third pair of fricatives, /s/ and /z/, are produced by bringing the tip of the tongue close to the alveolar ridge and squeezing air through a narrow gap at that point. /s/ is voiceless, /z/ is voiced. The fourth pair, /ʃ/ and /ʒ/, are produced with a much flatter configuration of the tongue behind the alveolar ridge close to the hard palate. /ʃ/ is the initial consonant of *ship*, *shoe* and so on (another single unit represented by two letters in the orthographic system). /ʒ/ is its voiced counterpart and has a very restricted distribution in English. It occurs in a relatively small number of words, such as the following:

ORTHOGRAPHIC	PHONEMIC
leisure	/lɛʒə/
pleasure	/plɛʒə/
treasure	/trɛʒə/
seizure	/siʒə/

Some people pronounce the words *garage* and *beige* with this element in final position: /gærɑʒ/, /bɛɪʒ/. It does not occur word-initially in English, although it does so in French—the French word *je* is pronounced /ʒə/. Finally, the glottal fricative /h/ is produced with an open vocal tract,

Table 5.4: Fricatives

	Labio-dental	Inter-dental	Alveolar	Palatal	Glottal
Voiceless	f (*f*at)	θ (*th*atch)	s (*s*ip)	ʃ (*sh*ip)	h (*h*at)
Voiced	v (*v*at)	ð (*th*at)	z (*z*ip)	ʒ (vi*si*on)	

increased air pressure from the lungs causing general turbulence. The various fricatives are given in Table 5.4.

There are three remaining minor classes of phonemes: 'affricates', 'liquids' and 'glides'. Each of these consists of a pair of elements:

affricates: /tʃ/ the initial sound of *church*
/dʒ/ the initial sound of *judge*
liquids: /l/ the initial sound of *light*
/r/ the initial sound of *right*
glides: /w/ the initial sound of *wet*
/j/ the initial sound of *yes*

I will not discuss the articulatory properties of these sounds here, since they play only a marginal role in the later discussion of phonological development. (A full description of all the English phonemes is given in e.g. Gimson 1970.)

One of the striking points about English phonology is the remarkable symmetry of the system. (The same point tends to hold for other languages too.) The nine stops are associated with just three positions—lips, alveolar ridge, velum—for each of which there is a voiceless member, a voiced member and a nasal. Eight of the nine fricatives are also associated with three positions—the top teeth, the alveolar ridge and the hard palate—with the teeth interacting either with the bottom lip (for /f/ and /v/) or with the tongue (for /θ/ and /ð/). For each position there is a voiceless and a voiced member. We will see that the symmetrical nature of the system plays a part in child language. Again, it will be clear from this discussion that the degree of control exhibited by human beings in producing the sounds of speech at high speed is quite remarkable. Speech is controlled by a constant stream of signals from the brain to those organs involved in articulation—the muscles of the chest, which compress the lungs, the musculature surrounding the vocal cords, the uvula, the tongue, the lips. The movements of each of these organs must be co-ordinated with each other in the most intricate way, in order to produce intelligible speech. There is very clear evidence here of the richness of the human being's biological endowment for language.

THE SPEECH-CONTROL MECHANISM

Let us now consider some of the psychological implications of the previous discussion. We have noted that the articulatory mechanism is controlled by a constant stream of signals sent out from the brain to the articulators. These signals co-ordinate the various articulatory organs, so that the sounds which the speaker intends to produce are in fact produced. (The system relies on the feedback of tactile and acoustic information from the vocal tract and through the ear, a point to which we will return in Ch.6.) All this means that for each word in a speaker's vocabulary, she must have some stored internal representation which she calls upon when she wishes to produce that word. For example, if I decide that I want to express a particular meaning encoded by the word *stone*, I need to locate immediately the information in my brain that the word I require consists of a /s/ sound, followed by a /t/ sound, followed by /əu/ and ending with /n/. Once I have located this information, it is immediately converted into the form of a set of signals which are then transmitted to the articulators. First, a signal is sent to the tongue, instructing it to move to the area of the alveolar ridge, but not to touch it yet, for the pronunciation of /s/. A few milliseconds later a signal is issued instructing the tongue now to make contact with the alveolar ridge and to adopt a general shape which will effect closure. Then a further signal arrives causing the tongue to withdraw rapidly, the result of which is the production of /t/. This brings the tongue downwards to a central position for the beginning of the diphthong, and a new signal then causes it to move upwards and backwards to complete the vowel. It is then brought back to the alveolar ridge in preparation for /n/, which is produced by a final signal causing rapid withdrawal. The whole operation is rather reminiscent of a complex military operation, in which the actions of different units need to be carefully and continuously monitored by the commander-in-chief.

There are, in fact, further complexities. To take a case in point, when adult speakers of English pronounce a /p/, they pronounce it in slightly different ways, depending on its position within the word. The /p/ in the word *pie*, for example, is pronounced with a certain amount of 'aspiration'. This means that the puff of air which accompanies the release of the closure is a significant one. On the other hand, this aspiration is much weaker in the pronunciation of /p/ in *spy*. If you hold your hand in front of your mouth and say these words in succession, the difference is quite noticeable. This variation is systematic in the sense that every word-initial stop in English is strongly aspirated in contrast with those stops which occur after /s/ in a 'consonant cluster'. This means that the signals sent from the brain which produce the /p/, /t/, /k/ in such words as *pie*, *pool*, *pun*, *tie*, *ton*, *tone*, *cool*, *key*, *come* differ from the set of signals sent to produce the same phonemes in such words as *spy*, *spool*, *spun*, *sty*, *stun*, *stone*, *school*, *ski*, *scum*.

The kind of differences just cited apply to other sound units besides the stops. For example, there are systematic differences between the /l/ in a word like *leaf* and the /l/ in *feel*. Phoneticians refer to word-initial /l/ as a 'clear' /l/ and to word-final /l/ as a 'dark' /l/. (For details see Gimson 1970: 201–5.)

We have noted above that a human being must have some internal representation for the pronunciation of each word that she knows stored somewhere in the brain. When she wishes to utter a particular word, she draws on this lexical representation in order to construct the set of signals to be sent to the articulators. (Certain types of brain damage can interfere with this access mechanism, so that a person may know a word in the sense of being able to recognise it when heard and know what it means but nevertheless be unable to pronounce it.) I will refer to this internal representation as the 'mental representation' for a particular word.

Now, we have observed that the mental representation for the word *stone* must contain the information that it consists of /s/, followed by /t/, followed by /əu/, followed by /n/. One question arising at this point is whether the information concerning the /t/ contains the specification that it is not only a voiceless alveolar stop but also that it is unaspirated. This seems unlikely. For one thing it would be extremely uneconomical for the brain to store for every stop in every word the information that it was either aspirated or unaspirated. It seems much more likely that the information that initial stops are aspirated and that those following /s/ are unaspirated is stored separately from the mental representation for individual words. Presumably, this separate store of pronunciation rules is then consulted when the mental representation for a particular word is accessed in the construction of the signals to be sent to the articulators.

One piece of evidence suggesting that this is indeed how it works is that, when children produce nonsense words, these follow the same pattern as other words in the language. Thus, if a child decides to invent a person called *Tiffy*, she will pronounce the word with an aspirated /t/. However, since she has not heard this word from an adult, she cannot have obtained the information that it begins with an aspirated /t/ from outside. There must be a piece of information in her brain to the effect that any initial /t/ is aspirated; that is, she must have formulated a general rule to this effect, separate from the mental representations for particular words. We can now suggest therefore, that the mental representations for particular words may not be identical to the phonetic form in which they appear. The mental representation for *stone*, for example, does not contain the information that the /t/ is unaspirated. This is stored separately. The idea that there can be a discrepancy between the mental representation for a particular word and its phonetic characteristics will show up again in the following chapter in the discussion of child-language development. I will therefore close this chapter with one or two more examples illustrating this point and elaborating on it.

Let us consider a question arising with respect to the mental representation for such words as *soar*, *roar* and *fear*. For me, as for many other speakers of English, these words end in a vowel rather than a /r/ sound in speech. That is, I normally pronounce *soar* as /sɔ/, *roar* as /rɔ/, *fear* as /fɪə/. At first sight, then, it seems reasonable to suggest that my mental representation for these words must be /sɔ/, /rɔ/ and /fɪə/, respectively. This, however, may be an overhasty conclusion. Consider now my pronunciation of the forms *soaring*, *roaring* and *fearing*. I pronounce these respectively as /sɔrɪŋ/, /rɔrɪŋ/, /fɪərɪŋ/. Grammatically, these forms are the present-participle form of the verbs in question. The present participle is used after the verbal auxiliary *be* in such structures as *he is walking slowly*, *he is taking a bath*, *he is soaring into the air*, *he is roaring in anger*, *he is pouring some milk*. Now, the general grammatical rule is that, in constructing the present-participle form of any verb, the suffix /ɪŋ/ is added to the mental representation for that verb. So /wɔk/ (walk) becomes /wɔkɪŋ/ (walking), /tɛɪk/ (take) becomes /tɛɪkɪŋ/ and so on. But if /sɔ/ is the mental representation for *soar*, then we would expect /sɔɪŋ/ rather than /sɔrɪŋ/ to be the present participle. (For me /sɔɪŋ/ is the present participle of the verb *saw*, as in *I was sawing some wood*.) On the other hand, if my mental representation for the word *soar* is /sɔr/, then the fact that I pronounce the present participle as /sɔrɪŋ/ would follow quite naturally. It would also explain certain other features of my speech; for example, the fact that I pronounce the sentence *we soar up* as /wisɔrʌp/, with a /r/ sound between the /ɔ/ of *soar* and the /ʌ/ of *up* (whereas I pronounce *saw up* in *saw up the wood*! as /sɔʌp/).

All this leads to the conclusion that my mental representation for the word *soar* is different from my normal pronunciation of it. My mental representation is /sɔr/; my normal pronunciation is /sɔ/. This in turn means that, before we pronounce words, we consult other areas of information in our brain besides the mental representation. In this case

I must have a rule somewhere to the effect that word-final /r/ is not pronounced (i.e. that it is 'deleted'), unless it is immediately followed by a vowel. This would explain why I pronounce *pour* as /pɔ/ in *we pour tea* but as /pɔr/ in *they pour in*, why I pronounce *fear* as /fɪə/ in *I fear nothing* but as /fɪər/ in *I fear an explosion* and so on.

Again, then, we have a situation where the mental representation for a particular set of words is different from their phonetic form—or, more precisely, from ONE of their phonetic forms. This case differs from the preceding example involving aspirated and unaspirated stops, in that in this case the mental representation contains information which may not appear in the phonetic form. The final /r/ of /sɔr/, /pɔr/, /fɪər/ and so on is often deleted when the word is pronounced. The situation discussed above was the converse one, since the mental representation did not contain all the information that appeared in the phonetic form. The information that the /t/ of *stone* is unaspirated is not present in the mental representation for the word but is added by a general rule. Thus we see that even the articulatory aspects of speech can be satisfactorily described only if we take speech to be the product of an intricate interaction between various rules operating at a number of levels.

In summary, a model of some of the steps involved in the pronunciation of *pour* in *they pour tea* is as follows:

1. The speaker decides that she wishes to pronounce the word *pour* in *they pour tea*.
2. In order to send out the correct set of control signals to the articulators, she consults her mental representation for the word *pour*. The information obtained is that the word consists of the following sequence:

$$\begin{bmatrix} \text{voiceless} \\ \text{labial} \\ \text{stop} \end{bmatrix} + \begin{bmatrix} \text{mid} \\ \text{rounded} \\ \text{long} \\ \text{back} \\ \text{vowel} \end{bmatrix} + \begin{bmatrix} \text{alveolar} \\ \text{liquid} \end{bmatrix}$$

3. Before sending out appropriate signals for producing this sequence, she checks to see if there are any general rules which might involve adding elements to or deleting elements from these signals. She finds the following:
   (a) Since the first stop is word-initial, it should be aspirated. This information is added to the set of signals designed to produce that item.
   (b) Since the alveolar liquid is word-final, the whole item should be deleted, unless the sound immediately following is a vowel. The following sound is a /t/, so the final unit of /pɔr/ is deleted.

These processes convert the sequence:

$$\begin{bmatrix}\text{voiceless}\\ \text{labial}\\ \text{stop}\end{bmatrix} + \begin{bmatrix}\text{mid}\\ \text{rounded}\\ \text{long}\\ \text{back}\\ \text{vowel}\end{bmatrix} + \begin{bmatrix}\text{alveolar}\\ \text{liquid}\end{bmatrix}$$

into the sequence:

$$\begin{bmatrix}\text{voiceless}\\ \text{labial}\\ \text{aspirated}\\ \text{stop}\end{bmatrix} + \begin{bmatrix}\text{mid}\\ \text{rounded}\\ \text{long}\\ \text{back}\\ \text{vowel}\end{bmatrix}$$

This set of information is then converted into the signals which are finally sent out to the articulators, resulting in the pronunciation /pɔ/.

I will close with just one more example of a rule which converts a mental representation into a different phonetic form. This time we will take an example from a language other than English. (The following discussion is based on Schane 1968: Ch. 1.) It is a well-known fact that French adjectives 'agree' with the noun which they qualify. This phenomenon is usually illustrated by such examples as the following:

(1) Le livre est petit.	'The book is small.'
(2) La table est petite.	'The table is small.'
(3) L'homme est grand.	'The man is tall.'
(4) La femme est grande.	'The woman is tall.'
(5) Le garçon est gros.	'The boy is fat.'
(6) La jeune fille est grosse.	'The girl is fat.'

The rule is generally said to be that, if the adjective is predicated of a feminine noun, it adds an *e* to the masculine form—*petit* becomes *petite*, *grand* becomes *grande*, *gros* becomes *grosse* (with a doubling of the *s* here) and so on. This statement of the rule is a description only of the written language, however. In the spoken language the situation is a little more complex.

Let us consider the way these forms are pronounced. In (1) the adjective is pronounced /pəti/; in (2) it is pronounced /pətit/. In the spoken language, then, it seems as if the feminine form /pətit/ is derived from the masculine form /pəti/ by adding not an *e* but a /t/. In (3) the adjective is pronounced /grɔ̃/, where /ɔ̃/ represents a nasal vowel; in (4) it is pronounced /grɔ̃d/. In this case the feminine is apparently derived from the masculine by adding a /d/ sound. In (5) the adjective is pronounced /gro/; in (6) it is /gros/. Here it looks as if the feminine is formed by adding /s/ to the masculine form. Does all this mean that we have in spoken French a whole set of idiosyncratic rules for creating feminine forms, with a different consonant being added for each adjective? Remember that French children have to construct their internalised grammar on the basis of these spoken forms—not on the basis of the written language—so that we are really asking a question about the nature of the child's mental grammar here.

There is a way of avoiding the conclusion that the rules for relating the masculine and feminine forms in French are idiosyncratic. Let us suppose that, although the French speaker normally pronounces the masculine form of *petit* as /pəti/, his mental representation for this form is really /pətit/, with a final consonant. Suppose similarly that his mental representation for *grand* (which he normally pronounces /grɒ̃/) is /grɒ̃d/ and the internal form for *gros* (pronounced /gro/) is /gros/. This would mean that he must also have an internal rule to the effect that word-final consonants are usually deleted. If we then add to this rule a condition that it does not apply if the next sound is a vowel (like the rule for final /r/ deletion in English, discussed above), this would explain why the masculine form of these adjectives may be pronounced with a final consonant in such phrases as *le petit ami*. As far as the feminine forms are concerned, we could say that these are derived from the masculine forms in the way that the written language suggests—by the addition of an *e* (more precisely an /ə/) to the mental representation. This would convert the masculine forms /pətit/, /grɒ̃d/, gros/ into the feminine forms /pətitə/, /grɒ̃də/, /grosə/.

There is in fact a good deal of evidence in French to support this postulated final consonant deletion rule. It would explain why the plural form of the French article, written *les*, is pronounced /le/ (with a final vowel) if the next word begins with a consonant and /lez/ (with a final consonant) if the next word begins with a vowel. Thus in *les garçons* and *les femmes* it is pronounced /le/, whereas in *les amis* and *les oranges* it is pronounced /lez/. Similar considerations apply to other words such as the possessive forms *mes*, *tes*, *nos*, the pronouns *nous*, *vous* and so on. We would say that in all these cases the mental representation for the word ends in a consonant: /lez/, /mez/, /nuz/ and so on, which is deleted if the following word begins with a consonant.

CONCLUSION

In this chapter we have examined the basic characteristics of the sound structure of English and explored some of the psychological implications. We have identified forty-five sound units: twenty-one vowel sounds, produced with a relatively open vocal tract, and twenty-four consonants, produced with various kinds of closure or constriction.

Speech is produced by very rapid transitions of the articulatory apparatus from one state to another—a mechanism that is actuated by a rich array of muscles, controlled by a stream of signals emitted from the motor control centre in the brain. In order to compose the appropriate set of signals for a particular utterance, the motor control centre needs to have access to the mental representations for the pronunciation of the words which make up the intended utterance. However, the control centre also has to consult other networks of information in the brain concerning pronunciation. We surmise that this is the case because the information which appears to comprise the mental representations for the words in question does not always correspond with the pronunciations we observe. It seems unlikely that the information concerning whether a particular stop should be aspirated or unaspirated, for example, is contained in the mental representation for each word. It is drawn, rather, from the network of information that we call the phonological component of the grammar. In other respects the mental representation may be richer than the form produced on a particular occasion. This situation is illustrated by such words as *soar*, *pour*, *fear* in English or *petit*, *les*, *nous* in French, which often lose the final consonant of their mental representation. Again, we would account for this fact by postulating a general phonological deletion rule in the grammar. All this indicates that the articulatory process is far from being the least complex aspect of language use.

6 Phonological Development

THE CONSTRUCTION OF THE SPEECH-CONTROL MECHANISM

In this chapter we turn to the question of how the child sets about the task of constructing the mental systems described in the previous chapter which underlie the native speaker's ability to pronounce words and sentences.

Infants, of course, are vocal from the outset. In the very early weeks of life their major vocal activity consists in crying. As time goes on, their vocal activity becomes more differentiated. They begin to produce various types of cry-expression—hunger, discomfort, frustration, tiredness and so on—and also to produce vocalisations which express other types of feelings, like pleasure and excitement. At about the age of 6 months most children begin to produce noises which sound much more like language than the previous cryings, cooings and gurglings. It is possible to hear vowel-like and consonant-like sounds, and many fond mothers convince themselves that their child is saying things like *mama* or *dada* at this stage. This activity is known as 'babbling'. It is unlike language in that it does not express meanings, except in the very broad sense that it is a general indication of contentment. The activity is informative rather than communicative (see p. 22). However, although nobody is quite sure how important babbling is as a precursor to speech, there are certain considerations which suggest that it may play a part in the development into language.

We have established that in order to pronounce a word such as *stone*, a human being needs to send a rather complex series of signals to the articulators—signals which are constructed in the motor-command centre of the brain. Now, the very young infant does not know how to construct such signals. Recall that even the production of a /t/ sound involves a complex series of mechanisms, in which air is gently squeezed out from the lungs and fully directed into the vocal tract by raising the uvula; the air flow is blocked by placing the tongue against the alveolar ridge, so that pressure builds up at that point and is then suddenly released by bringing the tongue smartly away; during all this the muscles of the larynx must keep the vocal cords open, so that they do not vibrate. Infants cannot co-ordinate these movements in the way that older children or adults can, partly because they have had no practice as yet in doing so. No matter how many times an adult might say *stone* to the infant, she is unable to repeat it. It is rather as if a concert pianist were to play repeatedly a musical phrase and then ask a rank beginner to copy it. Neither the child nor the musical novice has yet constructed the neural networks which are called upon by the motor command centre when it sets out to compose the required series of signals. It seems likely that babbling helps the child to construct such networks for speech.

In order to see how this may be so, let us consider a simple model of what happens when a sound is produced. Figure 6.1 represents such a model. When the brain sends out signals along line A, causing the articulators to move, two effects follow. The first effect is that an acoustic signal is produced. This is perceived by the ear of the speaker (as well as by the ear of the listener) and information concerning the acoustic character of the signal is sent back to the speaker's brain (line B). The second effect is that the articulators themselves send information back directly to the brain (line C). For example, suppose my brain sends out control signals causing the tongue to move up to the alveolar ridge. When the tongue hits the alveolar ridge it will send signals back to the brain conveying the information that it has touched something. These signals will include information concerning the extent of the contact at the tongue (e.g. whether just the very tip has touched or whether a larger area of the blade of the tongue is involved), as well as

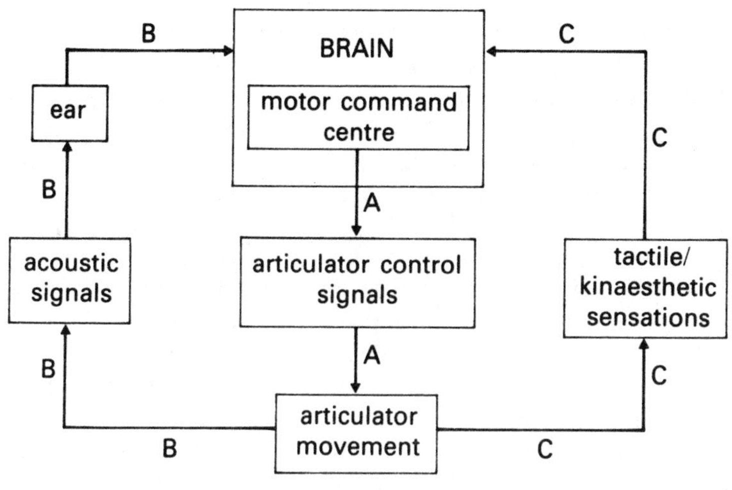

Figure 6.1

(This diagram is based on Fry's (1966: 189) concept of the 'auditory feedback loop'.)

information about the pressure of the contact, about the time the contact was maintained and so on. Signals will also be fed back to the brain by the alveolar ridge itself, giving further information about the extent of the contact.

There is, therefore, both an acoustic and a tactile feedback system concerning articulator movement. Either of these systems can be interfered with, sometimes to the detriment of speech production. The acoustic feedback system can be affected by partial or total deafness, so that a person may, for example, speak more loudly than she intends because she is not receiving full information about the acoustic effect of her articulatory gestures. The tactile feedback mechanism can be interfered with by a dental anaesthetic, for example, so that one may not know exactly what one's tongue is doing. In both these cases interference with the feedback mechanisms can cause the motor control centre to send out a different set of control signals from the ones needed to produce the desired effect. The result is some distortion of speech.

Now it is precisely this association between the nature of the control signals and the nature of the feedback signals which the child needs to establish in order to produce specific sounds. She needs to know that, when she sends out such and such a set of commands, then this is the kind of sound that is produced and this is how it feels in the mouth. Babbling would seem to have an important part to play in the construction of this kind of knowledge. For example, let us suppose that an infant is happily lying in her cot, concentrating on producing a gentle singing or humming noise by causing her vocal cords to vibrate. Suppose that she now brings her lips together and then pulls them apart to see what happens. The general effect will be a /m/-type sound. Since she finds this an interesting noise, she may repeat the gesture several times in rapid succession, producing a /məməməmə . . ./ signal. She may then, perhaps by accident, raise the uvula, blocking off the nasal cavity. The effect of this will be to change the /məməmə . . ./ sequence into a /bəbəbə . . ./ sequence. 'How did that happen?' she may wonder. 'Let's try to do that again': /məməməmə ... bəbəbə ... məmə .../ and so on. Gradually she is beginning to learn how to produce some of the crucial sounds of speech. This information is then stored in the brain. When at some later time the mother says *mama* or *baba*, the infant may draw on the information gained from babbling in order to imitate the mother's sounds.

At this point the child has reached the stage of being able to match an acoustic signal produced by the mother with acoustically-related information stored in her own brain—information which is paired, as a result of the babbling experiences, with a set of motor control signals. Deaf children are prevented from establishing these connections. Most deaf infants produce babbling sounds but they do not receive acoustic feedback from their own experiments with the articulatory apparatus. This prevents them from establishing a connection between any specific motor control signals and the corresponding acoustic information. They cannot therefore learn how to produce specific sounds. Nor, of course, does a deaf child receive acoustic signals from outside, so that there is no way in which she can establish associations between the noises made by others and her own articulations.

Some observers have claimed that many children appear to gain articulatory control over a vast range of sounds during the babbling period. Roman Jakobson, for example, has written about it in the following terms (Jakobson 1968: 21):

> The actual beginning stages of language, as is known, are preceded by the so-called babbling period, which brings to light an astonishing quantity and diversity of sound productions. A child during his babbling period can accumulate articulations which are never found within a single language or even a group of languages—consonants of any place of articulation, palatalized and rounded consonants, sibilants, affricates, clicks, complex vowels, diphthongs etc. According to the findings of phonetically trained observers and to the summarising statement of Grégoire, the child at the height of his babbling period is 'capable of producing all conceivable sounds'.

More recent studies of children would lead us to treat these claims with some caution, but there is certainly little doubt that children do obtain articulatory control over a wide range of sounds during this period.

This now bring us to the first true words produced by the child; that is, the child's pronunciation of such recognisable adult words as *mummy*, *daddy*, *teddy*, *train* and so on. Here we come to a paradox. We have just observed that the child appears to gain articulatory control over a very wide variety of sounds during the babbling period. Yet, in very many cases, the child appears not to be able to use the full range of her skills in the pronunciation of these words. For example, a child who was observed to produce fricative-type sounds such as /s/, /z/, /ʃ/ frequently during the babbling stage may substitute a /d/ for these sounds when they occur in words. So a child who can imitate the sounds /səsəsəsə . . ./ or /dədədə . . ./ quite happily may pronounce *see* as/di/ or *zoo* as /du/. Before we can offer any explanation for this phenomenon, we need to consider in a little more detail the phonological patterns and processes which show up in early child language.

PHONOLOGICAL PROCESSES

When we look at the way in which children pronounce adult words, we notice that their so-called 'mispronunciations' are often surprisingly systematic. For example, a particular child might pronounce the word *zip* as /dɪp/, *zoo* as /du/, *Lizzie* as /dɪdɪ/ and *cheese* as /tid/. In other words, the sound /z/ in an adult word is systematically replaced by /d/ in the speech of this child, whether it occurs at the beginning of the word (*zoo*, *zip*), in the middle (*Lizzie*), or at the end (*cheese*). There is no a priori reason to expect this kind of systematicity. One might have expected a young child to begin by setting up some rather vague mental representations for the early words. For example, on first acquiring the word *zoo*, she might set up a mental representation containing the information that the initial consonant in this word is some kind of alveolar consonant. One would then expect her to produce various pronunciations of it—any of /tu/, /du/, /nu/, /zu/, /su/ would fit with her vague internal specification. If she did the same for the medial consonant of *Lizzie* and the final consonant of *cheese*, then one would expect a vast range of pronunciations for these three words, even if all the other sounds in the words were fully specified:

zoo: /tu/, /du/, /nu/, /zu/, /su/
Lizzie: /lɪtɪ/, /lɪdɪ/, /lɪnɪ/, /lɪzɪ/, /lɪsɪ/
cheese: /tʃit/, /tʃid/, /tʃin/, /tʃiz/, /tʃis/

This potential variability is further increased by what we might call the environmental interference effect. A child hears particular words in all kinds of environments. She might encounter one word—*cheese*, for example—in the quiet environment of the home at lunchtime. On the other hand, she might hear *Lizzie* in the noisy environment of kindergarten, hearing the word much less clearly than she had heard *cheese*. This could lead her to set up a mental representation for *Lizzie* in which the /z/ sound was specified only as some kind of consonant. In that case we would expect her to produce a very wide range of pronunciations. All of the following would be compatible with her internal representation:

/lɪpɪ/, /lɪbɪ/, /lɪmɪ/, /lɪtɪ/, /lɪdɪ/, /lɪnɪ/, /lɪkɪ/
/lɪgɪ/, /lɪŋɪ/, /lɪfɪ/, /lɪvɪ/, /lɪθɪ/, /lɪðɪ/, /lɪsɪ/
/lɪzɪ/, /lɪʃɪ/, /lɪʒɪ/, /lɪwɪ/, /lɪjɪ/, /lɪlɪ/, /lɪrɪ/

Even this list is not exhaustive—there is no particular reason to expect the child at this stage to pronounce only the consonants of English.

Given these a priori possibilities, it is rather surprising that children's speech shows the kind of regularity and systematicity that it does. This is not to deny that there is variation in the way that children pronounce individual words and individual sounds at a particular stage in their development. They are far from exhibiting total consistency here. Part of this variation is no doubt due to a certain lack of specification in their mental representations, for individual words, and environmental factors undoubtedly play some part in this. However, children's speech is much more systematic than one might expect, suggesting that from an early stage they have a relatively stable and a relatively fully-specified representation for individual words. In a moment we will discuss the relationship between this mental representation and that of the adult in a little more detail.

The (relatively) systematic nature of the child's system goes further than that of pronouncing the same word in approximately the same way from one occasion to another, or pronouncing the same sound in the same way in different words. Many children go through a stage where pronunciations such as /du/ for *zoo* and /tid/ for *cheese* are simply part of a more general pattern, illustrated by the following examples:

Word	Adult pronunciation	Child pronunciation
fish	/fɪʃ/	/pɪt/
phone	/fəʊn/	/pəʊn/
van	/væn/	/bæn/
tooth	/tuθ/	/tut/
that	/ðæt/	/dæt/
see	/si/	/ti/
zoo	/zu/	/du/
ship	/ʃɪp/	/tɪp/

The general pattern here is that any fricative is replaced by its corresponding stop. Thus a voiceless labial fricative /f/ is realised in the child's speech as the voiceless labial stop /p/ (fɪʃ/ → /pɪt/, /fəʊn/) → /pəʊn/); a voiced labial fricative /v/ is replaced by a voiced labial stop /b/ (/væn/ → /bæn/); voiceless lingual fricatives such as /θ/, /s/, /ʃ/ are realised as the voiceless lingual (alveolar) stop /t/ (/tuθ/ → /tut/, /si/ → /ti/, /ʃɪp/ → /tɪp/); and the voiced lingual fricatives /ð/ and /z/ are realised as the voiced lingual (alveolar) stop /d/ (/ðæt/ → /dæt/, /zu/ → /du/).

The replacement of fricatives by their corresponding stops—a process known as 'stopping'—is a very widespread phenomenon in children's speech in any language. The interesting point about the phenomenon is that it applies to a particular 'feature' of a sound, not to the whole sound unit as such. It is not that a /f/ is being replaced by a /b/ here. If we were to see it in these terms, we would have to regard all these substitutions as separate processes: /v/ → /b/, /s/ → /t/, /z/ → /d/ and so on. Rather, it seems more satisfactory to say that it is the 'continuant' feature of /f/ that is changed by the child to the feature 'non-continuant' or 'stop', and that this is in fact a general process applying to all fricatives. In other words, the process applies at a surprisingly abstract level.

Stopping is just one of a set of processes which characterise early child speech. (Not all children exhibit all the processes to be mentioned by any means, but they are all sufficiently widespread in children learning a wide variety of languages to deserve mention.) Another typical process is known as 'voicing/devoicing'. Its most common form is when a child voices all word-initial and all word-medial stops but devoices all word-final stops. It is illustrated by the following pronunciations:

Word	Adult pronunciation	Child pronunciation
potty	/pɒtɪ/	/bɒdɪ/
teddy	/tɛdɪ/	/dɛdɪ/
cup	/kʌp/	/gʌp/
apple	/æpəl/	/æbəl/
kitten	/kɪtən/	/gɪdən/
pocket	/pɒkət/	/bɒgət/
bib	/bɪb/	/bɪp/
head	/hɛd/	/hɛt/
egg	/ɛg/	/ɛk/

Here the child realises the voiceless stops /p/, /t/, /k/, at the beginning of the words *potty*, *teddy*, *cup* as their voiced counterparts /b/, /d/, /g/, respectively. That is, a voiceless labial stop /p/ is realised as a voiced labial stop /b/; a voiceless alveolar /t/ as a voiced alveolar /d/; a voiceless velar /k/ as a voiced velar /g/. The same applies to the /p/, /t/, /k/ sounds in the middle of the words *apple* (pronounced /æbəl/ by the child), *kitten* (/gɪdən/) and *pocket* (/bɒgət/). However, when these phonemes are in word-final position the reverse process applies. The /b/, /d/, /g/ sounds at the end of the words *bib*, *head*, *egg* are realised as /p/, /t/, /k/, respectively.

The two processes—stopping and voicing/devoicing—can interact with each other to produce quite complex patterns in the child's speech. Thus a /v/ sound might be realised as /b/ at the beginning of a word (e.g. adult's /væn/ becoming (/bæn/) but as /p/ at the end of a word (adult /wɛɪv/ (*wave*) becoming /wɛɪp/). That is, /v/ is subject to stopping in both cases but is further modified by voicing/devoicing in *wave*, because of its word-final position. Similarly /f/ might be realised as /p/ in *leaf* (pronounced /lip/ by the child) but as /b/ in *fish* (pronounced /bɪt/), since in this latter case the sound unit is modified not only by stopping but also by voicing/devoicing (word-initial stops being voiced).

A rather different type of phonological process very widespread in early child language is known as 'cluster reduction'. It is exemplified by such pronunciations as the following:

WORD	ADULT PRONUNCIATION	CHILD PRONUNCIATION
spoon	/spun/	/pun/
stone	/stəʊn/	/təʊn/
skate	/skɛɪt/	/kɛɪt/
play	/plɛɪ/	/pɛɪ/
blanket	/blæŋkət/	/bækət/
prune	/prun/	/pun/
break	/brɛɪk/	/bɛɪk/
train	/trɛɪn/	/tɛɪn/
drive	/drɑɪv/	/dɑɪv/
biscuit	/bɪskət/	/bɪkət/
post	/pəʊst/	/pəʊt/

In these examples consonant clusters such as /sp/, /st/, /sk/, /pl/, /bl/, /pr/, /br/, /tr/, /dr/ are simplified to a single phoneme. Clusters usually consist of a stop such as /p/, /b/, /t/, /d/, /k/, /g/ and a fricative (e.g. /s/) or a liquid (e.g. /l/, /r/). In clusters consisting of a stop and the fricative /s/, the stop occurs after the fricative (/sp/, /st/, /sk/); in those consisting of a stop and a liquid, the stop comes first (/pl/, /br/, /pr/ /tr/, /dr/). In both situations, however, the cluster tends to be pronounced as a simple stop—the fricative or the liquid being deleted. The process can apply to clusters irrespective of their position in the word. Most of the examples above involve word-initial clusters, but /sk/ can be reduced to /k/ in the middle of a word (cf. the child's pronunciation of *biscuit* as /bɪkət/) and /st/ may be reduced to /t/ at the end of a word such as *post* (child: /pəut/).

Cluster reduction can also interact with other rules such as stopping or voicing. Thus, if a child pronounces the words *fly, frog, throw* as /paɪ/, /pɒg/, /təu/, respectively, she is applying both cluster reduction and stopping. Cluster reduction eliminates the liquid /l/ or /r/ from the cluster:

/flaɪ/ → /faɪ/
/frɒg/ → /fɒg/
/θrəu/ → /θəu/

and the initial fricative is converted to its corresponding stop by stopping:

/faɪ/ → /paɪ/
/fɒg/ → /pɒg/
/θəu/ → /təu/

If she pronounces the words as /baɪ/, /bɒg/, /dəu/, respectively, then she has applied the further process of voicing to all the initial stops.

We have noted that cluster reduction is a different type of rule from stopping or voicing. This is because it involves a process applying to a unit in a particular phonological context. A /s/ sound would normally be realised as a /t/ or /d/ by a young child, but in the specific context of a cluster such as /sp/, /st/, /sk/ it is often deleted. Context plays a part in another widespread process: assimilation. Consider the case of a child who produces the following pronunciations:

WORD	ADULT PRONUNCIATION	CHILD PRONUNCIATION
top	/tɒp/	/tɒp/
take	/tɛɪk/	/kɛɪk/
tea	/ti/	/ti/
tick	/tɪk/	/kɪk/
dirt	/dɜt/	/dɜt/
dog	/dɒg/	/gɒg/
drink	/drɪŋk/	/grɪŋk/
duck	/dʌk/	/gʌk/

At first sight this looks rather chaotic. The child sometimes pronounces /t/ as /t/ (/tɒp/ for *top*, /ti/ for *tea*), sometimes as /k/ (/kɛɪk/ for *take*, /kɪk/ for *tick*); she sometimes pronounces /d/ as /d/ (/dɜt/ for *dirt*), but some as /g/ (/gʌk/ for *duck*), /grɪŋk/ for *drink*). On closer examination there turns out to be a regular pattern. All the words in which /t/ and /d/ are pronounced /k/ or /g/ are those which have a /k/ or /g/ sound in them in the adult form: *take*, *tick*, *dog*, *drink*, *duck*. In other words, we can say that an alveolar sound is realised as the corresponding velar (voiceless /t/ → voiceless /k/, voiced /d/ → voiced /g/) under the influence of a neighbouring velar. That is, the alveolar is assimilated to the velar in these examples.

We have noted that assimilation is a widespread process in child language, but it does not always manifest itself in the same way (Smith 1971: 759). Some children may go through a stage in which they assimilate the alveolars /t/, /d/ but not the labials /p/, /b/ to neighbouring velars. In others both alveolars and labials may be affected. Yet others may assimilate the velars to the alveolars, pronouncing *take* not as /kɛɪk/ but as /tɛɪt/. Neil Smith reports a very subtle example of assimilation in the speech of his son, Amahl. Amahl went through a stage where he pronounced the words /kwin/ (*queen*) and /skwiz/ (*squeeze*) as /kim/ and /kip/, respectively (Smith 1973: 164, 250). It is natural for a child to reduce the /kw/ and /skw/ clusters to /k/ here, but not at all obvious why the child should be realising the alveolar nasal /n/ in *queen* as the labial nasal /m/ nor why he should be using a labial stop /p/ for the alveolar fricative /z/ in *squeeze*. Smith suggests that the reason is that the final consonant is being assimilated to the labial glide /w/ in each case, even though the latter is not actually pronounced in the child's form. This constitutes another good example of the subtle way in which these various processes can interact with each other in the child's early speech.

The various processes discussed above do not constitute an exhaustive list. They are illustrative of the kind of systematic properties which, rather surprisingly, appear to characterise early child speech. It is important to stress that not all children exhibit all these processes. Some produce early pronunciations which are remarkably like those of adults. Where their pronunciations do differ from adult forms, however, the differences are often explicable in terms of such processes.

MENTAL REPRESENTATIONS

Let us consider now some of the consequences of this discussion concerning the nature of the child's mental representations. We will take the case of a child whose speech is characterised by some of the processes discussed above. The question arising now is whether his mental representations for the words he uses are identical to the forms he pronounces or whether they are more like the adult's form. For example, suppose that he pronounces the word *pretty* as /bɪdɪ/, a form characterised by cluster reduction and voicing. Does his mental representation for the pronunciation of this word correspond to (1) or to (2)?

(1) /prɪtɪ/
(2) /bɪdɪ/

For ease of discussion I will consider just these two possibilities, although there are of course others.

At first sight it would seem unreasonable to assume that anything other than (2) was the form of the child's mental representation. If the child pronounces the word as /bɪdɪ/, why should this not be the form in which it is stored in his mental lexicon? There are in fact a number of reasons for surmising that the child's internal form may not be identical to his produced form. The first piece of evidence concerns his ability to distinguish perceptually between forms that he produces identically. For example, Neil Smith's child, Amahl, passed through a stage where he pronounced identically such pairs as *jug* and *duck* (both pronounced /gʌk/), *mouth* and *mouse* (both /mɑʊs/) (Smith 1973: 134). To test whether Amahl was discriminating perceptually between the members of these pairs, Smith invented a game in which the child had to bring pictures of various objects from another room. These included a picture of a jug, a duck, a mouth and a mouse. Smith then observed that Amahl scored a near-perfect success rate when asked to 'bring the picture of the jug', 'bring the picture of the duck' and so on. Now, if the child's internal representation for each word is identical to the way in which he pronounces it, we would be unable to explain this observation. Suppose, for example, that his internal representation for both *jug* and *duck*, each of which he pronounces identically, is /gʌk/. When his father asks for 'the picture of the duck', he has to match the perceived pronunciation of *duck* with one of his internally represented words. The nearest form he has is /gʌk/, but this form is in fact shared by two words, denoting very different objects. One would therefore expect the child sometimes to bring one object, sometimes the other. The fact that this did not happen suggests at least that he had different mental representations for the two words and that these representations could be appropriately matched with the adult pronunciations /dʒʌg/ and /dʌk/. Although this does not prove that his internal representations were identical to the forms produced by adults, it does suggest that they were closer to those forms than his pronunciation indicated.

A second important piece of evidence bearing on this question concerns the 'across-the-board' nature of the acquisition process (Smith 1973: 138–40). Consider a child who produces the following pronunciations:

WORD	CHILD PRONUNCIATION
tip	/tɪp/
sip	/tɪp/
ship	/tɪp/
tea	/ti/
see	/ti/
top	/tɒp/
shop	/tɒp/
two	/tu/
shoe	/tu/

We have here a number of examples where the child uses the same pronunciation for two or more forms that are distinct in the adult's speech. Now let us suppose for a moment, in spite of the evidence from Smith's experiment discussed above, that the child's mental representation for each of these words is identical to his own produced form. That is, he has the same internal representation, /tɪp/, for *tip*, *sip* and *ship*. Now let us move to the stage where fricatives begin to appear in his speech. Suppose that the first word in which this happens is the word *sip*. One day, instead of saying *mummy tip* when his mother tastes his juice before giving it to him, he says *mummy sip*. Obviously, in order for this to happen, he must have changed his internal representation of the word from /tɪp/ to /sɪp/. This must have come about as the result of interaction with the environment. He must have heard his mother produce the word *sip* on some occasion and realised from the context of the utterance that this was the same word for which he had the mental representation /tɪp/. He therefore changed the latter to /sɪp/. However, there is as yet no reason to change his internal representation for other words such as *ship*, *see*, *shop*, *shoe*, for which, under our hypothesis, he has the mental representations /tɪp/, /ti/, /tɒp/, /tu/, respectively. He will change each of these only when he realises that his mental representation in a particular case is unsatisfactory. This realisation can also come about only as a result of interaction with the environment. Given his new-found ability to perceive fricatives, he now needs to hear someone produce each of these words before he can become aware of the incorrectness of his internal representation.

Obviously, a considerable period will elapse before he will have heard all these words from the lips of an adult. This all leads to the conclusion that under this hypothesis the diffusion of innovations will be very slow. A long period should elapse between the first appearance of a fricative and its complete spread throughout all the words where adults use it.

In fact, diffusions of this kind take place rather rapidly. The first appearance of a fricative in a particular word is quickly followed by its appearance in other words where it is appropriate. The most obvious explanation is that, even at the stage when the child is pronouncing *tip* and *sip*, *tea* and *see*, *top* and *shop*, *two* and *shoe* identically, he in fact has distinct mental representations for each word. If these correspond to the forms produced by adults, then the situation is as follows:

ADULT WORD	CHILD'S MENTAL REPRESENTATION	CHILD'S PRODUCED FORM
tip	/tɪp/	/tɪp/
sip	/sɪp/	/tɪp/
ship	/ʃɪp/	/tɪp/
tea	/ti/	/ti/
see	/si/	/ti/
top	/tɒp/	/tɒp/
shop	/ʃɒp/	/tɒp/
two	/tu/	/tu/
shoe	/ʃu/	/tu/

This means that when the child begins to produce fricatives the advance involves his ability to produce distinctions of which he is in some sense already aware.

One minor qualification should be placed on the foregoing argument. Children's pronunciations of particular words do not change overnight, as the previous discussion may have suggested. A child does not switch abruptly from pronouncing *sip* as /tɪp/ to pronouncing it as /sɪp/. The normal pattern is for a period of variability to intervene between the two major stages, as follows:

Stage I: The child pronounces *sip* relatively consistently as /tɪp/.

Stage II: The child begins to pronounce the word on occasions as /sɪp/ (or as t^sɪp/) but also often produces the old pronunciation /tɪp/.

Stage III: The new pronunciation becomes almost fully established, with the old pronunciation occurring rarely and finally disappearing.

The crucial point, however, is that with the onset of stage II, fricative-type pronunciations appear very rapidly in a wide range of appropriate words, irrespective of whether the child has heard them produced by an adult since the onset of that stage. This in itself is sufficient to support the alternative hypothesis, that the child's internal representations for these words incorporated distinctions which did not show up in his speech at stage I.

The general significance of this discussion is that the alternative hypothesis provides some explanation for the fact that the child's overall phonological development is as rapid as it is. If we were to assume that his speech is an accurate mirror of the forms stored in his brain, it would be very difficult to account for the fact that the child seems to make sudden leaps forward in a manner which is relatively independent of environmental stimulus. This means that we cannot concentrate exclusively on the surface forms of the child's speech—we need to concern ourselves with the nature of the underlying psychological structures.

EXPLANATIONS

We turn now to the difficult problem of offering some kind of explanation for the major characteristics of phonological development identified in the foregoing discussion. Why do children simplify the structure of adult words? Why do they not simply imitate the sounds which they hear? And why do the simplificatory processes have the particular properties that we have observed?

Let us begin by noting that we have already rejected one possible explanation, that children do not produce the same pronunciations as adults because they do not have the same perceptual abilities as adults. One might have assumed that they pronounce *see* as /ti/, either because that is how they hear it or because they hear it only vaguely. In the previous paragraphs we have in effect discarded this explanation in light of the evidence suggesting that the child's mental representations are richer than the forms produced.

The second possible explanation lies not in the perceptual but in the articulatory process. A child pronounces *sip* as /tɪp/, one might argue, because it is easier to say /tɪp/ than /sɪp/. At first sight this appears to be a very plausible explanation. There IS a sense in which it is easier to produce /t/ than /s/. To produce /t/, we make complete closure at the alveolar ridge with the tongue and then withdraw it abruptly. This is not a particularly delicate operation, at least by the standard of other articulatory gestures. In the production of /s/, on the other hand, the tongue has to be shaped into a grooved configuration and held at a critical distance from the alveolar ridge, so that turbulent air flow is created. If the tongue is placed too close, a stop rather than a fricative is produced; if it is not held close enough or is not correctly shaped, insufficient turbulence is created to produce the intended acoustic signal. There is, then, something to be said for the view that, relatively speaking, /s/ is a more difficult sound to articulate than /t/.

There are, however, a number of objections to the 'ease of articulation' theory as a total explanation of the child's pronunciations. The first point is that, as we have seen, the infant appears to achieve during the babbling stage a considerable degree of articulatory control over a wide variety of sounds. He has no difficulty in producing /s/ sounds in such nonsense sequences as /səsəsə . . ./ or in imitating hissing noises of trains, kettles and so on. It is only in WORDS that the /s/ sound often does not appear at first.

A second point, noted by Neil Smith, is that the patterns in the child's pronunciations are much more complex than the ease-of-articulation hypothesis suggests. Take the example of a child who pronounces the word *light* as /daɪt/. It is tempting to say that this pronunciation is due to the fact that the child cannot pronounce /l/. However, one might then find—as Smith did with his son Amahl—that the child does pronounce /l/ in other words. There were too many occurrences of /l/ in the word *lorry*, for example, which Amahl pronounced /lɒlɪ/ (Smith 1973: 137). A second example quoted by Smith concerns the word *puddle*. Like many other children, Amahl pronounced this not as /pʌdəl/ but as /pʌgəl/. Is this due to some articulatory problem concerning the pronunciation of /d/ in this environment? This proved not to be the case, since Amahl could perfectly well produce the pronunciation /pʌdəl/, but not for the word *puzzle*; /pʌdəl/ was his pronunciation for the word *puzzle*.

Considerations of this kind lead one to look for other factors which might help to explain the child's patterns. Here again, we must stress the point that even at the early stages the child's phonology is much more systematic than one might have expected. The existence of processes such as stopping, voicing/devoicing, cluster reduction, assimilation—and the particular way in which they apply—illustrate this point. One is therefore led to seek alternative explanations in the nature of the system itself.

It should be remembered that, in the early stages of building up a vocabulary, the child is doing more than simply acquiring a list of words. Each word is constructed out of a sequence of sound units; the word *tap*, for example, consists of a sequence of the units /t/, /æ/, /p/. These same units can combine with each other in different sequences. In the reverse sequence—/p/ + /æ/ + /t/—they form another word *pat*. In a third sequence they constitute the word *apt* (although this is not one that the young child is likely to use).

The same units combine individually with other units to form other words—/t/ combines with /i/ to form *tea*; /p/ combines with /i/ to form *pea* and so on. That is, as part of the process of constructing a list of words, the child is beginning to identify a certain number of sound units or phonemes.

Now these units constitute a system within which various kinds and degrees of relationship obtain. For example, the units /t/ and /s/ are very closely related to each other, in that they are both voiceless alveolar consonants. They differ with respect to only one characteristic: /t/ is a stop, /s/ is a continuant. On the other hand, /t/ and /ɑ/ are much more clearly differentiated from each other. They differ, in fact, with respect to nearly every feature: /t/ is voiceless, /ɑ/ is voiced; /t/ is characterised by closure, /ɑ/ is an extremely open vowel, produced with the tongue in a low back position. In general, for any pair of units within the system as a whole, we can evaluate their relative degree of relatedness in comparison with other pairs of units. Roman Jakobson has suggested that it is these structural relationships which play an important part in determining patterns of phonological development in the child. In particular, he argues (Jakobson 1968) that it is the units that are involved in the maximal contrasts, the elements that are, so to speak, at the extremes of the system which appear early in child language.

Perhaps the clearest illustration of his argument is provided by the vowel system. As we noted in Chapter 5, the vowels /ɑ/, /i/ and /u/ lie at the extremes of the system, in that these are the vowels that are maximally distinct from each other. /ɑ/ is a low back vowel, /i/ a high front vowel and /u/ a high back vowel. Other vowels occupy an intermediate position between these extremes. Now, it is these vowels—/ɑ/, /i/ and /u/—which tend to appear early in child language, the others appearing a little later. It would be difficult to find a satisfactory articulatory explanation for this. As far as consonants are concerned, we have noted that the main feature of consonants in general is that they involve some degree of closure. In this sense the stops are the most typical—the most extreme—examples of consonants, in that they are characterised by complete closure. Fricatives, on the other hand, involve only partial closure. From a structural point of view, therefore, fricatives occupy an intermediate position between stops (complete closure) and vowels (no closure). It is perhaps for this reason that they tend to appear later than stops in child language.

The foregoing is a greatly simplified account of Jakobson's theory, which he develops in greater depth in a number of works. For our purposes here, however, this is as far as we need to go. In essence, Jakobson's theory provides a psychological rather than a physiological explanation for phonological patterns in language development. Although the nature of the structural relationships between the various sound units is closely connected with their articulatory properties, it is the fact that these relationships are seen as part of a psychologically-structured system that makes the approach an explanatory one.

Clearly, Jakobson's theory only provides an explanation for some of the very general facts of phonological development. In order to explain the pronunciations of a particular child at a particular stage, it is necessary to construct a grammar which accounts for his observed behaviour. The phonological component of this grammar will include postulated mental representations for the words which he produces and understands, together with rules which relate these to his pronunciations. For example, Neil Smith hypothesised that his son Amahl pronounced *puzzle* as /pʌdəl/ because his internal grammar contained a stopping rule, converting the alveolar fricative /z/ in his mental representation /pʌzəl/ to the alveolar stop /d/. This process applied to all fricatives in Amahl's mental representations. Similarly, he suggested that Amahl pronounced *puddle* as /pʌgəl/, because his grammar contained an assimilation rule which converted the alveolar /d/ in his mental representation /pʌdəl/ to a velar stop /g/ under the influence of the final velar /l/. Again, this rule was general in that it also applied to words like *beetle*, *pedal* (pronounced /bikəl/, /pɛgəl/ respectively).

This kind of detailed explanation will then give rise to new questions. For example, why does the assimilation rule not interact with the stopping rule in the way that we have seen other rules interacting with each other? That is, if the child's mental representation for *puzzle* is /pʌzəl/, we would expect stopping to convert the /z/ to /d/, which would then become /g/ by the assimilation rule. The child should then pronounce this word also as /pʌgəl/. Smith suggests that the reason why he actually pronounces it /pʌdəl/ is that some phonological rules, like some grammatical rules (transformations in particular), are ordered with respect to each other. Suppose, for example, that the assimilation rule is ordered before the stopping rule. Now, the assimilation rule affects only alveolar stops, making them velar when they are in the neighbourhood of other velars, such as word-final /l/. Thus it changes the medial /d/ of /pʌdəl/ to /g/ before the velar /l/. However, it does not effect any change to the medial /z/ of /pʌzəl/, since /z/ is not an alveolar stop. The stopping rule then applies to convert this alveolar fricative to an alveolar stop, giving the pronunciation /pʌdəl/.

Amahl: *puzzle* and *puddle*

A. Incorrect rule ordering	*puzzle*	*puddle*
Child's mental representations:	/pʌzəl/	/pʌdəl/
(i) Stopping rule: (fricatives → corresponding stops)	↓ /pʌdəl/	↓ /pʌdəl/
(ii) Assimilation rule: (alveolar stops → velar before /əl/	↓ */pʌgəl/	↓ /pʌgəl/

B. Correct rule ordering	*puzzle*	*puddle*
Child's mental representations:	/pʌzəl/	/pʌdəl/
(i) Assimilation rule: (alveolar stops → velar before /əl/)	↓ /pʌzəl/	↓ /pʌgəl/
(ii) Stopping rule: (fricatives → corresponding stops)	↓ /pʌdəl/	↓ /pʌgəl/

Figure 6.2

If Smith's explanation is right, in the sense that it proves to account for a wide range of phenomena in child language, then we have here another rather surprising finding. It indicates that the phonological component of the child's grammar, like the syntactic component, works in a surprisingly abstract, complex but systematic way.

In the preceding paragraph a parallel was drawn between the operation of phonological rules and the application of syntactic rules such as transformations. There is certainly one respect in which the kind of phonological rules discussed here differ from transformations. If the child's grammar does indeed include transformations at some stage, then they have been constructed by the child in order to account for patterns in adult speech. However, the motivation for these phonological rules is presumably to be sought within the child himself rather than within the patterns of speech addressed to him. Although he appears able to set up mental representations for words which involve many—perhaps most—of the sound units of adult speech, he is unable to convert these directly into phonetic form because of constraints on his system. These constraints result in some simplification of the sounds produced, but it is a simplification which is imposed from within rather than from without. It would be misleading to suggest that these rules are learned in the sense that transformations are learned. Rather, they have to be unlearned in the process of phonological development. This situation can be interpreted as lending further support to Chomsky's argument that children are equipped with an innate 'language-acquisition device' which leads them to process linguistic material in a particular way. Here we see them imposing certain systematic processes of simplification on the phonological material of the adult language. It would be extremely difficult to explain these processes by reference to the nature of the environment, since there do not appear to be any characteristics of adult speech which would lead children to produce the kind of patterns discussed.

CONCLUSION

In this chapter the process of phonological development has been traced back to the babbling period. Here the child learns how to produce particular sounds, how to construct the command signals that are sent from the brain to produce complex co-ordinated movements of the various articulatory organs. Given the degree of motor control achieved at that stage, it is rather surprising that the range of sounds which appear in the child's early words is relatively restricted. This suggests that factors other than purely articulatory ones are at work here, and the relatively systematic nature of the patterns in the young child's speech confirms this. Generally, processes such as stopping, voicing/devoicing, cluster reduction and assimilation characterise the speech of children learning any language, and these processes often interact with each other in intricate and in some respects rather abstract ways.

Once we have noted the existence of these processes, the question arises as to whether they operate as part of the child's perception of language or as part of production. If the child's mental representations for individual words correspond to the forms which she produces, then the processes in question must have to do with perception. On the other hand, if these mental representations correspond more closely to the forms produced by adults, then the processes must operate as part of the child's production of language. In fact there seems to be a good deal of evidence connected with the child's discriminatory abilities and with such phenomena as the rapid diffusion of innovations to support the latter position.

Once again then we find in the area of phonological development a similar situation to one we encountered earlier in semantics and syntax, such that the child's underlying system proves to be considerably more complex than her surface behaviour would indicate. The nature of the processes involved and the way in which they operate suggests that there may be certain general principles of language design, possibly innate in the child, which impose their own simplicatory patterns on early language.

7 Sociolinguistics

VARIATION

So far we have been concerned principally with the early stages of language development. In this final pair of chapters we turn to aspects of language which are more relevant to the later stages—particularly to the child in the school. We will be concerned with the role of language as a social instrument.

The field of sociolinguistics is one which has developed very rapidly in the last twenty years or so. There are now several distinct branches of the subject, and again my discussion will inevitably be selective. For many sociolinguists the most important characteristic of language (and here we continue to focus primarily on the spoken language) is that it exhibits variation. It varies from one region to another (in the form of different dialects), from one social group to another, from one age-group to another and—in some respects—from one sex to another. Some sociolinguists have seen their main task as being to investigate variation across all these parameters, in order to arrive at an understanding of how language operates across the social spectrum and thereby to obtain a deeper insight into the significance of variation for the field of language studies in general.

Before we can look at the ways in which sociolinguists have set about the complex task of analysing linguistic variation, there is one possible source of confusion which needs to be cleared up at the outset. Language, more so than perhaps any other area of human behaviour, is highly susceptible to prescriptive attitudes. Particular grammatical forms or particular pronunciations are thought to be intrinsically 'right' or 'correct' in some sense, and other forms are thought to be 'wrong'. If someone says *I done it yesterday* or *it was Jack what said it*, or if they pronounce the word *train* as 'trine', or *I* as 'oi', they are often said to be producing a form that is 'incorrect'. Moreover, such 'errors' or 'solecisms' are often regarded not only as being wrong but also as somehow ridiculous. The amused, condescending attitudes that are occasionally expressed by the members of one social group with respect to the language of another have their roots here. It is a phenomenon which is by no means exclusive to English speakers. Speakers of Dutch in Holland, to take just one example, have been known to express attitudes of this kind to the speakers of Dutch in Belgium—an attitude which is sometimes reciprocated.

In the British context the varieties which tend to attract attitudes of this kind are those associated with certain urban areas such as Birmingham, Manchester, Liverpool, Leeds and so on. Children are likely to encounter these attitudes first in the primary school, particularly if this is the first occasion on which they meet with children and adults from other social groups. There is obviously a danger that a child with what is usually called a 'strong' regional accent or dialect might experience problems of both an educational and social kind when she encounters such attitudes, and that these problems may have a profound and lasting effect on her subsequent educational and social career.

Now, linguists have become concerned about this kind of situation because they take the view that the notion of 'correctness' cannot legitimately be applied to language in any straightforward way. It is difficult, for example, to argue that the forms *I did it*, *he came late*, *they saw it* are INTRINSICIALLY superior to such forms as *I done it*, *he come late, they seen it*, or that 'trane' (phonemically /trɛɪn/) is a 'better' way of pronouncing *train* than 'trine' (phonemically /trʌɪn/). This point will be developed directly within the context of a more general discussion of variation. It is, however, desirable to make it clear from the outset what linguists are not saying. Most linguists would not take the view that 'anything goes'. In particular, they would probably agree that, if a child writes *I seen it happen* in a school essay, then this should be 'corrected' to *I saw it happen*.

They would, however, suggest that corrections of this kind should take place within the broad context of some understanding on the part of both teacher and child concerning the general issue of variation in language.

Such a topic, in fact, is one that can be fruitfully explored in the classroom. Children obviously need to be made aware that the use of such forms as *I done it* may work to their disadvantage in certain contexts, just as certain pronunciations—rightly or wrongly—may work against them. The extent to which one should modify one's behaviour in light of these considerations is very much a personal matter, but the option to do so should be open to the individual. It is presumably part of the educational process to make this option available. As far as the educational process itself is concerned, we need to do all we can to ensure that the child is not disadvantaged within the school by her own language variety. Teachers have a particularly delicate role here in that their attitudes to individual children are inevitably often strongly influenced by the child's speech (Seligman *et al.* 1972). Since teacher attitude has such an important bearing on the child's performance in school, it is obviously important that teachers be aware of the factors which underlie attitudes towards language in society as a whole.

It is useful in any discussion of linguistic variation to bring in, however briefly, a historical perspective. The fact that most people living in contemporary Britain speak a language that we call 'English' is due to a whole series of historical events dating back to about AD 450. At about this time a number of Germanic peoples—Jutes, Angles and Saxons—living in areas that we now know as Denmark and northern Germany, invaded Britain and settled there (Williams 1975: 53). They brought with them their language—or perhaps one should say their languages, since there were already a number of different but closely related linguistic varieties, that were to develop into what we now refer to as 'Old English'. Much of Scandinavia had already been settled by these Germanic peoples, and in these areas the process of linguistic change gave rise to the Scandinavian languages, linked to English by a common ancestry. German, Dutch,

Frisian also belong to this family. English has, of course, been strongly influenced by other languages such as Latin and French, the latter largely as a result of the Norman Conquest, and a significant proportion of its vocabulary and certain aspects of its grammar come from these sources. Its basic character, however, is Germanic.

One of the most important mechanisms in language change is sound change. The discovery of sound change and the description of how it has operated in the history of the Germanic language family was one of the major scientific achievements of the nineteenth century. As a small example of the effect it produces, consider the words for *stone*, *bone*, *home* in English and German, cited below in their phonemic forms:

English	German
/stəʊn/	/ʃtɒɪn/
/bəʊn/	/bɑɪn/
/həʊm/	/hɑɪm/

There are obviously systematic correspondences here, indicating that each pair of words in these languages is derived from a common source word. As far as we can tell, the sources for this set of words are the following Old Germanic words: /stɑn/, /bɑn/, /hɑm/. In the development of (High) German a relatively simple change has taken place. The vowel of these words has become 'diphthongised' from /ɑ/ to /ɑɪ/. In English it underwent 'raising' from the low back vowel /ɑ/ to the higher back vowel /o/. (The latter is a simple vowel, as in French *l'eau*, not a diphthong.) In many southern varieties, /o/ later underwent diphthongisation and centralisation to /əʊ/. What happens in sound change, then, is essentially that a particular sound unit undergoes a change in a large number—sometimes all—of the words in which it occurs. A stop may change to an affricate or a fricative, or vice versa. A liquid may become a vowel or it may disappear. (The partial disappearance of the final liquid from words such as *soar*, *pour*, *fear* has given rise to the patterns discussed on pp. 135–7.) A vowel may be raised or lowered, diphthongised or simplified, reduced to /ə/ or deleted. Very often these processes are influenced by the linguistic environment in which the phoneme is situated in a particular word—a stop may be converted to a fricative at the beginning of a word but remain unchanged at the end of a word. A stressed vowel often behaves very differently in sound change from the same vowel in an unstressed syllable in a particular word.

Changes of this kind, operating throughout the history of English, have given rise to the rich patchwork of regional varieties that we observe in the language at the present time. The vowel of words such as *stone*, *bone*, *home* is one which exhibits particularly marked variation within the British Isles, not to mention other English-speaking countries. Only in some varieties of English did the /ɑ/ of /stɑn/, /hɑm/, bɑn/ undergo raising to /o/ and subsequent diphthongisation to /əʊ/, as described above. Diphthongisation did not take place at all in many northern varieties, in which a long /o/ is still used. In the north-east of England the vowel was diphthongised not to /əʊ/ but to /ɔə/, so that many Tynesiders pronounce these words as /stɔən/, /bɔən/, /hɔəm/. Other pronunciations heard around Britain for this vowel include /ʌʊ/ (Cockney), /u/ (some parts of East Anglia) and /ɛʊ/ (used by some southern upper-class and middle-class speakers).

Now, it is partly because linguists have this kind of perspective on regional and social variation that they refuse to take seriously the claim that certain pronunciations are inherently 'correct'. Even the most 'educated' speech has come about as a result of the same kind of historical processes that have given rise to other varieties, so that it is difficult to take seriously any claim that its users may make to inherent superiority. Where then does the idea come from that one particular variety is the correct or proper form of the language? It derives principally from the fact that in any society there is always a group of powerful people who share a particular way of speaking. Their social prestige becomes associated with their speech, so that in time it comes to be regarded as the correct form. In England it was a southern variety that acquired this status, because for a variety of social, political and economic reasons people who were educated, prosperous and powerful were more likely to be southerners than northerners. The Royal Court became established in the south, and this was undoubtedly also a factor in the emergence of a prestigious southern variety. For similar reasons a northern variety of French emerged as the recognised form of the language in that country. The prestige of these varieties was enhanced by the spread of printing and by the development of the educational system. Thus the forces that lead to the emergence of a particular variety as pre-eminent are largely social, political and economic—not linguistic.

The process whereby a particular linguistic variety comes to be regarded as the correct form of that language is known as 'standardisation'. In some cases standardisation may start out as a subconscious process. Without being too aware of it, people begin to react favourably to certain grammatical and phonological forms, since they are the ones which are used by high-status people. Other forms, with other connotations, are stigmatised. In certain circumstances these subconscious attitudes may have more tangible consequences. In England the development of printing gave rise to the need for a certain degree of uniformity in the spelling conventions and grammatical forms that were to be used. This in turn led to the compilation of grammatical treatises and dictionaries, which became an important source of authority for those involved in the preparation and printing of books, legal documents and pamphlets. Inevitably, the compilers of grammars and dictionaries took the language of those who wielded social and political power as the model for their prescriptive statements concerning which forms should and which forms should not be used. In this way the standardisation process can become subject to conscious as well as subconscious influences.

In contrasting conscious and subconscious influences on the process of standardisation, we should make the point that conscious influences tend to bear more directly on the lexical and syntactic aspects of language than on pronunciation. Those who wrote traditional grammars were more concerned to outlaw non-standard grammatical forms than non-standard pronunciations. One is much more likely to find in a traditional grammar a claim that *did* rather than *done* is the correct past tense form of *do* than that /treɪn/ rather than /trʌɪn/ is the correct pronunciation of *train*. For a sociolinguist interested in linguistic variation, however, there is no essential difference between the kind of variation exhibited in *I did it* versus *I done it* and the kind illustrated in /treɪn/ versus /trʌɪn/. Although sociolinguists reject the idea that the notion of 'correctness' can be legitimately applied to such instances of variation, they would argue that variation of both kinds can function as a social marker. That is, there may be differences of social status between those groups of people who use *did* as the past tense of *do* and those who use *done*, and very similar social differences may exist between those who use the pronunciation /treɪn/ for *train* and those who use /trʌɪn/. Sociolinguists are interested in developing systematic methodologies for investigating variation of this kind, free from traditional preoccupations with the inappropriate concepts of correctness and incorrectness. In this way they see sociolinguistics as a branch of sociology—making its own specialised contribution to our understanding of social structures and social processes.

This discussion has a number of implications for children, particularly concerning their progress through the educational system. Here children are expected to master certain aspects of the appropriate standard variety, particularly those of its grammatical features that show up in the written form. This task will obviously be a little easier for those who are accustomed to using at home a variety that is close to the standard than it will be for those whose natural variety is more distant from it. It seems reasonable to suggest that the different degrees to which children feel comfortable with the standard variety may be one of the elements at work in the degree of educational success achieved by children in various social groups. This question will be discussed in more detail in the following chapter. Before we can pursue it, we need to look a little more closely at the kind of methodology developed by sociolinguists in recent years to study linguistic variation.

SOCIOLINGUISTIC METHODOLOGY

Some of the most important pioneering work in developing sociolinguistic methodology in the last twenty years was done by the American linguist, William Labov. Labov's approach has since been energetically applied and elaborated by a number of sociolinguists working in various communities around the world. Labov's early work was concerned largely with investigating the social significance of phonological variation. It started out from the informal observation that in New York City there were a number of sound units which were pronounced in different ways by members of different social groups. For example, if we consider such words as *think*, *thought*, *thing*, we would normally say that the initial phoneme in these words is the interdental voiceless fricative for which we have used the symbol /θ/. Labov noticed that although most middle-class speakers do in fact use /θ/ in these words, many working-class speakers use a different sound—the alveolar stop /t/. The same variation occurred in this sound unit in other positions in the word; for example, when it was in word-final position as in *bath*, *both*, *path* and so on.

Anybody will recognise this kind of observation as one which applies to all communities. In London, for example, there is similar variation in the pronunciation of the vowel of words such as *late*, *pale*, *take*, *tape* etc., with middle-class (MC) people tending to use the diphthong /ɛɪ/ and working-class (WC) people favouring the pronunciation /ʌɪ/. (To middle-class ears *late* pronounced with an /ʌɪ/ vowel sounds like *light*.) In many areas of northern England the vowel of such words as *dull*, *cut*, *mud* varies in this way—some speakers (predominantly MC) use /ʌ/, others (mainly WC) use /ʊ/ (so that *cut*, for example, rhymes with *put*). In Australia there is variation in the vowel of *line*, *cry*, *pipe* and so on; some speakers use the diphthong /ɑɪ/, others the diphthong /ɒɪ/. (Non-Australians often hear the latter pronunciation of *line* as *loin*.) Here, too, the variation seems to correlate to some extent with social class (Mitchell and Delbridge 1965: 43; Scott 1982; Horvath 1985: 69).

Class-related linguistic variation is, then, a widespread phenomenon, and it is designated in everyday terms by the traditional concept of 'accent'. Those who pronounce *thing* and *think* as /tɪŋ/ and /tɪŋk/ are said to have a different accent from those who pronounce them as /θɪŋ/ and /θɪŋk/; the same holds true for the other examples discussed. Labov decided that it might be fruitful to investigate this phenomenon more carefully and more systematically than had been done before, in the hope of discovering new insights.

Here we can sketch in only the general outlines of the methodology, leaving any interested readers to follow it up in more detail elsewhere. (For general surveys of sociolinguistic methodology, see e.g. Hudson 1980; Trudgill 1983; Downes 1984.) The first step is to identify a representative sample of the community one wishes to study, ensuring that it includes members of different social-class groups (defined largely in terms of different kinds of occupation), different age groups, different ethnic groups (if appropriate) and, of course, both sexes. Essentially, Labov's survey of New York (Labov 1966) was based on the kind of random-sampling techniques used by sociologists. The next step is to collect a sample of the speech of each individual in the survey; these samples need to be tape-recorded so that they can be carefully analysed later. In the New York study Labov attempted to obtain a range of different speech styles from each informant by dividing the interview into various sections. He began by working through a specific set of questions about the informant's background and situation, thus eliciting a rather formal speech style from the interviewee. Even more formal styles were elicited by asking informants to read aloud a text and a list of words. Later in the interview he attempted to make the interview situation much less formal by moving towards a more casual atmosphere. One technique which he found to be reasonably successful in eliciting casual speech was to ask his informants to tell him about any occasion when they had been in danger of death. People tend to become emotionally involved in telling this kind of story and to relax any constraints they impose on their speech in more formal situations. (Peter Trudgill 1974, found in his survey of Norwich, England, that his informants could not on the whole remember any occasion in which they had been in danger of death, but he achieved the same general result by asking them to tell him about anything funny or embarrassing that had happened to them!) In this way, Labov succeeded in obtaining samples of speech not only from different individuals across the social spectrum but also for different styles—casual speech, formal speech, reading-passage style, word-list style—for each individual.

The next step was to investigate carefully the patterns of variation in these speech samples for the specific sound units in which he was interested. We have noted that one of the elements that Labov decided to study in New York was the sound unit which occurs at the beginning of such words as *thing* and *think*, and at the end of *bath* and *both*. Let us represent this unit as (th). He would begin by listening to the speech sample for one individual at the beginning of the interview (formal speech), making a note of the words in which the sound unit occurred. For each occurrence he would note whether the speaker used the fricative /θ/ or the stop /t/. He immediately noticed that although some speakers use one or the other pronunciation consistently, there are many whose usage is variable in the sense that they will sometimes use the fricative and sometimes the stop. Successive occurrences of the same word may even be pronounced differently by the same speaker—*thing*, for example, being pronounced /θɪŋ/ on one occasion and /tɪŋ/ a few seconds later. Labov realised that this observation poses problems for the traditional concepts of accent and dialect. If we say that a particular individual speaks with such and such an accent, or in such and such a dialect, the implication is that he uses the sounds characteristic of that dialect consistently. Labov's observations were not compatible with this view.

Labov was therefore faced with the problem of how to describe satisfactorily a situation in which individuals exhibited variable patterns of pronunciation even within a single style. His approach was to adopt a fairly straightforward statistical solution. This can best be illustrated by an example. Let us suppose that there are twenty occurrences of words containing the sound unit (th) in the speech of a particular individual during that early section of the interview in which he is producing formal speech. If he uses the pronunciation /θ/ for fifteen of these instances and the pronunciation /t/ for the other five, then this situation can be expressed in percentage terms as follows:

/θ/ : 75 per cent /t/ : 25 per cent

An individual who used /θ/ consistently in this situation would give the following result:

/θ/ : 100 per cent /t/ : 0 per cent

One who used /t/ in all occurrences of the sound unit would give:

/θ/ : 0 per cent /t/ : 100 per cent

(In Labov's early work these patterns were expressed by means of a single index, but more recent work has shown the desirability of giving a percentage for each form—(Romaine 1980: 189–90.)

A number of important technical terms can be introduced at this point. The sound unit itself is called the 'variable' and the different pronunciations of it are the 'variants'. Thus, we can say that in New York City the sociolinguistic variable (th) can be 'realised' either as the variant [θ] or as the variant [t]. (From this point on I will follow Labov's practice of using the symbol ( ) to represent variables and the symbol [ ] to represent variants.) For London speech we might say that the variable (ā)—the vowel of *late*, *tape* etc.—can be realised as the variant [ɛɪ] or as the variant [ʌɪ]. The percentage score for a particular variant is known as the 'index'. The examples discussed above involve a relatively simple situation in which a particular variable is realised by only two variants. There may, of course, be many more than two in particular situations, but this does not pose any major problems in the calculation of indices.

The major benefit arising from the advent of this methodology was that it enabled a number of discoveries to be made and new questions to be raised. Some of the discoveries were not in themselves particularly surprising.

These consisted in the more precise identification of patterns which were already known informally to exist. Others, however, were less obvious.

The first point which the methodology established was that there was a clear correlation between linguistic patterns and aspects of social structure. If one compares the (th) index across different individuals in the same style (e.g. formal speech), one finds that the index for the [θ] variant rises and that for the [t] variant falls as one moves up the social scale. A typical result might well be as set out in Table 7.1. (I will not enter into detail here concerning the criteria used by Labov to assign individuals to particular social class groups—they have to do with such factors as occupation, education, income and so on.) These figures mean that UMC people use the [θ] variant consistently in this style, whereas MWC people, for example, use it on average for 47 per cent of the occurrences of the variable, using the [t] variant for the other 53 per cent.

Table 7.1: (th) variable (Formal Speech)

class	UMC	MMC	LMC	UWC	MWC	LWC
[θ] index:	100	93	87	65	47	33
[t] index:	0	7	13	35	53	67

These figures represent average frequencies of each variant for groups of people belonging to the same social class.
'UMC' = 'upper-middle-class', 'MMC' = 'middle-middle-class', 'LMC' = 'lower-middle-class', 'UWC' = 'upper-working-class' and so on.

The second finding was that within the speech of each individual the index for the [θ] variant tended to rise as the style became more formal. A typical illustration of this pattern is given in Table 7.2. This table shows that the proportion of times [θ] rather than [t] used by this speaker rises significantly as the formality of the situation increases. Similar results were obtained for other variables in the New York survey and in more recent studies carried out in other

Table 7.2: [θ] index for one individual

Casual Speech	Formal Speech	Reading Passage Style	Word List Style
30	63	84	100

communities by other researchers. The general finding is that there are many variables for which one variant, [x], is favoured by MC speakers and a different variant, [y], by WC speakers, and that for all speakers variant [x] is the one that occurs more frequently in formal contexts than in informal ones. This correlation between patterns of variation across the social-class spectrum and across the situational spectrum has led sociolinguists to distinguish between a 'standard' variant ([x] in the case just cited) and a 'non-standard' variant ([y]).

Again, the point should perhaps be emphasised that no qualitative judgements are associated with these terms. A standard variant is not intrinsically 'better' than a non-standard variant; it is simply that the two have different social distributions and therefore need to be distinguished terminologically.

These kinds of sociolinguistic patterning have also shown up in studies of the speech of children and adolescents. As far as class-related variation is concerned, the results illustrated in Table 7.3 were obtained in a study of 11-year-old Edinburgh schoolboys carried out by Euan Reid (reported in Romaine 1984: 92–3). The figure of 55 per cent for the (ing) variable for class-I (MC) children means that in words such as *walking*, *going*, *talking* this group used the non-standard [n] variant (i.e. the pronunciation usually represented orthographically by *walking'*, *goin'*, *talkin'* etc.) 55 per cent of the time and the standard [ŋ] pronunciation the other 45 per cent of the time. The boys in class III (WC), on the other hand, used the non-standard variant 78 per cent of the time in the same situations. The (gs) variable represents the frequency of use of a glottal stop (represented phonemically by the symbol [ʔ]) rather than a [t] in the

Table 7.3
Edinburgh schoolboys: average percentage frequencies of non-standard variants for (ing) and (gs) (glottal stop). (Reid 1976).

variable	(ing)	(gs)
Class I	55	18
Class II	74	66
Class III	78	74

The social class membership of the boys was assessed on their father's occupation, using the Registrar–General's classification.

middle of such words as *water* and *city*. Thus the boys in class I used the non-standard [ʔ] pronunciation only 18 per cent of the time, whereas those in class III used it no less than 74 per cent of the time. (The use of a glottal stop in these words is also characteristic of Cockney speech.)

These results are not, perhaps, particularly surprising, since one would have expected the speech of children to reflect fairly accurately that of the social group to which they belong. What was perhaps rather more surprising was the finding that, in some cases at least, children's speech also shows the same kind of stylistic variation that characterises adult speech. When Reid analysed the speech of these children in various situations, the results illustrated in Table 7.4 were obtained. The situations here involved (a) reading a text, (b) face-to-face interview, (c) peer-group speech and (d) playground interaction. Again the figures represent the average frequency of non-standard variants. It can be seen quite clearly that in (ing) use of the non-standard [n] variant as against that of [ŋ] increases dramatically as the situation becomes less formal, and that the same pattern is found in (gs).

Similar results have been reported in a number of studies, discussed in Romaine 1984, Chapter 5. These indicate that awareness of the social significance of language develops at a surprisingly early age. Children very quickly become sensitive to the fact that patterns which are appropriate

Table 7.4
Edinburgh schoolboys: average percentage frequencies of non-standard variants for (ing) and (gs) in four styles. (Reid 1976).

variable	(ing)	(gs)
Reading	14	25
Interview	45	71
Peer-group	54	84
Playground	59	79

to one social context are not appropriate to another. In pioneering his methodology, Labov has provided linguists with a tool for identifying and accurately charting this phenomenon.

Another rather surprising discovery to have emerged from the application of Labovian methodology is that in many cases there are systematic differences between the speech of men and women. (For a general review of the relationship between language and gender, see Cheshire 1984.) One interesting finding has been that the proportion of standard to non-standard variants tends to be higher for women than for men from the same social group. Since this kind of result has been obtained time and again in studies in different parts of the world, it obviously requires some explanation. Perhaps one of the most significant factors concerns the contrasting images that are associated with the different speech varieties. Non-standard speech is associated with working-class life and is therefore surrounded with an aura of toughness and ruggedness that is perhaps more attractive to men than to women (Trudgill 1972). Standard speech, on the other hand, given its association with the middle class, may symbolise values which are more appealing to women. There are undoubtedly other factors at work here, however. It seems more likely that the basis for these contrasting patterns is laid down in childhood and adolescence. Roger Shuy has suggested that it may have to do with the fact that girls find it easier to identify with the general ambiance of the primary school than boys, and that since the speech of primary school teachers tends to be characterised by the occurrence of more standard than non-standard variants, this may give rise to different speech patterns across the sexes (Shuy 1969). It has also been argued (Maltz and Borker 1982) that differences with respect to peer-group interaction patterns may play a part. Boys tend to form peer-group networks comprising many individuals, groups which have their own value systems, often in opposition to those of the school. In these networks the function of (non-standard) speech is to maintain and reinforce the norms and values of the group. Girls, on the other hand, generally do not form groups of this kind but tend to establish close friendships with just one or two others. These friendships are usually not in opposition to school values and speech style does not therefore carry the same kind of in-group meanings as it does in the boys' networks. In other words, Maltz and Borker are arguing that different speech patterns reflect the fact that boys and girls undergo different socialisation processes.

Whatever the merits of these various explanations, we have here a good example of the way in which the advent of a new, precise methodology gives rise to observations which it was not possible to make within the earlier framework. These observations require explanations which may involve the setting up of new hypotheses and new techniques of investigation. This is one of the ways in which Labov's approach has led to the development of fruitful new avenues of enquiry.

Perhaps the most important aspect of this new work in sociolinguistics has been its contribution to our understanding of the process of linguistic change. Linguists have always been intrigued by the way in which a particular phoneme could change through time into a different phoneme through a whole series of words, as mentioned earlier (see pp. 167–8). How does this kind of change come about? Clearly, it cannot be the case that a whole group of people switch their pronunciation overnight. The answer to this question eluded linguists for so long, because they did not devote a great deal of attention to linguistic variation. They tended to study languages and dialects as if they were fixed, static systems, abstracting away from the fact that language is produced by people and that variability is one of its most salient characteristics. Labov's focus on variability has made it clear that change in language—like change in biology—must operate through variation. One of the discoveries he made was that in some variables there were significant differences between the relative frequencies of particular variants for different age groups. Older people may favour one way of pronouncing a particular sound unit, younger people may favour a different variant. The point about this situation is that the contrast is not an all-or-nothing one. It is not that older people all use one variant and younger people another. Most people use each of the variants on occasion, but in different proportions. This means that, in general, people are not consciously aware of the differences, which show up only in careful analysis by the linguist. It is clear, however, that if this pattern were to be repeated through several generations, then one variant would gradually be replaced by another, even though it would not be at all obvious at any particular stage in the process that a change was taking place. (There is, of course, a great deal more to be said about the complex process of linguistic change and its interaction with variation, but we will not pursue it further here, since it is tangential to our main concerns.)

One of the interesting questions arising out of any discussion of standard and non-standard varieties is why sociolectal variation persists. Why is it that non-standard speakers do not modify their speech in the direction of what everybody appears to perceive as a more prestigious speech pattern? To the extent that there was a traditional answer to this question, it was that non-standard speakers 'do not know any better'. This view was probably largely influenced by the fact that people tended to think of non-standard speech as a corrupt form of the standard variety—that non-standard speakers had not succeeded in learning their language properly. Intensive recent studies of non-standard varieties have shown that this view is untenable. Non-standard varieties are just as systematic and viable in linguistic terms as standard varieties. This means that those who use them have demonstrated just as much ability for language learning as anybody else. Moreover, Labov's work has shown that many non-standard speakers can and do use standard variants on certain occasions when circumstances seem to require it. One major theme of his work on variability is that most people's usage fluctuates between different variants—often involving both standard and non-standard forms—in response to changes in the social context. The point is, then, that there are situations in which many people PREFER to use non-standard rather than standard forms. Why should this be?

We have in fact already sketched out the beginnings of an answer to this question in the preceding discussion of linguistic variation across the sexes. There we noted that standard and non-standard speech styles are associated with different 'images' or value systems. In particular, although standard speech clearly has its own kind of prestige, associated with relatively high social status, non-standard speech also has its own positive connotations. It is associated with the stereotypical values of working-class life—toughness, resilience, frankness, friendliness. It is associated particularly with informality. Many people tend to shift their speech in the direction of non-standardness in more informal, more relaxed social contexts, as Labov demonstrated very clearly in the analyses of his sociolinguistic interviews. The use of non-standard phonological or grammatical features may therefore convey all kinds of positive social meanings. These positive connotations of non-standard speech have come to be known as 'covert prestige' (Trudgill 1972), in contrast with the 'overt prestige' of standard speech. The prestige is covert because people are often unaware of it at a conscious level and are generally apt to disparage non-standard forms, even when they know that they themselves use them. People will often say that their own speech is 'bad', 'ungrammatical', 'full of mistakes' and so on. If pressed, however, they can often indicate covert prestige by admitting, for example, that they would not really want to change their speech, in case others thought that they were 'putting on airs'.

The concept of covert prestige has received striking confirmation from another strand of sociolinguistic work pioneered by Wallace Lambert, Howard Giles and others (Giles and Powesland 1975; Fasold 1984: Ch. 6). This has set out to investigate the way in which hearers react to different accents and varieties. People are asked to listen to tape recordings of a number of voices and to rate the speakers with respect to various criteria such as social status, intelligence, friendliness, sincerity, persuasiveness and so on. Unbeknown to the hearer-judges, a number of apparently different voices all belong in fact to the same individual, speaking the same material in different accents. (The technique is known as the 'matched guise' technique.) This means that any differences between the way in which a hearer-judge rates one voice and the way he rates another one produced by the same individual must have to do with his reaction to the different accents involved rather than to other features, such as its pitch or voice quality. One important finding to have emerged from studies of this kind (again carried out in many parts of the world) is that, although speakers with standard accents tend to be rated highly in terms of such criteria as social status and intelligence, they are often rated less highly than non-standard speakers in terms of criteria such as friendliness, likeability, trustworthiness, honesty and so on. This constitutes striking confirmatory evidence for the concept of covert prestige and thereby confirms the view that non-standard speakers remain so, not because they cannot shift towards standard speech, but because they do not wish to do so.

This discussion has a number of implications for our consideration of the child in the educational process. It is a well-established fact that children from middle-class backgrounds fare much better on average in school than do children from working-class homes. There are no doubt many reasons for this, but it seems reasonable to suggest that language may have some part to play here. There are a number of ways in which the linguistic differences between middle-class and working-class children could affect their work in school. By definition, middle-class children are likely to be standard speakers and working-class children non-standard speakers. Teachers are likely to use a standard rather than a non-standard variety (a) because the middle classes are proportionally more heavily represented in the teaching profession than the working classes and (b) because the fact that they have had some tertiary education will often have influenced their speech patterns in the direction of the standard variety. One result of this situation is that, from the outset, middle-class children may feel more at ease in the school than do working-class children. This in itself could be an advantageous factor for them.

The second point concerns the attitude of teachers to the children. We noted above that most people react favourably to standard speech, at least on certain parameters. In particular, there is a general tendency, from which teachers are not immune, to regard standard speakers as more intelligent. This may set up expectations on the part of teachers with respect to their middle-class pupils. Now, it seems highly likely that teacher attitudes will have an important influence on their pupils' achievement. Those who are expected by their teachers to do well must have a good chance of becoming high achievers. The converse, of course, must also apply.

The third point is that the forms that children are expected to produce in writing English are standard forms. This point will be unimportant in a community where the linguistic differences are phonological (differences of accent) rather than grammatical (dialectal). There are, however, very few situations in which differences are only phonological. Even in the south of England there are non-standard grammatical forms used by a large proportion of the population of particular communities. (See, for example, Jenny Cheshire's 1978 study of the speech of adolescents in Reading.) As one moves into the midlands and north of England and into Wales and Scotland, so the grammatical differences between the local non-standard varieties and standard English become more marked. Throughout Britain, therefore, there are large numbers of children—particularly working-class children—who need to use a different variety in their writing (in any school subject) from the one which they use at home or with their friends. This again can constitute an area in which circumstances work against the working-class child.

One would guess that the sum total of these factors, interacting with each other, can in many circumstances lead to educational disadvantage. In the next chapter we will pursue this question in greater detail with reference to variation in both Britain and the USA.

THE ETHNOGRAPHY OF COMMUNICATION

In the first two sections of this chapter we have tended to concentrate on the techniques that have been developed in recent years to investigate variation in language in terms of such concepts as standardness and non-standardness. It would be wrong to conclude this chapter without giving some brief indication of other areas of enquiry within sociolinguistics. Although this work is perhaps not yet as well-developed as the work referred to above, its importance will certainly increase in the coming years, and it is highly relevant to our concerns here.

One important question is whether there are differences other than those concerning variation in accent and dialect between the language used by one social group and that used by another. The first point to make here is that, just as an individual may have control over different accents or varieties of a language, so he may have control over different 'registers'. The term 'register' is used to denote those features of language that are specifically oriented to a particular function or subject-matter. The most obvious characteristic of a particular register is a specialised vocabulary. There is a legal register of English, for instance, which includes such words as *trial*, *prosecution*, *attorney*, *counsel*, *infringement* and many more. This is not to say that these words will occur only in texts or conversations concerning legal matters, but their probability of occurrence is much higher in such a context than in others. Other registers are associated with such topics as car maintenance, religion, soccer, education, philosophy, politics, economics and so on, for each of which it would be easy to think of a number of key words. Specialised registers of this kind may be characterised by grammatical features as well as by vocabulary. In legal documents it is possible to find types of sentence structure which (fortunately!) are not to be found in any other area of usage. In scientific reports—particularly those concerned with experiments—one will often find a much higher incidence of passive structures (e.g. *the copper sulphate was then added* . . .) than in other types of text.

How might the concept of register relate to possible linguistic differences between children? Clearly, there may be important differences concerning the nature and range of topics to which children are exposed in their home or peer-group environment. Boys are more likely to have been exposed to the soccer register than girls, and this may be especially true of working-class boys. The latter may therefore have a particularly rich set of words and concepts for this area in comparison with other groups. There may, however, be other registers where their vocabulary and concepts are less well developed than those of other groups. Different reading habits between working-class and middle-class children may be a factor here. If it proves to be the case that these areas are also those which are important or useful in school, then again the working-class child may be at a disadvantage.

There may be other important social differences besides register concerning language use. One's social identity is often signalled by the kind of meanings one expresses in a particular situation, by the way in which one sets out to achieve one's aims in some particular linguistic interaction. In Britain a good deal of friction between members of different ethnic groups is caused by differences of this kind. Consider the following example of an Indian worker in Britain asking his foreman for a week off work:

Supervisor: Hello H. Good morning!
Worker: Hello, good morning! I want to ... one week off, please. I ... my brother is coming to the ... India ... And ... want one week off.

Contrast this with an example of a British worker making the same request:

Worker: Good morning! Uh, well, I got a request to make, actually.

Supervisor: Yes?
Worker: Um, it's very important to me. I wonder if you could possibly give me one week off?

(These examples occurred in role-play situations involving Indian and British participants, cited in Gumperz 1982: 55.) There are of course different levels of fluency and control of sentence structure in these two examples, which may have some bearing on the way the requests would be received. The more important point, however, is that the speakers are using different strategies for making the request in each case. The second speaker is adopting a strategy characteristic of many Western cultures; before actually making the request, he tells the supervisor that he is going to do precisely that—he warns his addressee that he is about to produce a particular type of speech act. He also indicates the status of the forthcoming request in his eyes ('it's very important to me . . .'). The role of this preparatory material is crucial. It sets up certain expectations in the supervisor's mind and also indicates the relative status of the two participants in the speech event, in particular the relative power of the addressee. This is reinforced by the way in which the request is actually expressed: ('I wonder if you could possibly . . .') and by the explicit reference to the supervisor's authority in terms of his being able to 'give' the speaker something; that is, to exercise (benevolently) his power. Indian norms of politeness are different, however, and the first speaker adopts quite a different strategy. His approach involves making the request explicitly at the outset, intending to adduce the reasons for it and to express appropriate politeness meanings later. This technique is unlikely to be as successful if the supervisor is used to Western norms—indeed, the approach is likely to be interpreted as rude or even offensive.

This example illustrates well the fact that the successful use of a foreign language involves far more than the acquisition of a vocabulary and grammar. It involves a knowledge of the norms adopted in the community for achieving a wide range of social goals—norms which may be significantly different from those used in one's own community. That is, the successful use of foreign language involves the acquisition of an extensive repertoire of sociocultural skills in addition to purely linguistic knowledge. Yet these skills are not separate from language. In order to acquire them, one has to learn what kind of meanings are to be expressed and how these meanings are to be organised in specific situations.

Eades 1982 provides another example, from a rather different sociocultural context, illustrating this point. She is concerned with an important discrepancy involving the use of language between the norms of some Australian Aborigines and those of many white Australians. Her study focuses in particular on Aborigines living in south-east Queensland and is concerned with the ways in which individuals use language in order to obtain information from others. She begins by noting that, whereas whites are usually quite happy to answer questions expressed by means of an interrogative structure such as 'were you very young then?', 'where was your husband from?', Aborigines are less likely to answer questions expressed in this way, as the following example shows:

Eades: Were you very young then?
A: Eh?
Eades: You were very young?
A: I was about 14.

The following extract from a later part of the interview illustrates the same point:

Eades: Your husband was a Batjala man?
A: He was a Batjala.
Eades: And where was he from again?
A: Beg pardon?
Eades: He was from further south, was he?
A: He's ... he's from here, not far from X station.

This Aboriginal woman is clearly much more comfortable with questions expressed in a declarative form ('you were very young then?', 'he was from further south, was he?') than with interrogative questions. Eades suggests that there is in fact much more to this than a preference for one particular kind of syntactic form over another. She argues that there is a contrast between white Australian (especially middle-class white Australian) society and Aboriginal society in south-east Queensland in that in the latter the communication of information is very much a two-way process. Anyone requiring information should also ideally be in a position to offer it. The idea of someone approaching a stranger with the intention of obtaining personal information is one that is totally alien to this culture. Rather, information should normally be exchanged, with first one individual contributing to the conversation, then another, each in their own good time and as they judge appropriate to the developing situation. The reason why the declarative form is preferred is that it approximates more closely to the ideal situation in that the questioner expresses a proposition which the other may choose to confirm, qualify, elaborate or correct, if it seems appropriate at that point to do so. By contrast, the interrogative form openly expresses the fact that there is a lack of shared knowledge, a social distance between the individuals concerned and is not therefore conducive to creating the kind of atmosphere in which information can be communicated comfortably.

Clearly, differences of the kind discussed above relate to fundamental differences between the social structure of Aboriginal communities and those of many Western communities. The former are characterised by tight-knit social structures, in which each individual is related to the community as a whole by extensive ties of kinship. Many Western-type communities are much looser by comparison. Clearly, too, when there are contrasting social norms of this kind within a society which embraces different cultures, there arises the possibility of lack of understanding between the groups involved. For example, one can see in these contrasting norms some explanation for the fact that (white) school-teachers often complain that Aboriginal children do not take part in activities involving questioning, which play a vital role in Western-style teaching. They are often said to be verbally lazy or deficient in this way. There are also reports that Aborigines often fail to do themselves justice in the legal system, by failing to understand or comply with the question–answer routines on which the whole legal process is based (Eades 1982: 70–1).

The examples of cross-cultural differences concerning the use of language discussed above are only a tiny sample of the kind of ethnographic differences which distinguish one society from another. (For a much more complete description, see Saville-Troike 1982.) These observations raise the question of whether there may be subtle differences of this kind not only across different societies, but also across different social groups—for example, different class groups—within a particular community. If such differences do exist, perhaps they too constitute a factor which might help to explain the overall discrepancy between the educational achievements of middle-class children and working-class children. The issue is one that has been debated in some detail in recent years and is one that is far from being resolved. We take it up in the final chapter.

CONCLUSION

In this chapter we have noted that a language is above all a variable phenomenon. This means that there may be important differences between the mental grammars of one group of speakers and those of another group if the two groups are separated regionally or socially. Those who speak non-standard varieties possess a linguistic system which is just as rich and complex as that possessed by speakers of standard varieties, but this fact is often not widely recognised. Non-standard speakers can therefore be disadvantaged within a given society, particularly since it is in general the standard variety that is accorded prestige in the educational system. In recent years sociolinguists, following the pioneering work of Labov, have made remarkable progress in coming to grips with the complex phenomenon of variation and in developing our appreciation of the value of non-standard varieties.

Although most attention has been devoted so far to variation in accents, there is a growing realisation among linguists that the phenomenon has a much broader range. One important and developing sociolinguistic approach sets out to describe and explain the different strategies used by different social or ethnic groups in their ways of expressing meaning. One would hope that in time this work will lead to a greater awareness and tolerance of linguistic variation in all its manifestations.

8 Social Aspects of Language Development

THE LANGUAGE-DEFICIT HYPOTHESIS

In this final chapter we examine in more detail the question of whether there is any linguistic basis for the undoubted disadvantage which appears to operate against children from underprivileged social backgrounds. The debate has been raging for some time. In Britain the discussion tends to centre on the concept of class: do working-class children suffer from some linguistic disadvantage by comparison with middle-class children? In the USA the focus has been on ethnicity: do linguistic differences have some role to play in explaining the relatively poor performance of many black children in the educational system? The issue is a complex one and deserves some discussion in depth.

Let us begin by looking at the debate as it has been carried on in the American context. The most straightforward version of the so-called 'language-deficit hypothesis' is associated with the American educationalists Carl Bereiter and Friedrich Engelmann. Their work has been concerned mainly with the situation in urban centres such as New York City. They argue that there are important differences between the language of many black children coming into the educational system at the age of five and white children of the same age. In their view these differences put the black children at a disadvantage at the very beginning of their school career—a disadvantage from which most never fully recover. (See e.g. Bereiter and Engelmann 1966: 33–43.)

Now, the first point to make is that there are certainly clear differences between the speech of blacks and whites in New York City. This is not to say that all blacks use one dialect and all whites another—the discussion in the previous chapter indicated that linguistic variation in any community is far more complex than this. It is true, however, that there are certain grammatical and phonological forms that are used more extensively by blacks than by whites and vice versa. This has led a number of sociolinguists to suggest that it is useful to recognise the existence of a social dialect called 'Non-standard Negro English' (NNE) or 'Black English Vernacular' (BEV). This variety has been the subject of intensive study over recent years. Like other varieties of English, including the one that we refer to as 'Standard English', BEV is a highly systematic, rule-governed variety. It does not have the kind of overt prestige associated with Standard English but, like any other non-standard variety, it does enjoy a very high degree of covert prestige.

The following extract from Labov's article 'The Logic of Non-standard English' (Labov 1969) gives us some idea of the nature of BEV. One of the speakers—Larry—is a typical speaker of this variety:

JL: What happens to you after you die? Do you know?
Larry: Yeah, I know.
JL: What?
Larry: After they put you in the ground, your body turns into—ah—bones, an' shit.
JL: What happens to your spirit?
Larry: Your spirit—soon as you die, your spirit leaves you.
JL: And where does the spirit go?
Larry: Well, it all depends . . .
JL: On what?
Larry: You know, like some people say if you're good an' shit, your spirit goin' t'heaven . . . 'n' if you bad, your spirit goin' to hell. Well, bullshit! Your spirit goin' to hell anyway, good or bad.
JL: Why?
Larry: Why? I'll tell you why. 'Cause, you see, doesn' nobody really know that it's a God, y'know, 'cause I mean, I have seen black gods, pink gods, white gods, all color gods, and don't nobody really know

that it's a really a God. An' when they be sayin' if you good, you goin' to heaven, tha's bullshit, 'cause you ain't goin' to no heaven, cause it ain't no heaven for you to go to.

JL: Well, if there's no heaven, how could there be a hell?

Larry: I mean—ye..eah. Well, let me tell you, it ain't no hell, 'cause this is hell right here, y'know!

JL: This is hell?

Larry: Yeah, this is hell, right here!

JL: . . . But, just say that there is a God, what colour is he? White or black?

Larry: Well, if it's a God . . . I wouldn' know what color, I couldn' say—couldn' nobody say what color he is or really WOULD be.

JL: But now, jus' suppose there was a God—

Larry: Unlessn' they say . . .

JL: No, I was jus' sayin' jus' suppose there is a God, would he be white or black?

Larry: . . . He'd be white, man.

JL: Why?

Larry: Why? I'll tell you why. 'Cause the average whitey out here got everything, you dig? And the nigger ain't got shit, y'know? Y'understan'? So—um—for – in order for *that* to happen, you know it ain't no black God that's doin' that bullshit.

This extract illustrates some of the major differences between BEV and Standard English (SE). Where SE uses the construction *there is NP* (*there's a God*, *there's no heaven* etc.), BEV uses *it is NP* (*it's a God*, *it ain't no heaven* etc.). Another difference is that BEV uses two negative markers where SE uses one:

(1) You are*n't* going to Heaven. (SE)
You ai*n't* goin' to *no* Heaven. (BEV)

(2) There is*n't* any God. (SE)
It ai*n't no* God. (BEV)

In certain constructions where SE uses the order: noun phrase + verb phrase (e.g. *nobody knows* . . .), BEV uses an auxiliary verb in the position preceding the noun phrase (e.g. *doesn' nobody know . . .*). This particular structure occurs only under very precise grammatical conditions, one of these being that the noun phrase in question has to be negative. Speakers of BEV would use *can't nobody say . . .* where speakers of SE would use *nobody can say*, for example, but would not use *can't Larry say . . .* for *Larry can't say . . .*. A fourth systematic feature of BEV is the non-occurrence of the verb *be* under certain conditions. Examples in the text above include *your spirit goin' to heaven*, *if you bad*, *your spirit goin' to hell*, *if you good*, where SE speakers would say *your spirit's going to Heaven*, *if you're bad*, and so on. There are, however, certain grammatical environments in which speakers of BEV would always use *be*. In the conversation above, note that Larry says *couldn' nobody say what color he is*, with the verb *be* occurring (in the form *is*) in final position. Under no circumstances would a BEV speaker omit *be* here. There is a general grammatical rule at work in BEV, which in fact is very similar to one in SE. The point about examples like *your spirit is going to Heaven*, *if you are bad* is that speakers of SE can use either the full form of the verb *be* here (as in the examples just cited) or the 'contracted' form as in *your spirit's going to heaven*, *if you're bad*, where the contracted form *'s* or *'re* is attached to the preceding word. However, it is not possible in SE to use the contracted form in an example like *nobody could say what colour he is*. That is, no speaker of SE would say **nobody could say what colour he's*. There is a rule which speakers of SE subconsciously follow here, preventing contraction of *be* in this situation (King 1970; Zwicky 1970). The point is that exactly the same rule applies in BEV, except that in that variety the rule prevents deletion rather than contraction of *be*.

The BEV characteristics illustrated above, along with many others, are prominent in the speech of many black New Yorkers, adults and children (and incidentally of some whites who have been brought up in predominantly black areas). Now, it has often been argued that at least some of these features constitute a severe handicap to the intellectual development of the child in the educational process. One of the most widely cited characteristics is the double-negative structure, illustrated above at (1) and (2). The suggestion is that two negatives cancel each other out: *I couldn't not voice my opinion* means 'I could (and did) voice my opinion'. This principle (that two negatives cancel each other out) is said to be a rule of logic. Speakers who use the double-negative structure, when they obviously don't mean the negatives to be interpreted as cancelling each other out, are therefore thought to be expressing themselves 'illogically'. The claim is that they mean one thing but are saying the opposite. Clearly, if this argument were valid, then the logical, rational modes of thought which the education system sets out to inculcate would be at odds with the thought processes associated with the BEV dialect. Little wonder, the argument runs, that so many black children make slow progress in school.

Another feature which has been used in support of this line of argument is the omission of the copula verb *be* in examples like those discussed above. The meaning of the SE sentence *they are mine* is thought to be composed of a number of what we might call conceptual or semantic units. *They* designates the objects in question; *mine* expresses the concept of speaker-possession; *be* establishes the link between these two major concepts, so that the hearer interprets the concept of speaker-possession as applying to the objects in question. If this linking word is left out, so the argument runs, the logical relationship between the concept of speaker-possession and the objects designated by *they* is not expressed, with the result that each major concept is somehow left floating around, alone and unattached. Again the suggestion is that the linguistic characteristics of BEV do not lead the child to establish crucial logical relationships between entities in our conceptual world.

Now, linguists would argue that there are serious flaws in these arguments. As far as the double-negative structure is concerned, the argument that it inhibits the development of logical thinking collapses in the face of the fact that there are many (standard) languages in the world which use two negative markers. The Spanish for 'he said nothing' is *no dije nada*, with two negative elements, *no* and *nada*. A literal translation would be *not he said nothing*. In French both *ne* and *pas* can be used independently as negative markers, as in the following examples:

(3) Je ne sais. ('I don't know')
(4) Pas un mot. ('Not a word')

However, in most negative sentences they are both used, so that here too there is a kind of double negation:

(5) Il ne vient pas. ('He isn't coming')

This situation is common in many languages, yet it would obviously be absurd to argue that speakers of French, Spanish and so on are inhibited from logical modes of thought by the structure of their languages. The fallacy involved here is the failure to recognise the fact that languages (and language varieties) are independent systems, in which the relationship between meaning and form is an arbitrary, conventionalised one. There is no intrinsic reason why any given language should use only one marker to represent negation.

As far as the copula-less construction illustrated by *they mine* is concerned, a number of points can be made. The first is that, again, there are many (standard) languages in the world which lack an element corresponding to the copula *be*. This indicates that its contribution to the meaning of the sentence as a whole is not significant in the way that has often been suggested. When a speaker of BEV says *they mine*, there is no confusion in his mind as to the nature of the relationship between the objects designated by *they* and the speaker. Nor is there any problem of interpretation for the hearer. The fact that the relationship is one of possession, with the speaker as 'possessor' and the objects as 'possessed' is expressed by a number of grammatical features. The crucial ones are (a) that the speaker has selected the possessive pronoun *mine* rather than other forms available for referring to himself such as *I* or *me* and (b) that he has selected the form *they* to designate the objects rather than *them*, *their* or *theirs*. Word-order is another relevant factor, since it is conventional in this kind of structure to place the 'possessed' before the 'possessor'. In other words, the copula verb does not in fact make any contribution to the expression of meaning here, which is no doubt why it is absent from a number of varieties of English and from many languages. In particular, it plays no significant role in the expression of logical relationships.

Another point that should be made in this context is that most individuals who would be regarded as typical speakers of BEV do not in any event use the BEV forms on each and every occasion. In formal contexts they tend to use a greater percentage of standard grammatical forms than they do in informal contexts. This is a convention across all members of the community, although individuals obviously differ in the degree to which their usage does vary in this way, just as they differ with respect to the relative proportions of standard and non-standard phonological forms which they use in any given context. The same point holds for white New Yorkers who are not typical speakers of BEV, in that in informal contexts some individuals use features of BEV like the double-negative structure or the copula-less structure (features that are of course found in any event in other non-standard varieties besides BEV). If one held the view that such structures are the expression of non-logical modes of thinking, one would have to draw the absurd conclusion that the quality of thinking of many white New Yorkers deteriorates in informal situations and that of speakers of BEV improves in formal ones. In the context of the studies described in the previous chapter, there is clearly a much more plausible explanation—namely, that speakers are changing their surface style in response to changes in the social context. There is no more reason to associate this kind of grammatical variation with cognition than there is to connect the patterns of phonological variation described in Chapter 7 with cognitive processes.

One illustration of the fact that variation here is a surface phenomenon is provided in a study by Jane Torrey (cited in Labov 1969: 20), comparing the speech of 10-year-old black children with that of older individuals from the same community. Torrey found that the black adolescents of about 17 years of age in the study were using non-standard structures like the double negatives and copula-less examples much more frequently than the 10-year-olds. This would be an extremely surprising observation if the non-standard forms correlated with lower levels of cognitive development. One would expect precisely the opposite pattern. On the other hand, if variation here is connected with social factors, then the pattern falls into place. For most of these boys the period between the ages of 10 and 17 involves a process of progressive integration into the local peer-groups, which are characterised by markedly non-standard speech. The change in their speech patterns over that period simply reflects this social development and expresses their identification with the values of the peer group.

For these reasons contemporary sociolinguists argue that the association which is often made between non-standard speech and illogical modes of thought is itself irrational. Labov has argued that it is also dangerous. Those who hold this view will inevitably, from the best of motives, argue that the educational process should aim to modify the speech of young non-standard speakers in the direction of the standard variety. This would be an essential part of inculcating logical thinking. In fact, however, what they are unwittingly setting out to do is to change the personality of the child. By asking him to distance himself linguistically from his peer group and perhaps from his family, they are seeking to distance him socially from the background and culture in which he has grown up and where he feels at home. Certainly, a general shift in his language would be interpreted in this way by his family and peers. In other words, the process inevitably encounters the full counter-pressure of covert prestige. What the child is in fact being asked to do is to adopt a different surface style, one which is associated, both in his own view and in the view of those close to him, with a social group to which he does not belong. Moreover, the latter is a group which he is likely to see as unjustly privileged and perhaps even as oppressive with respect to his own (as Larry's argument clearly indicates). Inevitably, then, the process is doomed to failure in the vast majority of cases, particularly as there are in fact no cognitive benefits to be gained from it anyway. For Labov the danger here consists in the interpretation that (white) observers might put upon this failure. They may see it as a failure on the child's part to develop 'better' modes of thinking and may therefore be led to the conclusion that there is a genetic difference between black children and white children concerning the development of cognitive processes. It is for this reason that linguists like Labov have so vehemently attacked the assumptions behind some of the remediation programmes that have been tried in the schools, based on the language-deficit hypothesis.

Although the identification of non-standardness with unsatisfactory modes of thinking is irrational, the fact that it is widespread in society is an important point to recognise. We have already noted that teachers' expectations can play an important role in the child's progress (or lack of it) in school. If a teacher is influenced by a child's non-standard speech into formulating low expectations for that child, because of the general framework of ideas discussed above, then this factor could easily come to reinforce those general processes of disadvantage operating against the working-class child. Indeed, it is difficult for ANYONE to resist making judgements of this kind. Sociolinguists clearly have an important role here in making us subject our prejudices to rational scrutiny. In the previous chapter I suggested that children do, of course, need to become aware of the distinction between standard and non-standard forms and that teachers should encourage them to use standard forms on appropriate occasions, particularly in written English. What is important is that all those involved should distinguish between the good reasons and the bad reasons for doing so. Issues connected with language constitute a particularly sensitive area, since they are so closely bound up with questions of social identity, and they therefore need to be treated with particular delicacy and understanding.

THE LANGUAGE-DISADVANTAGE HYPOTHESIS

I turn now to a more complex version of the language-deficit hypothesis, associated with the British sociologist

Basil Bernstein. There is in fact some doubt as to whether Bernstein's ideas really do constitute a language-deficit theory. He himself believes that they do not. Yet his view certainly does involve seeing language as a factor involved in differential levels of achievement in school. Bernstein's argument is that, although there is no intrinsic qualitative difference between the linguistic KNOWLEDGE of his advantaged group and that of his disadvantaged group, certain differences involving the USE of language can lead to a discrepancy in the way they fare in the educational process. Perhaps, then, it would be more accurate to call Bernstein's a language-disadvantage hypothesis rather than a language-deficit hypothesis. (For a general review of Bernstein's work, see Lee 1973.)

I noted above that it is a well-known fact that working-class children perform less well on average in the educational system than do middle-class children. The initial observation which led Bernstein to suggest that this might have something to do with language was the fact that working-class children often do less well in certain types of IQ test than do middle-class children of the same level of intelligence. This may seem paradoxical at first sight. If they do less well in the IQ tests, on what basis can it be asserted that they have the same level of intelligence? In fact this assertion is based on the observation that a working-class child may achieve the same score as a middle-class child on a non-verbal IQ test (i.e. one which does not involve the use of language) but achieve a lower score on a verbal (i.e. language-based) test. This suggested to Bernstein that working-class children do not demonstrate their full potential in language-based exercises. There are in fact a number of reasons for doubting the usefulness of verbal IQ tests as an indicator of a child's general language capacities. However, since this is somewhat marginal to the main tenor of Bernstein's argument, I will not pursue the point here.

Let us for the moment follow Bernstein in his hypothesis that there are differences in the way in which working-class and middle-class children use language. In what might these differences consist? The first point is that, in spite of the interpretation put on Bernstein's arguments by many educationalists and teachers (Gordon 1980), the question has nothing to do with the differences between standard and non-standard English. Bernstein, like other sociolinguists, views these as alternative varieties of equal status, each capable of expressing the same range of meanings and the same kinds of logical thought. This is where Bernstein's theory differs from that of Bereiter and Engelmann. For Bernstein, the differences between what we might (rather oversimplistically) call middle-class language and working-class language have to do not with the superficial characteristics that differentiate standard from non-standard varieties but with deeper questions of meaning and use. In order to illustrate this point, I need to present some details of the sociological aspects of Bernstein's argument.

At the heart of Bernstein's theory is a hypothesised opposition between two different family types—what he calls the 'positional' family (the archetypal working-class family) and the 'person-centred' family (the archetypal middle-class family). Bernstein is not saying that every working-class family is positional and that every middle class family is person-centred, nor that any particular family can be wholly assigned to one or another category in all respects. Rather, he is setting up the terms 'positional' and 'person-centred' as the two poles of an axis, with working-class families tending to cluster towards the positional pole in most respects and middle-class families tending to cluster towards the person-centred pole. The alleged differences between working-class and middle-class language are traced back to the contrast between these two family types.

The two family types are characterised, in Bernstein's view, by quite different attitudes to the role of the individual, both within the family unit and within the larger context of society as a whole. In the positional family, each individual is seen primarily as fulfilling a certain role, which is defined independently of the individual by general social conventions. There will be certain tasks associated specifically and exclusively with each role. As far as the relationship between parents and children is concerned, the main factor here will be the concept of authority. A mother will inform her child of the behaviour that is required of him on some specific occasion, but the main rationale for this behaviour is the position of the mother vis-à-vis the child. Since the mother is in authority over the child and since she wishes him to perform a certain action, then he should do it, for that reason. Failure to comply necessarily means a challenge to the mother's authority. In the person-centred family, by contrast, the concept of authority plays a smaller role. Here the rationale for the behaviour required of the child needs to be made much more explicit. It is not sufficient for the mother simply to tell the child what to do and to rely implicitly on authority as the rationale for that action. Rather, the considerations that have led her to require the action in question need to be formulated explicitly.

Here in Bernstein's view we find the source of important differences involving the use of language. In a positional family, language will be predominantly concerned with the concrete elements of the here-and-now situation. It will be devoted to the expression of what he calls 'particularistic' meanings. In the person-centred family, by contrast, much more attention will be given to establishing the link between specific actions and general principles governing behaviour. Relationships will need to be established between the here and now and other events that may have happened in the past or the consequences that might be expected to follow in the future. These more general meanings are called 'universalistic' meanings by Bernstein.

In school the major concern will be with universalistic meanings. Specific events and situations are of interest only for their more general significance, for the principles that they illustrate. This is an inevitable preoccupation of the school, since its role is to prepare the child to cope with new situations; this can be successful only if the child understands the relevant general principles. If, therefore, it is true that the middle-class mother devotes more of her time to expressing universalistic meanings than does the working-class mother, then it would appear that she is laying a more satisfactory basis for success in school.

The following passage from Joan Tough's book *The Development of Meaning* (1977: 63) is relevant here:

The position-oriented mother is likely to see the child as a child and to infer that there is little knowledge within his reach. She expects him to play with other children because this is a traditional activity for young children, so she releases him from her control quite readily. The parent may not see the child as a developing person to whom knowledge should be made accessible and so may be doing little to help him acquire basic, everyday knowledge.

The person-oriented mother will see her child as a developing individual who is learning to share in the interests of other members of the family. Thus, she tries to make knowledge available to him. She explains phenomena as they arise, they look at books, she is alert to what will interest him and it all becomes part of her control strategies: appeal to reason, appeal to interest, appeal to participation and to the basic principles that govern their relationship.

One might well ask at this point WHY differences of the kind outlined above might be expected to characterise the opposition between working-class and middle-class attitudes. In Bernstein's view the reasons have to do with the different social experiences of the two groups. In the past, working-class people for the most part have had little control over the kind of jobs they could do and over the nature of those jobs. In Joan Tough's words, 'work is generally for the lower working class a routine that requires no planning on their part' (1977: 29). On this view, language is thought to have little role to play in discrimination and organisation—its main role, rather, is in the perpetuation of relatively fixed social traditions. For the middle classes, however, a much greater range of occupations is available, and the situations which an individual encounters in each of these occupations are much more varied than are those experienced in most working-class occupations. Language may therefore have a much more important role as a social instrument in this context. More generally, the family as a whole is said to experience the need for long-term planning, where immediate pleasures and rewards may need to be sacrificed for some longer-term benefit. The use of language is essential here in formulating such goals, in establishing the connections between various potential chains of events and in evaluating the desirability of one course of action over another.

It should be said at this point that Bernstein's view of the life and attitudes of both working-class and middle-class people has been widely criticised as involving a number of gross oversimplifications. One of the main difficulties with Bernstein's argument is that it is couched in such general, abstract terms that it is very difficult to know what kind of evidence would clearly support or refute it. In the early stages of the development of the theory, Bernstein made the mistake of identifying certain syntactic criteria which he felt would exemplify the general contrasts that he was trying to draw. For example, he suggested that what he called 'elaborated code' (the kind of language supposedly used by person-centred families) was characterised by such grammatical features as complex sentences and a relatively high frequency of passive structures (Bernstein 1974: 55). The reason for specifying the contrast between 'elaborated code' and 'restricted code' in these terms was no doubt the fact that these criteria lend themselves to verification. A number of studies were then carried out (e.g. Lawton 1963, 1964; Robinson 1965a, 1965b; Poole and Field 1972) to see if middle-class children do in fact use more complex sentences and more passives than working-class children. However, the problem is that the link between 'universalistic meanings' and complex sentences or passives is a very tenuous one. Complex sentences can be used to talk solely about the here and now; that is, to express particularistic meanings. Conversely, a series of short, grammatically simple sentences can be used to express universalistic meanings. Anyone who has written an essay will be familiar with the experience of finding that the presentation of ideas and arguments can often be greatly improved by simplifying some of the sentence structures of one's original draft. There is no straightforward link between cognitive complexity and grammatical complexity. The point about Bernstein's theory is that it is essentially semantic rather than syntactic in nature. He is arguing that there are differences between the kinds of meanings expressed by members of different social groups in the same situation. The suggestion that these differences are reflected in syntax was unfortunate. It was no doubt made because of the fact that until recently the tools that we possessed for describing semantic categories were much more primitive than those that were available for the description of syntactic ones.

For a number of years, then, Bernstein's theory came under very heavy attack from linguists and others (see e.g. Labov 1969; Rosen 1972; Gordon 1976, 1978). They criticised confusions introduced into the debate by some interpreters of Bernstein, who mistakenly took his arguments to apply to the standard/non-standard contrast. They criticised the abstractness of the argument, the lack of clear verificational criteria. They criticised many of the experiments performed by Bernstein and his followers. These often involved the use of questionnaires, so that any alleged differences between the reaction of a middle-class mother and that of a working-class mother to a particular situation were usually based on how they said they would react rather than on actually-observed behavioural differences. They criticised the confusion which developed at one point involving syntax and semantics, which made Bernstein's theory appear to be concerned with relatively superficial aspects of language use. For these and other reasons, many linguists remain wholeheartedly opposed to Bernstein's theory.

For others, however, the issues raised by Bernstein remain open. This is due in part to the recent growth of interest in semantics. Work in the area of the ethnography of communication (see p. 184) has also focused on the fact that there are differences involving the use of language across different communities and social groups. Joan Tough's work (1977) constitutes one example of the continuing interest in Bernstein's ideas. She has argued that there ARE circumstances in which certain semantic differences can be identified in the use of language by working-class and middle-class children. In one study of 3-year-olds she found that the middle-class children used language more often to 'project beyond the limits of the immediate situation'. For instance, a child playing with a doll exclaimed 'oh . . . she's had an accident' when the doll fell off a toy car. Another child said 'get an ambulance . . . you've got to get an ambulance if you have an accident', and the first child replied 'and a doctor . . . doctors make people better' (Tough 1977: 75). In each of these cases—and she cites many more examples from her recordings of children at play—we see the child assigning particular events to general categories such as 'having an accident', specifying the general rules for behaviour in a particular situation, such as getting an ambulance in the case of an accident, and identifying the cause–effect relationships between the phenomena of experience: 'doctors make people better'. These meanings are much more akin to Bernstein's category of universalistic meanings that to his particularistic meanings. In the group of working-class children, on the other hand, she found that there was a tendency for the child to use language a great deal of the time to 'monitor the ongoing situation in order to be alert to any threat to his position' or for it to be directed towards 'the successful maintenance of his position in relation to others'. The middle-class children did this too, of course, but to a lesser extent. They were much more inclined to relate the present experience to past experiences and to future possibilities—to seek for explanations and associations, to survey the range of possibilities open to them. It was this kind of result that Bernstein's theory predicted, and it can be argued that there is some empirical support for it in this study of children at the age of 3.

Tough carried out further studies on the same group of children when they reached the age of 5½ (1977, Ch. 8). Once more she found differences between the way in which the children from the two social groups used language. For example, there are different ways in which a child presented with a picture may respond to the question 'could you tell me all about what's happening there?'. Some children tend to list or label the various elements in the picture separately. Others establish connections between elements in the picture; for example, 'the boy's going to stroke the cat'. Others impose a structure on the whole scene or look for a central meaning. Tough found that 19 of the 24 middle-class children placed an overall interpretation on the scene and the other five established connections between elements within it. In the group of 24 working-class children only 4 placed an overall interpretation on the scene, 6 established connections between various elements within the picture and

14 responded by simply listing all the elements separately. (All the children had, incidentally, been matched for IQ.)

There could, of course, be all kinds of reasons why the majority of the working-class children responded differently from the middle-class group. Their attitude towards the task may have been less positive; they may have felt less comfortable about being asked to talk about a picture and therefore have been less inclined to make the task interesting by responding to it creatively. Tough is cautious in interpreting the results, but she does comment that all the children seemed intrigued by the way in which the picture was presented (as a peepshow) and that there were no indications in their behaviour that they were not well motivated to respond.

Similar results were obtained when the same children were studied again at the age of 7½. The middle-class children evinced a strong tendency to place interpretations on the behaviour of people in the scene (which concerned an imminent street accident), whereas the working-class children produced a large proportion of utterances concerned simply with listing or labelling the elements in the scene. It may not be the case that the children actually see the pictures differently. All the children demonstrated their perception of the central meaning of the picture. Where they differed was in the kind of meanings they chose to make explicit spontaneously. The middle-class children were much more ready to express complex meanings concerning relationships, causes and effects, without being prompted. Such meanings could be elicited from the working-class children by questions such as 'what do you think the bus driver's thinking?' or 'why shouldn't the boy be on the road?' but they did not express them as frequently in their initial reaction to the picture. It is in fact difficult to say whether the child sees these underlying patterns only when prompted to do so or whether she does not feel the need to express them in her initial response. In any event, there does seem to be a difference here between the two groups in terms of their readiness to use language in the explicit exploration of underlying meanings and relationships.

In the same study, Tough explored a number of other

situations comparing the linguistic response of the two groups of children. We will not look at these in detail; suffice it to say that in each case the results were predictable from Bernstein's hypothesis. Middle-class children were more ready to refer to past experiences in relation to the current topic and to explore the future consequences of a particular situation. In a problem-solving task they expressed explanatory meanings more readily and produced logical justifications for their suggestions. Again, it is not a question of fundamental differences in cognitive development or linguistic knowledge here. Most of the working-class children could produce explanatory meanings when prompted (although there were in one case certain differences involving their ability to support their judgements with logical explanations), and they could certainly produce sentence structures of the same degree of complexity as those produced by the middle-class children. The differences relate rather to the way in which children use their language spontaneously and the kind of meanings they choose to express in a particular situation.

Again, the point should be emphasised that extreme caution is needed in interpreting results of this kind. The number of relevant studies in this area is still very small. The descriptive framework on which the semantic categories are based is not as clear-cut as are other areas of linguistic description. Above all, there are possibly important differences between the way in which various groups of children respond to experimental situations, however carefully designed, which may well mean that children's responses here cannot be taken as a reliable indicator of their linguistic potential in natural situations. (Note, however, that the study of 3-year-olds was based on the language used spontaneously in informal play sessions with other children.)

Labov (1969) has put forward quite a different explanation from that advanced by Bernstein for the different achievement levels of the various social groups. He argues that one of the major determinants of the child's performance in school is his degree of integration into the local peer-group network. Those who spend most time in these peer groups and most strongly identify with their value systems (which are usually in opposition to those of the school) will tend to be those whose performance in school is worst. Children in this category are often very intelligent and have a considerable range of skills in the use of language—skills which are very useful to them in the vernacular culture but are not highly valued in the school system. Their speech also tends to be markedly non-standard, which is also not a helpful factor in the school situation. (Whether Labov's theory is as relevant to girls as it is to boys is doubtful, if Maltz and Borker (1982) are correct in arguing that adolescent boys and girls are subject to different socialisation processes—see p. 179.)

It is not my aim here to attempt to provide any definitive answer to the question of whether there is such a thing as language disadvantage and, if so, what form it might take. The question is still too open to be clearly resolved. Still less is it may aim to suggest what practical steps might be implemented in the school to mitigate any such disadvantage. What I have tried to do here is to clarify some of the issues which impinge on this debate and to indicate the kind of evidence that might be relevant to it. This seems to me to constitute an important prerequisite to any decisions that might be taken by educators in responding to the issue. Most linguists would argue that the important point is to recognise the magnitude of the achievement of children in the language-learning domain. By the age of 5 (and in many cases by the age of 3) most children, whatever their social background, have constructed a very highly developed phonological, grammatical and semantic apparatus for communicating successfully. If there are differences across children, these have to do with the way in which children use the linguistic resources available to them rather than in the nature of the resources themselves.

CONCLUSION

In this chapter we have examined two different versions of the thesis that some children begin their educational life with a disadvantage involving language. The most straightforward version is the so-called 'language-deficit hypothesis', associated primarily with Bereiter and Engelmann. They have argued that certain linguistic forms characteristic of the speech of many children—especially black children—in cities such as New York indicate an inadeqate level of language development. They have advocated the urgent use of remedial programmes in this situation to counteract what they see as a massive obstacle to the child's progress in school.

Whilst recognising that those who hold this view are concerned and well-meaning, sociolinguists have vehemently attacked the underlying premise. Labov in particular has argued that the forms in question belong to a systematic language variety that is of equal value in linguistic terms to the standard variety—one that is an equally effective vehicle for the development and expression of logical thought. On the other hand, Labov recognises that non-standard varieties are not respected in the general community, certainly not in the field of education. Unfavourable attitudes may therefore contribute to the undoubted social disadvantage that operates against children from economically depressed backgrounds. For Labov and others sociolinguistics has a crucial role to play in counteracting attitudes of this kind, by encouraging a more general awareness of the intrinsic value of all linguistic varieties. Linguistic variation, in effect, is not only a sign of vitality within a particular language; it is also a reflection of the complexity of the culture within which that language operates and which it helps to define.

A rather different view of the link between language and disadvantage has been espoused by Bernstein. Although he recognises that all children acquire a fully developed linguistic system (unless there is some specific disability such as total deafness or brain injury), Bernstein argues that there are, nevertheless, differences in the way the system is USED. In particular, he believes that some children find it relatively easy to express meanings that relate features of the context of utterance to general principles of cognitive or social organisation. Children from other backgrounds are thought to be able to do this much less readily.

This theory too has come under attack from some linguists. Their main criticism has been that Bernstein has failed to provide clear definitions of many of the central concepts in his theory, particularly the crucial concept of 'code'. Part of the problem undoubtedly has to do with the fact that, as yet, our understanding of the domain of semantics is severely limited. We therefore leave this question open in the hope that the recent upsurge of interest and research in this area will throw light on some of these issues in the years ahead.

Many sociolinguists feel that there has been far too great a preoccupation in the past with the negative aspects of linguistic variation such as deprivation and disadvantage. It is arguable that we should now be building a much more positive set of attitudes here. There are in fact signs that recent sociolinguistic work has taken place within a climate of growing tolerance in this area; one such indicator is the greater acceptance of non-standard speakers in the broadcasting media as reporters and (less frequently) announcers. There are also encouraging signs that sociolinguistic research is beginning to have practical benefits in such areas as educational policy (Labov 1982) and the law (O'Barr 1981; Gumperz 1982b; Milroy 1984). If this work makes a real contribution to reducing the waste of human potential that has resulted from negative attitudes in the past towards non-standard varieties, then linguists will have gone some way towards justifying the significant financial and human resources that have been invested in the subject in recent years.

Bibliography

Aitchison, J. 1976. *The Articulate Mammal*. London: Hutchinson.

Akmajian, A. and Heny, F. 1975. *An Introduction to the Principles of Transformational Syntax*. Cambridge, MA: MIT Press.

Anderson, E. S. 1975. Cups and glasses: learning that boundaries are vague. *Journal of Child Language* 2, 79–103.

Angiolillo, C. J. and Goldin-Meadow, S. 1982. Experimental evidence for agent–patient categories in child language. *Journal of Child Language* 9, 627–43.

Bellugi, U. and Brown, R. 1964. The acquisition of language. *Monographs of the Society for Research in Child Language Development* 29. Reprinted 1971, Chicago: University of Chicago Press.

Bereiter, C. and Engelmann, F. 1966. *Teaching Disadvantaged Children in the Preschool*. Englewood Cliffs, NJ: Prentice Hall.

Berlin, B. and Kay, P. 1969. *Basic Color Terms: Their Universality and Evolution*. Berkeley: University of California Press.

Bernstein, B. 1974. *Class, Codes and Control*. London: Routledge and Kegan Paul, vol. 1.

Bolinger, D. 1980. *Language: The Loaded Weapon*. London: Longman.

Bower, T. G. R. 1971. The object in the world of the infant. *Scientific American*, October, 225 (4), 30–8.

Braine, M. 1963. The ontogeny of English phrase structure: the first phase. *Language* 39, 1–14.

Brown, R. 1973. *A First Language*. Cambridge, MA: Harvard University Press.

Brown, R. and Fraser, C. 1964. The acquisition of syntax. In Bellugi and Brown 1964.

Carroll, J. B. (ed.) 1971. *Language, Thought and Reality: Selected Writings of Benjamin Lee Whorf*. Cambridge, MA: MIT Press.

Cheshire, J. 1978. Present tense verbs in Reading English. In Trudgill, P. (ed.) *Sociolinguistic Patterns in British English*, London: Arnold.

Cheshire, J. 1984. The relationship between language and sex in English. In Trudgill 1984.

Chomsky, C. 1969. *The Acquisition of Syntax in Children from Five to Ten*. Cambridge, MA: MIT Press.

Chomsky, C. 1982. *Ask* and *tell* revisited: a reply to Warden. *Journal of Child Language* 9, 667–78.

Chomsky, N. A. 1957. *Syntactic Structures*. The Hague: Mouton.

Chomsky, N. A. 1965. *Aspects of the Theory of Syntax*. Cambridge, MA: MIT Press.

Clark, H. H. and Clark, E. V. 1977. *Psychology and Language*. New York: Harcourt Brace Jovanovich.

Cromer, R. F. 1970. Children are nice to understand: surface structure clues for the recovery of a deep structure. *British Journal of Psychology* 61, 397–408.

Crystal, D., Fletcher, P. and Garman, M. 1976. *The Grammatical Analysis of Language Disability*. London: Arnold.

Dore, J. 1975. Holophrases, speech acts and language universals. *Journal of Child Language* 2, 21–40.

Downes, W. 1984. *Language and Society*. London: Fontana.

Eades, D. 1982. You gotta know how to talk . . .: information-seeking in south-east Queensland Aboriginal society. *Australian Journal of Linguistics* 2, 61–82.

Erreich, A., Valian, V. and Mayer, J. W. 1980. Aspects of a theory of language acquisition. *Journal of Child Language* 7, 157–79.

Fasold, R. 1984. *The Sociolinguistics of Society*. Oxford: Blackwell.

Fillmore, C. J. 1968. The case for case. In Bach, E. and Harms, R. T. (eds.) *Universals in Linguistic Theory*, New York: Holt, Rinehart & Winston.

Fry, D. B. 1966. The development of the phonological system in the normal and the deaf child. In Smith, F. and Miller, G. A. (eds.) *The Genesis of Language*, Cambridge, MA: MIT Press.

Geertz, C. 1960. *The religion of Java*. New York: Free Press.

Giles, H. and Powesland, P. F. 1975. *Speech Style and Social Evaluation*. London: Academic Press.

Gimson, A. C. 1970. *An Introduction to the Pronunciation of English*. London: Arnold.

Gordon, J. C. B. 1976. An examination of Bernstein's theory of restricted and elaborated codes. *University of East Anglia Papers in Linguistics* 2, 1–22.

Gordon, J. C. B. 1978. Folk linguistics and the essence of verbal deficit theories. *University of East Anglia Papers in Linguistics* 7, 11–21.

Gordon, J. C. B. 1980. A case study in misrepresentation: a note on some disseminations of Bernstein by educationalists. *University of East Anglia Papers in Linguistics* 12, 45–52.
Greenfield, P. M. and Smith, J. H. 1976. *The Structure of Communication in Early Language Development*. New York: Academic Press.
Greenfield, P. M. and Zukow, P. G. 1978. Why do children say what they say when they say it?: an experimental approach to the psychogenesis of presupposition. In Nelson, K. E. (ed.) *Children's Language*, New York: Gardner Press, vol. 1.
Gruber, J. S. 1967. Topicalization in child language. *Foundations of Language* 3, 37–65.
Gumperz, J. J. (ed.) 1982a. *Language and Social Identity*. Cambridge: Cambridge University Press.
Gumperz, J. J. 1982b. Fact and inference in courtroom testimony. In Gumperz 1982a.
Halliday, M. A. K. 1975. *Learning How to Mean*. London: Arnold.
Horvath, B. M. 1985. *Variation in Australian English*. Cambridge: Cambridge University Press.
Howe, C. J. 1976. The meanings of two-word utterances in the speech of young children. *Journal of Child Language* 3, 29–47.
Huddleston, R. D. 1984. *Introduction to the Grammar of English*. Cambridge: Cambridge University Press.
Hudson, R. A. 1980. *Sociolinguistics*. Cambridge: Cambridge University Press.
Jakobson, R. 1968. *Child Language, Aphasia and Phonological Universals*. The Hague: Mouton.
King, H. W. 1970. On blocking the rules for contraction in English. *Linguistic Inquiry* 1, 134–6.
Labov, W. 1966. *The Social Stratification of English in New York City*. Washington, DC: Center for Applied Linguistics.
Labov, W. 1969. The logic of non-standard English. *Georgetown Monographs on Language and Linguistics* 22, 1–22, 26–31. Also in Giglioli, P. P. (ed.) *Language and Social Context*, Harmondsworth: Penguin, 1972. Also in Labov, W. (ed.) 1972 *Language in the Inner City*, Philadelphia: University of Pennsylvania Press; Oxford: Blackwell (1977).
Labov, W. 1982. Objectivity and commitment in linguistic science: the case of the Black English trial in Ann Arbor. *Language in Society* 11, 165–201.
Langacker, R. W. 1972. *Fundamentals of Linguistic Analysis*. New York: Harcourt Brace Jovanovich.

Lawton, D. 1963. Social class differences in language development: a study of some samples of written work. *Language and Speech* 6, 120–43.
Lawton, D. 1964. Social class language differences in group discussions. *Language and Speech* 7, 183–204.
Lee, D. A. 1982. Do children infer underlying structures? *AUMLA* (Journal of the Australasian Universities Language and Literature Association) 57, 51–68.
Lee, V. 1973. *Social Relationships and Language: Some Aspects of the Work of Basil Bernstein*. Bletchley: Open University Press.
Lehmann, W. P. and Pflueger, S. 1976. *Workbook for 'Descriptive Linguistics (2nd Edition): An Introduction'*. New York: Random House.
Lock, A. (ed.) 1978. *Action, Gesture and Symbol*. London: Academic Press.
Lock, A. 1980. *The Guided Re-invention of Language*. London: Academic Press.
Lyons, J. 1977. *Semantics*. Cambridge: Cambridge University Press, vol. 1.
Lyons, J. 1981. *Language and Linguistics*. London: Fontana.
Maltz, D. N. and Borker, R. A. 1982. A cultural approach to male–female miscommunication. In Gumperz 1982a.
Mayer, J. W., Erreich, A. and Valian, V. 1978. Transformations, basic operations and language acquisition. *Cognition* 6, 1–13.
Miller, W. and Ervin, S. 1964. The development of grammar in child language. In Bellugi and Brown 1964.
Milroy, J. 1984. Sociolinguistic methodology and the identification of speakers' voices in legal proceedings. In Trudgill 1984.
Mitchell, A. G. and Delbridge, A. 1965. *The Speech of Australian Adolescents*. Sydney: Angus and Robertson.
O'Barr, W. M. 1981. The language of the law. In Ferguson, C. A. and Heath, S. B. (eds.) *Language in the USA*. Cambridge: Cambridge University Press.
Poole, M. E. and Field, T. W. 1972. Social class and code elaboration in written communication. *Language and Speech* 15, 1–7.
Reid, E. 1976. Social and stylistic variation in the speech of some Edinburgh schoolchildren. MLitt thesis, University of Edinburgh.
Robinson, W. P. 1965a. Cloze procedure as a technique for the investigation of social class differences in language usage. *Language and Speech* 8, 42–55.

Robinson, W. P. 1965b. The elaborated code in working class language. *Language and Speech* 8, 243–52.

Romaine, S. 1980. A critical overview of the methodology of urban British sociolinguistics. *English World-Wide* 1, 163–98.

Romaine, S. 1984. *The Language of Children and Adolescents*. Oxford: Blackwell.

Rosch, E. and Mervis, C. B. 1975. Family resemblances: studies in the internal structure of categories. *Cognitive Psychology* 7, 573–605.

Rosen, H. 1972. *Language and Class: A Critical Look at the Theories of Basil Bernstein*. Bristol: Falling Wall Press.

Saussure, F. de 1916. *Course in General Linguistics*. London; Fontana, 1974.

Saville-Troike, M. 1982. *The Ethnography of Communication: An Introduction*. Oxford: Blackwell.

Schane, S. 1968. *French Phonology and Morphology*. Cambridge, MA: MIT Press.

Scott, R. 1982. An investigation of (ay) in Australian speech. *Working Papers in Linguistics* (University of Melbourne) 8, 27–34.

Seligman, C. R., Tucker, G. R. and Lambert, W. E. 1972. The effects of speech style and other attributes on teachers' attitudes towards pupils. *Language in Society* 1, 131–42.

Shuy, R. W. 1969. Sociolinguistic research at the Center for Applied Linguistics: the correlation of language and sex. *Giornata internazionali di sociolinguistica*. Rome: Palazzo Baldassini.

Slobin, D. I. 1973. Cognitive pre-requisites for the development of grammar. In Ferguson, C. A. and Slobin, D. I. (eds.) *Studies of Child Language Development*. New York: Holt, Rinehart & Winston.

Smith, N. V. 1971. Puggles and lellow lollies. *The Listener*, December.

Smith, N. V. 1973. *The Acquisition of Phonology*. Cambridge: Cambridge University Press.

Snow, C. E. 1979. Conversations with children. In Fletcher, P. and Garman, M. (eds.) *Language Acquisition*, Cambridge: Cambridge University Press.

Soames, S. and Perlmutter, D. M. 1979. *Syntactic Argumentation and the Structure of English*. Berkeley: University of California Press.

Thomson, J. R. and Chapman, R. S. 1977. Who is 'Daddy' revisited: the status of two-year-olds' over-extended words in use and comprehension. *Journal of Child Language* 4, 359–75.

Tough, J. 1977. *The Development of Meaning*. London: Allen & Unwin.

Trudgill, P. 1972. Sex, covert prestige and linguistic change in the urban British English of Norwich. *Language in Society* 1. 175–95.

Trudgill, P. 1974. *The Social Differentiation of English in Norwich*. Cambridge: Cambridge University Press.

Trudgill, P. 1983. *Sociolinguistics: An Introduction to Language and Society*. Harmondsworth: Penguin.

Trudgill, P. (ed.) 1984. *Applied Sociolinguistics*. London: Academic Press.

Warden, D. 1981. Children's understanding of *ask* and *tell*. *Journal of Child Language* 8, 139–49.

Weisenberger, J. L. 1976. A choice of words: two-year-old speech from a situational point of view. *Journal of Child Language* 3, 275–81.

Werner, H. and Kaplan, B. 1963. *Symbol Formation*. New York: Wiley.

Wierzbicka, A. (forthcoming). Is language a mirror of culture?: evidence from Australian English. *Language in Society*.

Williams, J. M. 1975. *Origins of the English Language: A Social and Linguistic History*. New York: Free Press.

Zwicky, A. M. 1970. Auxiliary reduction in English. *Linguistic Inquiry* 1, 323–36.

Index